SECRETS OF
SUCCESSFUL GARDENING

A GARDEN MINGLING BEAUTY AND UTILITY

SECRETS
OF SUCCESSFUL
GARDENING

BY

RICHARD SUDELL, F.R.H.S.

ODHAMS PRESS LIMITED
LONG ACRE, LONDON, W.C.2

*Made and Printed in Great Britain
by Odhams (Watford) Ltd., Watford*

CONTENTS

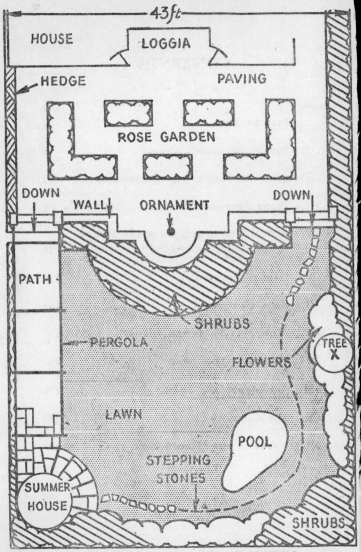

A GOOD LAYOUT FOR LAWN AND FLOWERS

INTRODUCTION

ONE of the most remarkable developments in modern recreation is the growth of gardening as a hobby. Nowhere is this growth so remarkable however, as in these islands; wherever you travel you will find that people cultivate gardens around their homes.

A variety of causes have contributed to this development, and perhaps the most important is the increasing urbanization of our life today; paradoxically the more people migrate to the towns in search of work, the more they long for a garden, however small, to remind them of the country. But, not only to remind them of the country; the rationalization of industry, so that workers spend their lives in performing largely mechanical tasks, has led to a vital psychological need for some outlet for creative activity in our spare time.

This outlet gardening, more than any other hobby, provides; you "make" your garden, and even the humblest gardener owning the tiniest plot knows that it depends on him whether it looks bright in Spring, Summer and Autumn, whether the various colours harmonize, whether in fact his flowers grow at all. Gardening provides the perfect opportunity for self-expression. Added to this creative activity is the competitive spirit in its best form. It is up to you to make your garden brighter, more original than your next door neighbour's, and each one of us is keen that this should be so, without hoping that our neighbour may fail.

Gardening can be made into an extremely complicated science. You can, if you wish, devote a lifetime to the cultivation of some rare plant. If your desires are more modest, then even the veriest beginner can reasonably expect success provided he follows certain simple rules. It is the chief purpose of this book to tell you what those rules are.

How to plan your garden according to the space available, how to make different types of paths, how to level a piece of ground, the different treatments needed by bulbs, annuals and perennials, the problems of the herbaceous border, the best times for planting, how to grow the most useful and simple fruits and vegetables, these are some of the problems you will find discussed in the following pages; while for the more ambitious, and for those with more space at their disposal there are chapters

7

on rock gardens, water gardens and greenhouses. The various types of soil are described and the classes of plants to which each is most suitable, and the numerous ways in which plants can be propagated anew are gone into in detail. In fact, every aspect of gardening is touched upon.

But though those with large gardens and money to spare will find much profit in this book it is intended not primarily for them, but for that great multitude who have much less than an acre of ground on which to experiment. For them, the main problem, after mastering the simple rules governing all plant cultivation, is how to achieve variety in a small space, and to this problem a major part of this book is devoted. There is, it cannot be too frequently stressed, no reason why the smallest garden should be dull.

There is no reason either, why a beginner should not rapidly become an expert in specialized plants. All over the country, each year, flower shows are held, from the local village affair to the great national shows, such as Southport or Chelsea. At the bigger shows valuable prizes are offered, and it is surprising how often the comparative beginner carries off many of these prizes. There is no reason, if you wish to become a specialist, why you should not be one such, and it is my hope that this book will help you on your way. It is my further hope that I have brought home to my readers the fact that gardening is one of the most pleasant and most rewarding of all occupations.

R. SUDELL.

CHAPTER I

DESIGN AND CONSTRUCTION

NEW garden owners are of two kinds. Some have had experience of garden happiness, perhaps in gardens they have previously rented, or in the old home garden. These owners approach the vacant plot with delight. They appreciate the fact that they can now make a garden to their own pattern, with features of their own choice and styles to suit their own taste. They probably also have some idea of how to attain their ideal.

Others view their rough grass and rubbish heaps with a sinking feeling. They do not know where or how to begin, nor what to aim at, and usually they pass the first few weeks in a sort of helpless bewilderment watching the efforts of their neighbours, and perhaps wondering how they did it.

I intend to write as if all my readers belonged to this second group, though I hope to deal so fully and comprehensively with the subject of garden making that there will be few amateur gardeners who will find nothing here to excite interest and add to their knowledge.

Here, in this first chapter, I want to outline the general principles of garden design. These principles are the same whatever the size of the garden, whatever its shape or aspect, its soil and its situation. A garden, using the word in its widest sense, is land brought under cultivation in such a way that it becomes a part of the home. It not only produces crops for use in the home—the allotment or farm would do that—but it must also be so arranged that the various domestic duties of the home can be carried out, and it must also contribute to the amenities of the household. In other, simpler words, you should be able in the ideal garden to grow vegetables and fruit, to dry washing, and to invite your friends to parties.

THE PROBLEM OF PLANNING

It is obvious that the first thing in garden design is to decide what you want the garden for, and then to allocate the various parts of the site to the various features that you decide to include. You must decide whether you want to play games or not, and what games you wish to provide for in the layout. You must decide how much, if any, of the garden space can be allotted to vegetable and fruit cultivation. You must decide whether much or little of the available space can be set aside for such domestic purposes as drying the weekly wash, cleaning mats and so on.

If the plot is large enough for every garden idea you want to be included, then it is probably so large that you will do well to call in a professional landscape architect. If it is smaller, then you must decide which of the desirable features can best be left out from your plan. Is it more important to have fresh vegetables for your table, or to have a garden for the children to practise cricket? Do you want a rose garden? If so, are you willing to dispense with the idea of a water garden in favour of roses? And so *ad infinitum*.

In planning, the following points should be borne in mind.

The first point for consideration, the arrangement of pathways, is linked up with convenience. Every part of the garden must be accessible, both for its use and for its development. That is

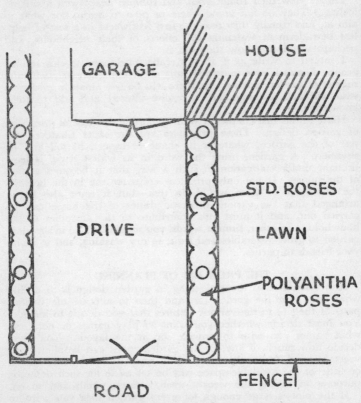

Fig. 1.   *A plan for an entrance from road to garage.*

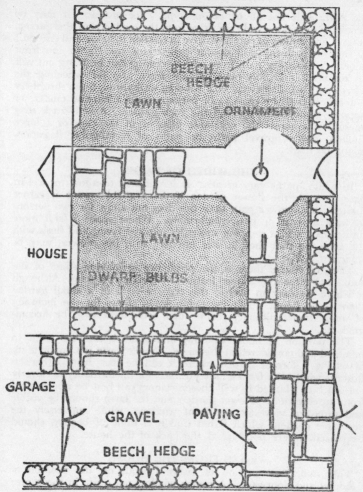

Fig. 2. A garage and small drive in relation to house and garden.

to say, there must be service paths to allow for the wheeling of manure, sand, composts and pots, as well as clean paths to allow for visits to each part of the plot in showery weather.

Paths are of many different kinds, and even in a small garden the paths will not all be of one type. For instance, it may be necessary to make a wide car drive from the roadway to the garage. (Figs. 1 and 2 show garage and drive in relation to house and garden.) A smaller pathway will do for pedestrians coming to the front door. A clean dry path from which washing can be hung out will be required, and this may perhaps serve also for wheeling the barrow. Then there may be a winding walk through the shrubbery —a gravel path or grass walk perhaps—and a narrow cinder, or stepping-stone track through the rock garden. A soil track may be sufficient across the vegetable plot, or in the case of a large kitchen garden gravel paths or paths of rectangular flagstones might be made.

THE WIDTH OF PATHS

In width, paths vary greatly. It is sufficient to allow for a 4-ft. path through the flower garden if the available space is rather limited : a narrower path than this does not allow for two persons to walk abreast or pass comfortably. Where space is still more limited, a track of stepping stones let into the lawn, and flush with the grass, so that they do not interfere with the mower, may be sufficient.

Then of course there is the possibility of making some of the walks into three-dimensional features by erecting pergolas. Although it would be easy to overdo this type of walk in a small garden there is no doubt about its usefulness: it allows for the inclusion of many more climbing plants than could otherwise be accommodated.

The position of house windows and doors is another point to be noted and considered at this stage. Never waste the opportunity of setting a formal garden where it can be seen from either an upstairs window or from a raised terrace, for the formality of cleverly cut out beds planted in well-chosen colours can best be appreciated from an elevation. Flower borders and the lawn should be visible and afford a view for the front windows, while conversely the vegetable garden, which is not usually a thing of beauty, should be placed, where possible, at the back of the house.

VISTAS FROM THE HOUSE

Then too, the question of vistas depends on the position of windows and doorways. A french window not quite in the centre of the house would suggest the position for a long straight walk dividing the garden into two not quite equal portions. A similar garden entrance on one corner of the house might ask for the long vista to be one side of the garden, instead of in the middle.

Aspect is very important. Flower borders need sunshine to bring them to the brilliance that most of us desire. True, some plants will flower quite well in the shade, but the shady border is never quite so full of colour over so long a period as the sunny border. Some vegetables will succeed in partial shade; most of them need open sunshine. Rock gardens need sun too, but a good rock and water garden can be made among trees and shrubbery, if a blaze of colour is not required. A tennis court needs a site to allow for the courts to run north and south, or nearly so, otherwise the players find the late afternoon sunshine very trying. A rose garden needs sun and an open situation, but not too strong winds. A heath garden, and a carnation and pink garden both do well on the windy hill-top.

Natural features control the garden design to a large extent, and are inseparable from the question of aspect. An exposed spot with peaty, heath soil for instance, would immediately suggest to the experienced gardener an opportunity for a heath garden. Similar soil on a valley site would perhaps suggest a garden of rhododendrons and azaleas. A heavy loam over chalk is ideal (when well cultivated) for orchard fruits, and for roses. An undulating stretch of ground would easily be converted to a rock garden. A naturally boggy site, or ground near a natural stream would be converted without much expense into an ornamental water garden.

COUNTING THE COST

Into all of these questions another problem intrudes, that of expense. This is not a mere matter of the initial outlay. Often features that cost little at first mean heavy expenditure over a number of years, while features that are considerable items in the contractor's estimate will need almost no expense in upkeep.

Consider, for example, the difference in costs between a formal water garden planted with lilies and other aquatics, and a formal flower garden made by cutting beds of various shapes and sizes out of an existing strip of turf. In the one case it means excavation, the use of stone (or cement), possibly the cost of installing company's water mains, or alternately the cost of an electric motor to run a fountain by the repeated use of the same water. Such mechanism is described on page 48. In the other case it may mean nothing more than a few hours labour, plus the cost of a dozen boxes of bedding plants or a few seed packets. In less than six months, however, the formal flower beds will have to be refilled, and then the cost of bulbs and spring bedding plants will be added to another account for digging, and these costs will be repeated half-yearly. It does not take many years for the expense (including labour costs) of the formal flower beds to surpass the cost of laying out a water garden.

At the same time, of course, the owner who is prepared to cut labour costs by becoming his own gardener, may think the outlay on stone and cement unjustifiable.

This question of labour in upkeep is worthy of deep consideration from the very first, and perhaps it would be well here to run over a few types of garden, and to discuss their merits from this and other standpoints, and also their demerits, so that even the novice can judge between them.

The simple, common-because-it-is-good, type of garden layout, suited to the average small or medium-sized garden, is that which includes a lawn, mixed flower borders, one or two rose beds, an archway or pergola for climbers, one or two orchard fruit trees, and either some small bush fruits or a vegetable patch. To these features is added possibly a tennis court. Generally the lawn is near the house, surrounded by borders, separated from the vegetable or fruit plot by the pergola or by trellis screens. This type of layout is good because so long as the lawn is kept cut, and the flowers in the mixed borders are weed-free and staked, the garden is always reasonably tidy and pleasant. A lawn in this case should never be too large for the owner to run the mower over it two or three times a week in high summer. If there is more than a quarter of an acre of grass, a motor mower is an essential.

Rose Garden

A rose garden is a feature of the small or medium-sized garden which definitely gives character to a layout and does not add very much to the labour of upkeep. Roses will grow on any type of soil, though a rather stiff loam suits them best. On poor sandy soils certain varieties do better than others, and by the use of these, with a little extra care over soil preparation, a good rose garden can be made. Pruning, once a year, cutting during the flowering season, and an occasional hoe over the soil surface is all the upkeep required. Roses are grown in small beds for ease in management, and where these beds are separated by grass (a grass setting is far the best for roses) the care of the grass edges adds to the labour of upkeep.

Bulbs and Bedding Plants

Flowers other than roses vary enormously in the amount of labour needed for their upkeep. Bedding plants of slightly tender nature, such as the bedding geraniums and fuchsias, must either be re-purchased annually, or kept under glass during winter and propagated each season. This means the cost of heating (to exclude frosts), of upkeep of the greenhouse or frames, and possibly cost of hired labour. Spring bulbs to alternate with the summer flowers are also items of considerable expense.

Perennials

Perennial flowers of hardy kinds, such as lupins and delphiniums and irises, are not expensive after the first season, except in the matter of labour. Even that is not a heavy item, as the plants are only lifted for division about once in two years (on an average) and, properly cared for, their lifetime is almost unlimited. Here first cost is not heavy if the owner is not impatient, for the best varieties of many border plants can be raised from seed.

Shrubs—flowering shrubs in particular—are popular as border plants in many gardens. Their first cost is pretty high as compared with the cost of annuals and perennials of herbaceous nature, but as shrubs do not have to be replaced for many years, and even then can easily be replaced by cuttings, the first cost is justified and eventually proves an economy.

Hardy Annuals

Hardy annuals, the kind of flowers you can raise by simply scattering the seed where you want the plants, are the cheapest of all garden plants, and very showy : their fault is that they last only one brief season. But as they can so easily be re-sown each spring, annuals will always commend themselves to the garden maker. Some gardeners prefer to use them in beds by themselves, because of the ease with which the soil can be turned over as each batch of annuals fades. Other gardeners find them useful to fill odd bare or colourless places in the garden.

ROCK AND KITCHEN GARDENS

Rock gardens, like rose gardens, are generally popular. These can be of the " constant expense " type or of the " self-maintenance " type. That is to say, you can make a natural landscape, and plant it with the sort of plants that would be found on it in Nature's garden—ferns in the shady damp gullies, and saxifrages, houseleeks and stonecrops on the sunny dry slopes—and leave it to grow and flourish with no further attention. Or you can build up artificial screes, moraines, trickling streams, and in rock-supported pockets of special soils, plant rare alpines. On such a rock garden you may spend every minute of your time, even though the area of the whole rockery is but a few square yards. Also, you may, if you wish, spend a good deal of money on the valuable but small plants with which such a rock garden can be planted.

The kitchen garden is a feature which must also be looked at from many viewpoints. I do not think that the average small garden owner saves much on the actual cost of his vegetables and fruits by including just a few of each kind in a small corner of his garden. I do think, however, that the crops he raises himself come to the table in a better condition, fresher, and healthier, than any that have been through the turmoil of the modern packing shed and market, and for this reason alone, a kitchen garden is a desirable feature wherever there is any room for it. In any case, the kitchen garden should at least pay for itself, so that this

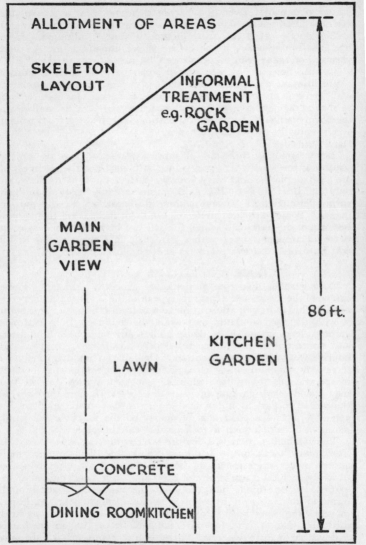

ALLOTMENT OF AREAS

SKELETON
LAYOUT

INFORMAL
TREATMENT
e.g. ROCK
GARDEN

MAIN
GARDEN
VIEW

86 ft.

KITCHEN
GARDEN

LAWN

CONCRETE

DINING ROOM KITCHEN

Fig. 3. How to plan preliminary allotment of areas in a small garden.

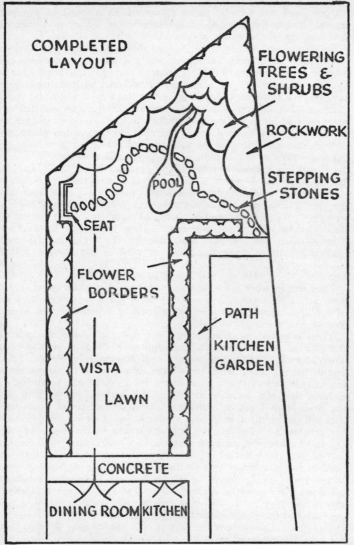

COMPLETED LAYOUT

FLOWERING TREES & SHRUBS

ROCKWORK

POOL

STEPPING STONES

SEAT

FLOWER BORDERS

PATH

KITCHEN GARDEN

VISTA

LAWN

CONCRETE

DINING ROOM KITCHEN

Fig. 4. The completed garden scheme developed from Fig. 3.

feature need not be one to be discarded on account of expense, though it may be thought undesirable where labour is a difficult problem, or where space is limited.

So, having roughly reviewed the possibilities, and decided whether you want a utilitarian garden or one that is merely ornamental; whether you want to finish its construction quickly, regardless of expense, or whether you would prefer to begin with a simple plan and gradually introduce such elaborate features as time and funds permit; whether you want to please the children, or whether you have only an adult family to consider—having settled in your mind these various problems, what is the next step in garden planning?

Well, the best thing to do at this point is to draw a plan of the garden. First a rough plan of the plot as it is when you take it over, with its various knotty problems indicated on the plan. By knotty problems I mean such points as a tree that overshadows some part of the plot, and which you may be able to work into the new garden plan to advantage, or a neighbour's ugly shed or garage that you will need to hide, or your own shed or garage that may be even more obtrusive. Then there may be manhole covers—there usually are, and usually, I think, in the most undesirable place from the point of view of the garden maker.

THE GARDEN'S MAIN FEATURES

Then set to work on a second plan, the plan of the garden that you intend to make. A good way to begin is to write out a list of the desirable features such as a lawn, a vegetable plot, a rock garden and so on.

Then take the most important one first, and select the part of the plot that is best for it, and outline it roughly on the plan. Then the next important feature will be similarly treated. You might, for instance, begin by allocating a part of the site near to the drawing-room doors as a lawn, or, if you want to include a terrace, and can happily introduce this feature, put it first near the door from house to garden. Then, if your heart is set on a rock garden, you might choose a sunny open spot for this—remember that it is useless to try rock gardening in the shade of trees unless you are just making a rock and water semi-wild garden.

You may have to try your various features in several different parts of the plot before you finally fix on the happiest arrangement. When very large grounds are to be laid out it sometimes helps if small plans are made on various coloured scraps of paper, and moved round the plan until the best position for each is decided, but generally in the home garden there is no need to go to this length. (Figs. 3 and 4 show how the layout of a garden may develop from a rough allotment of areas.)

When you have more or less decided on the positions of the

arious sections, think out the question of paths and internal division
edges or screens. It makes a garden more interesting if some
arts of it are not immediately visible, but have to be found by an
xcursion through winding paths, or behind hedges and screens.
t also adds interest if there is more than one walk through a garden,
nd the successful linking of various garden sections is a matter
f real significance. As an outstanding example of this point in
arden design I suggest you try to visualize the well-known sunk
arden at Hampton Court robbed of its iron gateway—the ideal
ntrance to an old-world formal garden.

Even while you draw the plan (if you do draw one, and of course
ou may prefer to keep your ideas in your head for the present)
ou will have to make some decisions regarding boundary hedges
nd internal divisions. Often the gardener begins with these
eatures, and even plants or builds them, before he fully makes
p his mind about other matters.

THE IMPORTANCE OF SCREENING

The chief reasons for the erection of such screens is privacy,
xcept in very windswept open districts where shelter may be even
1ore important. Often the two go together, and a boundary
edge that gives privacy will also serve as a windbreak, but this
; not always the case. A belt of deciduous trees, for instance,
1akes a fine windbreak, but a garden made in the shelter thus
fforded will not necessarily bo screened from view.

Another reason for screen planting is that harmonious back
grounds for the various garden pictures can be provided. A light
trellis, for instance, separating the formal rose garden from an
informal plot of grass and shrubs adds both to the beauty of the
rose plot and that of the lawn. Such a screen set between the
flower border and vegetable patch makes a decorative background
to the flowers, and hides from view the less beautiful vegetables.

It is because division boundaries also form backgrounds, and
because their beauty is important to the garden picture, that every
consideration should be
given to the choice of
suitable material. First
let us review the various
non-living materials of
which such screens can
be made.

First there is wood, in
the form of trellis. Trellis
can be very open, as in
the case of narrow strips
of wood nailed to form

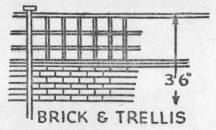

3' 6"

BRICK & TRELLIS

Fig. 5.   A good screening combination.

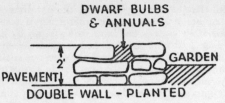

Fig. 6.   *Cross-section of double boundary wall.*

where a close screen is unnecessary, as for example between a orchard and flower garden.   It is also employed on walls, whe the training of climbing plants direct on to the wall is undesirabl Asbestos sheet bungalows can be successfully decorated by th erection of trellis of this kind, over which roses or clematis are traine

The common expanding trellis of diamond pattern, though n in itself so decorative as other kinds, is nevertheless useful in plac where climbers can be allowed almost to smother it.   Anoth popular type of trellis, frequently used for the upper half of fenc between suburban gardens, where a fairly close screen is preferre is made of inch square pieces of oak nailed together to leave thre inch square openings.   Even without the climbers this is a usef screen; stained with creosote, it is immediately unobtrusive, an settles well into the garden picture.

Another type of wood fencing is of closed boards, either set clos together, vertically, in the old fashioned way, or woven baske fashion.   The woven type is available from several firms, usuall in finished sections which can be easily erected by any quit inexperienced worker.   There seems to be nothing with which fault can be found in this type of fencing other than its rathe high initial cost, for its appearance is good, and it stands up to the strongest gales even in exposed seaside districts.

Stone, bricks, and tiles employed in various ways also come into the list of materials suitable for bound- aries.   Stone walls and brick walls are obvious possibilities where cost is no matter, or where these materials are to be ob- tained without difficulty, and a combination of brickwork and trellis, as is seen in Fig. 5, is very substantial, decorative and

The text running alongside the top figure:

foot squares, supporte by stout posts. Th type of open fencir is frequently used f rural gardens, whe the vista through th trellis is worth preser ing. Similar light oa trellis is used to divic parts of the garde

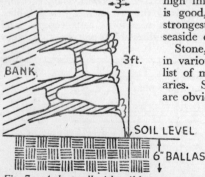

Fig. 7.   *A dry wall with soil between stones.*

fective. A cross-section of a double boundary wall is seen in
g. 6.

Dry walls, that is walls built without cement, are particularly
ecorative, since they are built with soil between the stones, and
is allows for the planting of the wall with suitable rockery plants.
hey are most used where there are different levels in the garden,
parated by a steep bank, and in this form they are called retain-
g walls (*see* diagram in Fig. 7). Retaining walls can, of course,
e made with cement joints, and can be quite formal, and con-
ructed of natural or artificial stone, bricks or tiles, without any
tempt at floral camouflage.

Stones and bricks can also be used in the erection of pergolas and
reens as in Fig. 8.

As a contrast to these various non-living screens and boundaries

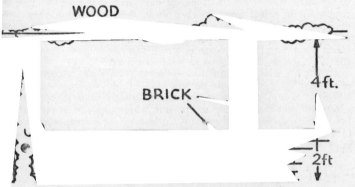

WOOD

BRICK

4 ft.

2 ft.

Fig. 8.   *Stone and brick screen with wood crossbar.*

ere are the ordinary evergreen hedges, screens of mixed hedging
ants, and several different methods of screening by rows of trees
belts of woodland.

The first matter to be considered by the new garden owner is
suitable type of hedge or screen for the outer boundary of the
arden. Naturally this depends a great deal on the size of the
arden and on the type of land that lies immediately beyond the
oundary. The large estate is often quite suitably surrounded by
a simple line of posts with a couple of wires strained to them at
distances of 18 in. and 3 ft. from the ground, or by a line of chestnut
pales. In the small garden, where other small gardens join it on
every side, neither wires nor chestnut paling can be considered
sufficient in themselves, but must be supplemented by a living
hedge. It is possible during the first season to cover a chestnut

paling fence with annual climbers, and it would be possible
continue to do this every subsequent summer, but that method
hardly satisfactory since it leaves the gardens open and the palir
bare during the winter months. An evergreen hedge which ca
be clipped back to a narrow wall of green is probably best in a
such cases.

HEDGES OF EVERGREEN

Privet, the first and most obvious suggestion, has the merit c
being particularly cheap, and it does stand clipping. Also it grow
rapidly. It is, however, for other reasons a poor choice becaus
there are other more decorative shrubs available, and because it
roots are such drastic soil robbers that a privet hedge will ruin al
other plants that are set near it.

Lonicera *nitida*, the small-leaved evergreen honeysuckle, has al
the merits of privet (even its cheapness, since plants cost very littl
and can be increased with extraordinary rapidity), and it does no
rob the soil quite so much. There are, however, a number o
other good evergreens that will grow quickly if well treated, and
that will stand clipping just as well as privet.

Unless the title deeds of the property specify that a certain type
of fencing or hedge is to be maintained, an evergreen hedge is
sufficient boundary without chestnut pales. If it is to be planted
where no non-living fence exists, but where the site is exposed to
keen winds, it would be well to use hurdles or a temporary screen
of some kind until the hedge is established. This would make a
considerable difference to the rate of growth.

COLOUR IN THE HEDGE

The alternative types of boundary hedges might be given more
consideration in new gardens if only because the trim clipped
evergreen wall is apt to become monotonous. A hedge of mixed
evergreens and deciduous shrubs, such as the one in Fig. 9, specially
if there are a good number of showy flowering shrubs among them,
makes a very attractive picture. Such a hedge can include ordinary
evergreens, and also some of the golden or silver foliaged varieties,
shrubs with purple or red foliage or with foliage that changes to
these tints in autumn, plants that flower in spring, summer, autumn
and winter, and plants that have decorative berries, or brilliant
winter bark.

From these few suggestions it will be seen that a hedge of mixed
shrubs could, in itself, have as much variety and as much beauty
as a mixed flower border, and in fact that is the position exactly.
A mixed hedge surrounding a well-kept lawn is sufficient to complete the layout of a front garden, and where labour is a serious
problem this helps to solve it in more than one sense. Mixed

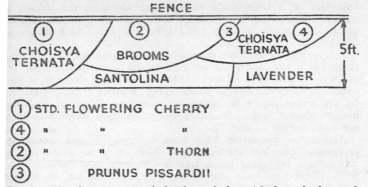

Fig. 9. *Mixed evergreen and deciduous hedge with fence background.*

shrubs need very little attention, whereas a clipped hedge needs attention almost weekly in the growing season.

When planning a mixed hedge it should of course be remembered that some plants are better suited to special soils than others. Rhododendrons, for instance, make an excellent and very decorative thick screen, and form a good boundary hedge. It is useless, however, to plant them where there is chalk in the subsoil.

A flowering hedge made of any one kind of shrub is a very good type of hedge for the not-too-formal garden. Berberis *stenophylla*, the narrow leaved evergreen barberry, is possibly the best of all plants for this type. It is thick and impenetrable, spiny enough to keep out dogs and prevent much wanton damage. Its arching stems are quite attractive all the year round and really spectacular in their beauty during April, when they are covered from end to end with small golden blossoms.

Since the planting of a boundary hedge is likely to be the very first garden operation carried out by a new owner, it shall be described here in detail.

THE SPACING OF SHRUBS

A decision as to the number of plants needed must first be made. If a neat formal hedge of clipped evergreens, thick from base to top, is wanted with all possible speed it is wise to be generous with the order, and to allow for a double row of plants, staggered, that is set in this fashion . ·. ·. ·. ·., as seen in Fig. 10. A double row is also advisable if such hedges as thorn, beech, hornbeam and cherry plum are planted. These hedges are exceedingly useful though they are not evergreen, for the thick mat of stems makes a good windbreak. As a rule, however, their place is along the boundary of a large estate rather than alongside the suburban garden. For a double row hedge the plants are generally spaced about 2 ft. apart in each row, 1 ft. if a very thick hedge is required.

When planting the more expensive type of shrub, such as berberis *stenophylla*, fewer plants can be used to the yard, in fact from 18 to 24 in. is generally allowed. This brings down the cost of the seemingly expensive hedges considerably, a point to be considered by the owner before he makes his decision. Diagrams showing how to plant a simple boundary hedge and also screen plantings are seen in Figs. 11 and 12.

As soon as the shrubs have been ordered, the site should be prepared. The best method on a fairly open boundary site is this. Begin by taking out a trench 1 ft. deep, and perhaps 2 ft. wide, where the shrubs are to be set. Turn the soil on to the garden side of the trench.

Get into the trench, and take out another foot of the soil, throwing this layer over on to the outer, boundary side. Pile this neatly,

SPACING FOR A LONICERA HEDGE

Fig. 10.   *This hedge is best planted in two rows in echelon.   Twelve inches between each shrub in one line and a total of eight shrubs to the yard, taking both lines is a good spacing.*

for it will remain where it is placed without further disturbance.

Break up the lowest layer of exposed soil, using a strong digging fork. Any small weeds, lumps of turf, leaves, rough stones and so on can be thrown into the trench as you break up the subsoil.

If you are not planting lime haters, dust hydrated lime along the soil that was taken from the trench first, using about four ounces to a yard. Naturally, if the subsoil is of chalk, and some of this has been brought to the surface during digging, the lime will not be needed, but on most soils there is no lime left in the top layer. Now return this top soil to the trench, and it will probably be found that it nearly fills it, owing to the increased space that broken soil takes as compared with that which has consolidated. In any case there will be left a shallow trench, filled with good top soil, protected on the outer side of the boundary by a ridge of subsoil.

Use a measuring stick to space the hedge plants evenly, i.e., a stick measuring exactly the space that you intend to leave between

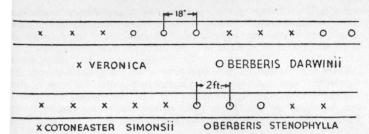

Fig. 11. *A boundary hedge of mixed shrubs showing correct spacing.*

the plants. Set out the small plants firmly in the prepared shallow trench, pressing soil well round and among their roots. Small plants are best. It is quite a false idea that tall hedge plants are worth buying. Though bushy plants in pots might perhaps establish themselves quickly and without losses, large plants of privet, lonicera or escallonia generally take so long to get established that parts of the tops die back. The result is a ragged hedge which can only be thickened and improved by drastic pruning. Even then the older plants have not quite the vigour of young specimens, so that in a few years a hedge planted at the height of 9 or 12 in. will far surpass one planted at the same time with specimens of 2 or 3 ft. high.

Firm planting has already been mentioned; it is most important, for loose planting is by far the commonest cause of failure among new gardeners. The shrubs should be set in a prepared hole and the roots spread out as much as possible. Then fine soil should be worked in among the roots, and over them, and *trodden* firm before the final top layer of soil is added. Plants treated in this way will more readily begin to grow, because their roots will be in actual contact with damp soil.

In a garden where something more than a hedge is required as a boundary screen, a line of formal trees, such as a line of conifers, or an informal belt of mixed trees and shrubs may be considered. On a very exposed site, such as on a seaside cliff, it would be best to plant a hedge in the manner already described

Fig. 12. *A screen for kitchen garden mingling beauty and effectiveness.*

—preferably a hedge of some quite hardy nature, such as sea buck-thorn, or tamarisk (which revels in sea breezes). This on the extreme outer boundary would sufficiently break the force of the gales so as to afford protection to such trees as might be chosen for the shelter belt.

Trees are planted in the same way as fruit trees or ornamental shrubs, that is in soil that has been dug to a depth of 2 ft. or more, keeping the top layer of soil at the top, but turning this layer over, and breaking up the lower soil well so as to encourage good drainage which is essential for tree cultivation.

TREES FOR SCREENING

It is not possible here to name all the various trees available for the purpose, nor to give full details of the amount of space they require. A good tip for an amateur to follow is this. Send for a shrub and tree catalogue from a specialist, and make your selections according to the descriptions (generally full and com-plete) in the catalogue. Then make a rough plan of your proposed plantings, and send it with your order to the nurseryman, and ask his advice. He will gladly tell you if you have not allowed enough room for the ultimate spread of the trees, or if there are other and better subjects for your purpose. It is wise to tell him a little of the soil and aspect of the garden when you inquire.

To make a satisfactory windscreen of hedging plants and trees, a strip of land at least 15 ft. should be allowed on the plan—more if it can be spared. A small garden plot could not well spare so much, but then a very small garden generally needs nothing more than a simple hedge which would occupy roughly about a yard strip and give adequate shelter to the other plants.

INSIDE HEDGES

Internal division hedges in a garden are sometimes desirable for the purpose of outlining the sections without completely screen-ing them. A hedge of lavender round a sunk garden serves as a frame to this feature, and gives a feeling of privacy without inter-fering with the view across it. A low hedge sometimes takes the place of a stone or wooden balustrade along the terrace wall, or one may be used to separate the entrance path from the lawn so that visitors (specially errand boys) are not encouraged to wear a track across the grass.

These low hedges vary in type just as do the taller ones. They can be quite informal, as when lavender is used and allowed to flower freely, or they can be strictly formal, as for instance a hedge of clipped box. Lavender, rosemary, dwarf polyantha roses, veronicas of several species, and ericas, also of several species, are useful subjects for this type of hedge. The plants should be small

when set out—generally about 9 in. high—and should be no more
than 1 ft. apart for the best results.

Pruning of different shrubs will be dealt with in a later chapter,
but as this affects the choice of hedging plants, a word or two
here must be included. The trim formal type of hedge requires
clipping frequently all through the spring, summer and early
autumn. It is a mistake to clip hedges too late in the season.
Sometimes it is actually harmful to the plants, sometimes it leaves
them with bare cut stems showing all winter, and either way it is
unsatisfactory. Cypress hedges, which can be extremely useful,
since they reach a sufficient height to give real privacy, are particularly susceptible to late pruning, and no cutting back should
be done later than August.

Flowering hedges, as a rule, need one or at most two prunings
annually—to prune more often would mean the loss of a season's
flowers. Flowering and fruiting (i.e., berrying) hedges rarely need
much regular pruning at all, and certainly do not need the secateurs
more than once during the year. It is obvious that flowering and
berrying hedge subjects are labour saving as well as more decorative
than strictly formal hedges.

One other point that concerns choice of hedging, and also
pruning. If a quick growing subject is chosen, it will want more
pruning than if a slow grower is planted, for obvious reasons.

WHEN SHOULD YOU PLANT?

The new gardener generally asks for one more item of information
concerning hedges—when is the best time to plant? As a rough
guide, September, April and May are good months for planting
evergreens, and the winter months between them for planting
deciduous shrubs. But hedging plants are generally pretty hardy,
and often can be purchased in pots. Also, as they are only small
when planted, they can be kept moist overhead by the use of a
hose or watering can. Therefore it is quite possible, if care is taken,
to plant a hedge at almost any season except high summer, with
reasonable prospect of success, and the garden maker is well advised
to get to work on boundary hedges, at least, as his first job on the
plot.

Main paths and entrance drives are usually considered early,
and in fact are often constructed by the builders. They make a
great difference to the garden plan, and for this reason the owner
who finds he has everything to do in this respect himself may smile
at his good fortune. Builders have seldom much respect for garden
design, and in laying down a path or drive their first consideration
is to make it as direct and convenient as possible with the least
possible outlay on material and labour. The result is that most
of the house entrances they construct are monotonously uniform.

Of course, if a gardener has a house built to order, he is able from the first to choose a position on the plot that will allow for convenience and privacy where desirable. If the house is already built his choice is limited, but it may still be possible to give a measure of privacy to the house windows by curving a path to the door. A curved path is often very useful in creating a semi-formal garden style that is suited to certain house types.

Most gardens have their own special problems, and it is idle to talk of " best " types of entrance or other paths. These, however, are the items that should be kept in mind in this connection :—

ESSENTIALS FOR ENTRANCE PATHS

1. No entrance path should wind so much that it becomes tortuous.

2. A path for pedestrians should be at least 4 ft. wide, and for a car 8 or 9 ft. wide.

3. All curves should be gradual—in the case of a long drive one or two very gradual curves allow for changes in the picture, but sudden curves are disconcerting.

4. The materials used in construction should be in keeping with the style of the house and that of the intended garden.

5. On entrance paths, particularly, no untidiness is permissible : the materials should be such as can be kept in perfect condition by the owner, according to the labour available.

6. In any type of garden, paths should be varied according to the amount of use they will receive. A path through the vegetable garden might be just a rolled soil track, while that from door to front gate should be finished with some clean, lasting surface material, such as tiles, paving stones or bricks.

CHOICE OF MATERIALS

The types of path, that is the materials employed in surfacing, can be selected from a very wide range. They include the well-known gravel path, which if properly constructed and finished with bitumen to divert rain, is quite satisfactory for walking or as a car drive; paving stones in variety, rectangular or crazy, real stone or artificial, plain or multi-coloured; cobbles laid to set patterns; tiles, bricks, grass and combinations of all these so arranged as to form decorative features in themselves. Figs. 13-16 show various types of paths.

Stepping stones let into the lawn surface take the place of the conventional path when convenient : they are ideal in the labour-saving garden, as they have no edgings to keep trim, and cannot become weedy. Coloured paths, which are popular in dull town gardens and can also find a place in certain types of formal garden, can be made of multi-coloured artificial stone or of gravel, tarred and then surfaced with various materials, grey, green, red, white, gravel-brown and so on.

Path construction is really a simple matter, but the utmost care must be taken over it, otherwise the path will be faulty, that is it will sink in places and leave an uneven surface, so that water will collect in rainy weather, and this will gradually add to the uneven settling. All paths, whether small or large (except the simple stepping-stone type) are made on the same principle, and the early stages of the work are the same.

The first thing to do is to excavate where the path is to be, taking off the top 10 in. or so of soil, and moving it to some other part of the garden. It is not exactly wise, especially when the garden is on rather dry gravel or chalk subsoil, to make up the flower beds alongside the path with this soil. That is to say, the beds should not generally be at a higher surface level than the path, otherwise they dry out too rapidly in the summer. Soil taken from the path sites can generally be put to good use in the potting shed, or greenhouse and frames, or used to build up a rock garden. Naturally, if the garden site is very wet, and raised beds are desired for that reason, the soil from the paths would be thrown at once on to the borders.

RANDOM & CRAZY PAVING

Fig. 13.

When about 10 in. of soil has been taken away, the site of the path should be tested for its levelness. The gardener should also note whether rains collect and remain stationary on the site. If they do, extra care must be given to drainage. If not, the path can be made without further digging. A slight slope from one end to the other is permissible, but if there is a very steep slope the possibility of introducing one or two steps should be considered.

DRAINAGE AND FOUNDATIONS

With regard to drainage, a simple agricultural drainpipe laid down the centre of the path or drive, and packed round with a hard core of open material—clinker for instance—so that it takes the surplus water, is sufficient even on a waterlogged site, but it must be remembered that if much water has to be carried away the pipe must have an outlet either to a sump or to a ditch or main drain. In laying this pipe a trench should be cut specially for it down the path centre, rather deeper than is needed to take the pipe, so that after it is laid, and covered with clinker, the path can be constructed in the usual way.

The method of construction is to lay first the roughest hard core available. Old tins beaten flat so that there is no further subsidence, flints, broken bricks and rough breeze blocks are good materials for this layer. They should be distributed evenly, and then rolled well, preferably during showery weather. A slight camber of an inch or two should be aimed at, so that the centre of the path dries quickly after rain.

This foundation is desirable whatever the path surface. After a satisfactory underlayer has been prepared a dressing of rather finer porous material is required. Where paving stone is to be laid, this layer can be of fine sifted ash, or sand, or very sandy soil. Paving, if of natural stone, is generally somewhat uneven in thickness, and a certain amount of packing below the thinner stones is required, so that the surface is dead level.

GETTING AN EVEN SURFACE

A good method with an ordinary 4-ft. garden path is to fix, temporarily, some edging boards between the path and border soil. The top edge of the boards should be dead level for a level path, and sloping gently for a sloping path, but the two opposite boards should always be level with each other, i.e., the path should not slope from side to side. A spirit-level, which can be bought for a few pence, is desirable to test the levels.

By laying a strip of quartering across from side to side, and moving it gradually down as the paving is laid, an even surface can be secured without much trouble. Gaps between the stones should not be more than 1 in. wide. There is really no need for any camber on a crazy paved path where the cracks are filled with sandy soil, and plants are grown, but if cement is used in the cracks, a camber is important. There are arguments for and against the use of cement. A cement-filled area of crazy paving is durable, and keeps its even surface, but where sandy soil is packed between the stones instead, and plants are set in the cracks, a less severe picture is created, and the opportunity is given to the gardener to grow many plants which are particularly at home in this situation. Plants are, however, growing things, and when they are allowed to grow so rampantly that they become large mounds, they make a pathway that is neither clean nor safe. This is an easily avoidable trouble. The plants can be set mainly in the cracks to the sides of the path, not in the centre where most of the walking is done. Also with a little attention occasionally, the plants will never get to the rampant, nuisance stage. A crazy paving design is seen in Fig. 13.

Some gardeners solve the problem by the use of cement between cracks in the middle of the path and soil and plants at the edges. A better plan is to use only the most dwarf of paving plants, such as arenaria *balearica*, cotulas and mentha *requieni*, which are unlikely to become troublesome.

Any plants to be used in making a crazy paving path can be set in place as the stones are laid. Or, if this cannot well be done, seeds may be used instead of plants. The succulent leaved annual mesembryanthemum *crineflorum*, perennial rock pinks, cotulas and thymes are paving plants that can easily be introduced as seed. This should be mixed with some sandy soil, pressed well into the cracks, and left to its own devices.

Rectangular paving stones are laid like crazy paving. They take a little less time to lay than crazy paving, but it is perhaps even more important that rectangular paving should have a perfectly level surface. These larger paving stones are frequently associated with other materials. For instance, rectangular paving stones are often laid alternately lengthways and crossways down a long path, with grass or cobblestones to fill the remaining areas (Fig. 14). If grass is used, the paving should be laid over fine cinders or ash, and turf can be laid over the same material. Where turf is not available, and seed

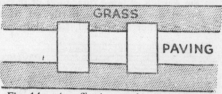

Fig. 14. *An effective combination of paving and grass useful in path making.*

must be used, prepared soil would be packed into position and levelled, and sown as for a lawn.

Cobblestones are laid into wet cement—not too wet, or it will be difficult to produce an even surface. The cobbles should be quite close to each other, and only enough cement used to fill the cracks between and come half-way up the sides of each cobblestone. Cement should not be smoothed off level with the tops of the cobbles, as is done by some amateur gardeners, as this spoils the beauty of this type of paving. Cobbles are decorative, rather than useful, being uncomfortable for walking.

Bricks used for paving should be rough surfaced. If they are not, the path becomes dangerous for walking. They are best laid on edge over a layer of sand, and the path maker should endeavour to pack the under layer very firm before laying the bricks. More sand should be used between the bricks if necessary, but the closer the bricks, the better the path. Cement can be used both under and between the bricks, but sand is better, as it allows for free drainage.

Bricks can be set in any sort of pattern, and if they are of a

good quality, sand faced, and not inclined to crumble wh
weathering, the path will improve in appearance as the years pa
They can be combined with paving, as in Fig. 15. Crumbli
bricks should never be used for paths.

Tiles are extremely decorative and neat, and for formal pat
near the house they are often chosen. They have the disadvanta
of being slippery, especially in wet weather. They are also ve
difficult to lay, since the surface must be absolutely true. Til
are, of course, set in cement.

Concrete paths at one time would have been dismisse
unreservedly by the garden artist as unworthy of consideratio
Today many delightful concrete paths exist to give the lie to th
belief. A good way to use concrete for paths is to set up
shuttering of boards on each side of a path site, and to lay
smooth run of concrete about 2 in. thick between them. The si
chosen need not be that of the actual path, and the concrete ca
be mixed and laid over and over again in the same odd corne
of the garden, if large quantities of paving have to be done.

When the concrete is partly set, it will be cut across with
spade or other sharp tool, into slabs of even size, or broken int

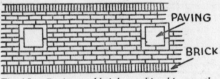

Fig. 15.   *Paving and brick combined in a path.*

pieces for use as craz
paving. In either cas
it must be left to dr
out completely befor
being moved. Then th
slabs are laid as alread
described for pavin
stone. It is possible t
use colouring material
in mixing the concrete, so that a very natural appearance can b
given to a concrete path where desired. A point worth notice i
that very smooth concrete is slippery, and the surface is best
roughened in some way. Watering with a rose-can while the
concrete is still wet is one way to make a non-slip surface.

The advantage of this way of making concrete paths over the
old, unsatisfactory way of pouring the concrete direct on to the
path site, is that planting can be done in the cracks, and this
does much to soften the artificial appearance of concrete.

THE MERITS OF GRAVEL

Gravel paths are not only simple and comparatively cheap to
construct, they are definitely attractive. In some kinds of garden
design they are even preferable to paving. Soundly constructed,
of good quality gravel, and finished with a waterproof surface, they
last for years in good weed-free condition.

Good gravel is a self-binding material. Watered and rolled

lternately as it is laid, it makes a really serviceable path or drive.
ix inches of rough clinker or bricks as already described for path
undation, with 4 in. of coarse gravel and a surface 2 in. of finer
ravel, is the ideal. Just before the final surfacing is given, a dress-
g of hot tar, or one of the tar preparations now on the market
hich are applied cold, should be given to the gravel, and this
n then be top dressed with pea gravel, to restore the colour of
e path. If preferred, white or grey stone chippings, or any of
e available coloured
p dressings (sold by
e makers of the cold
r preparations) can
e used. Grass paths,
metimes edged with
aving, are frequently
und in gardens
'ig. 16).

After you have
cided what sort of
aths you want and
here you want them,
u can begin pegging
em out. Then start
aking them. If

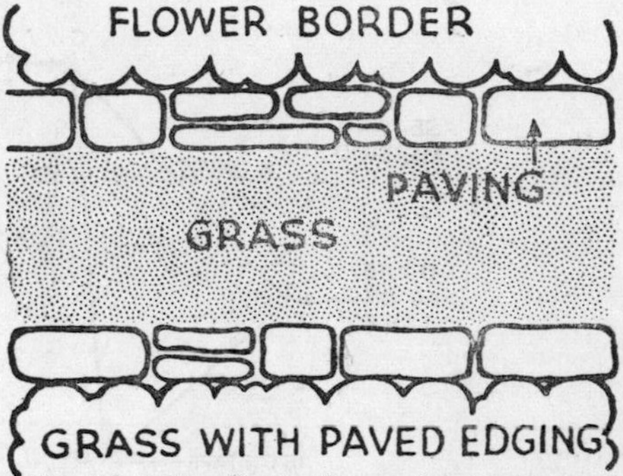

Fig. 16.   An effective layout for a grass path.

cessary, a path edging of non-living character will be set in position,
it the use of such edgings is not nearly so common as once it was. In
ct they are rarely used except in cases where gravel paths adjoin
orders.

When grass meets border, either the turf is cut and trimmed
egularly to keep a straight edge (in which case there must be a
lrop of 2 in. from turf to border surface) or small pieces of paving
tone are used to outline the turf, laid flush with the grass, so that
he mower passes over them and there is no need for constant edge
trimming. If a non-living edging is desired, bricks laid end to
end, 2 in. above the level of the path, are as good as anything.
They should be bound together with cement, for greater security.
Plants can, if desired, be allowed to creep a little over the bricks,
and so soften their hard outline. Now you will be in a position
to peg out lawn areas, and to mark the position of formal beds.
Lawn areas are not necessarily subjected to such deep digging as
are the sites for beds and borders, so that it is very useful to have
them clearly marked out, if not prepared, at an early stage so that
deep digging does not take place over their sites.

After this, procedure will vary. If terraces, sunk gardens, and
other features entailing the removal of large quantities of soil are
contemplated, these must be dealt with as soon as possible, but

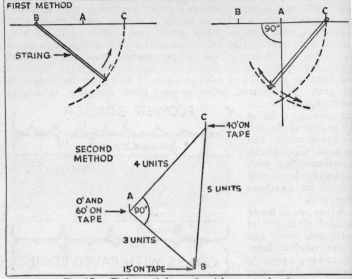

Fig. 17. *Fixing a right angle with pegs and string.*

of course, if levels are already roughly what they are required to be in the finished design, the question of precedence becomes unimportant. All such features as steps, terraces, pergolas, pools and fountains should, however, be carefully thought over, together with their effect on other parts of the plot, so that there need be no unnecessary labour.

What tools are necessary to begin with in the new, empty garden plot? On any new plot the tools that an experienced worker would take with him would be these :—

A measuring tape, some pegs, a mallet, a garden line, a spade and a large digging fork. Other tools might be desirable, but one could get along pretty well for a time with just these.

HINTS FOR THE BEGINNER

Now for a few hints that may be of use to the beginner. One of the things you will certainly want to do almost at once will be to set out a right angle. It sounds quite simple to peg out a path at right angles to the house, but on an irregular plot it may not prove so easy as it sounds. Fig. 17 illustrates two simple solutions. The first is as follows : Suppose you have a straight line, and at a given point (call it A) you want to erect another line at right angles. Measure an equal distance both ways, say a yard each way, and call these points on your original line B and C. Now drive in a wooden peg at B, and round this loop a piece of string just long enough to reach, double, to point C. Drive another peg in at point C. Use the string to describe an arc, first with C as the radius point and then with B. Where these two arcs meet will be a point on a line at right angles to A.

The second method is that known as the 3-4-5. If a path is to be made at right angles to the house, let us call the house the " straight line." At the point A on the straight line where the right angle is required, hammer in a thin peg. Place the metal loop that is at the beginning of the tape over this and measure 15 ft. along the straight line. Call this B. Hammer in another peg at this point and pass the tape round it. Taking the 60-ft. mark on the tape hold it at A. Then get a second person to hold the 40-ft. mark and pull the tape taut, so that it forms a triangle. Hammer in a peg C at this point. A-C is the required line at right angles to A-B. Any triangle whose sides are in the proportion 3 : 4 : 5 must be a right-angled triangle.

SHAPES FOR FLOWER-BEDS

With these same tools a variety of geometrical shapes can be drawn for the outlines of beds, fountains, etc. A circle is easy enough, and a square almost as simple, if care is taken over the right angles. An oval is made by driving in two pegs (*see* Fig. 18) along the middle line of the required oval, and throwing a loose circle of string over them : then with a third peg the line is drawn taut in all directions, thus forming the oval outline. Other geometrical forms are mostly variations of these, used in various different associations, so that a rectangular flower-bed may have semi-circular ends, or an eight-pointed star can be made from two squares, superimposed on each other at different angles.

Where a straight line is required, a line of string can be stretched between two pegs as a guide to the worker.

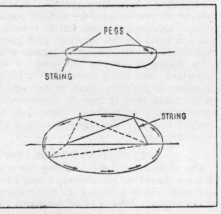

Fig. 18. *Constructing an oval. String looped round two pegs is drawn taut by another peg.*

Where the outline is curved, it must be marked with chalk or cu
with a spade as the pegs are moved round.

It is just as vital to determine levels at an early stage as to draw
the outline of beds and paths. As will be explained in Chapter II,
an important thing for a garden maker to know is that the top
spit (i.e., depth of the spade blade, or approximately 10 in.) of
soil is the most fertile, the underneath layers being either wholly
or partly infertile. Since most plant roots are found in the top
spit, it is obviously important that this fertile layer of soil shall be
kept in its position at the surface. Under cultivation it is turned
over and broken and mixed with manures and fertilizers, but it
is never buried under a layer of the subsoil, for if this were done
plants would not thrive in it.

THE TOP LAYER OF SOIL

It needs only a few minutes of reflection to realize that serious
harm can be done by moving soil from one place to another, unless
the work is done in such a way that the fertile top layer is still
available. If a sunk garden is contemplated, for instance, the
top layer of fertile soil must first be stripped off, and set aside for
future use, while the contours of the sunk portion are fashioned,
then it can be replaced as a top layer to receive grass or plants
as desired. Similarly, if much levelling has to be done to make
a lawn, the top soil should first be removed and kept on one side,
to be replaced after the subsoil has been levelled satisfactorily.

All this stripping and replacing of soil means a great deal of
labour over the initial stages of the layout, but it is worth while
to take all precautions, for though subsoil will, if brought to the
surface, gradually become fertile, it may take half a dozen or even
a dozen years for this to occur, and inevitably it will mean greater
expenditure on manures and labour during that period.

In certain cases the stripping of the top soil becomes less
important, one being when turf is to be laid on a levelled site.
Levelling is generally done, in the small garden, where a lawn is
to be made, but it may be necessary to level portions to form
terraces on a steep slope. Should it be intended to pave these
levelled surfaces, the position of top soil and subsoil are of no
importance.

ESSENTIAL TOOLS FOR LEVELLING

The tools needed for levelling are a straight-edge, i.e., a piece
of stout board or quartering, a spirit-level, pegs, spade and fork,
and rake. It is a great help if the spirit-level is first tied securely
to the straight-edge, so that both can be quickly moved from peg
to peg together. A further aid is to dip the top 6 in. of each
wooden peg (a pointed piece of wood 12 or 16 in. long that can be

easily driven into the ground) into white paint, so that it can be seen quickly from a distance. More elaborate instruments are used when large areas are to be levelled, but these simple items are quite sufficient for the average garden.

When the top soil has been stripped off (if this is thought necessary) and the uneven subsoil is to be levelled, the first thing to do is to determine roughly what parts of the plot are too high, and about how much of the soil must be moved from them to the lowest parts. As soil seems to multiply itself rapidly when it is loosened by the spade, it is as well to have a clear idea on this point before you begin.

Take first the procedure on a plot that slopes gently and fairly evenly from end to end. Drive in one of the wooden pegs at the highest point of the plot first, knocking it in right to the bottom of the 6-in. white top. Then drive in a second peg, as far down the plot as you can, but not farther than the straight-edge will reach, so that you can rest this on the tops of the two pegs. Drive in this second peg until the bubble of the spirit-level shows that the straight-edge is in a dead horizontal line. Drive in a third peg, still farther down the plot, and move the straight-edge to rest on pegs numbered two and three, again leaving the tops of the pegs dead level. Continue this all down the plot, if possible, so that you have a series of pegs, each standing a little farther out of the soil than its predecessor.

PEGGING ON AN EVEN SLOPE

If the slope is even, the middle peg or pegs will indicate the level that you must work to all over the plot, to secure an even surface. You can therefore note how far the middle peg stands from the soil, and knowing this you can proceed to move soil from the higher parts to the lower parts. Should you have to use a barrow for the purpose, which is probable, remember that a few planks laid down to take the weight of the barrow will not only save you trouble in wheeling, but may also prevent the trouble which would occur from uneven sinking of the soil after it has been rained on.

It does not pay the garden maker to hurry unduly over these tasks, for soil must be allowed to settle fairly well before the surface turf or paving is laid, otherwise there will almost inevitably be trouble later. In fact it is wise to level the subsoil in early winter, and then to leave it for a month or two before attempting to finish the work.

Although the description above concerns only an even slope, the procedure with a very uneven strip of land is much the same. Pegs are used to determine where soil is needed and where it can be spared, and by the exercise of some judgment any work of

levelling that falls to the lot of the average garden maker should
be carried through without trouble.

It is worth noting here, though further reference will be made
to this point in the chapter on lawns, that where soil is excavated
from a sloping bank to form a level lawn or terrace, there is always
a tendency for the end of the lawn where the excavations have
taken place to be wetter than the remainder, since this part receives
surplus water from the soil bank above. If the bank is supported
by a retaining wall, and this in turn is planted with rock plants,
there will be little trouble from surplus water, which will be claimed
by these wall plants. If, however, the bank is left as a sloping
bank of turf, it may be advisable to pay special attention to the
drainage of the part at the foot of the slope. When a high terrace
is left to overlook a flat lawn, and a great deal of excavation has
been done, it is sometimes found possible to include a wall fountain
in the design, with a formal pool below, and surplus moisture can
then be drained into the pool.

STEPS IN GARDEN DESIGN

Steps, sometimes a necessity in garden design, are also often
introduced deliberately in order to create interest in an otherwise
flat picture. I have seen even a little garden acquire character
in this way. I have in mind a garden where the entrance from
the french windows was by way of a small paved area, and a
narrow path between two rocky banks. The owner excavated the
area of the path to a depth of 10 in., and made two steps down
at one side and two up at the other side—this necessitating only
a little rebuilding of the rocky banks, and the relaying of the paved
pathway. The charm of the design was enormously increased,
partly because of the steps themselves, which were well-propor-
tioned and therefore picturesque, but also because the lower level
gave the visitor a more intimate acquaintance with the rock plants
on each side.

HOW STEPS ARE CONSTRUCTED

Step construction is not difficult, and steps can be of so many
different types that they can easily fit into any style of garden
design. The simplest of all the kinds of step that one encounters
is in a woodland walk, where the difference in levels is accentuated
here and there by a log pegged into position across the path. This
type of step can well be introduced where a shrubbery is planted
on a sloping site.

If a really formal step or steps are wanted, you should remember
the following points.

Risers (i.e., the back of the step, or height of each step above
the next) should not be more than 6 in., and the treads should

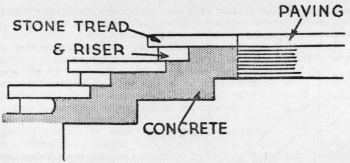

Fig. 19. *Step construction. The tread overhangs the riser. A good height for the latter would be about 6 in.*

be at least 12 in. wide. The wider the step, and the shallower the risers, within reason, the more dignified the steps appear. A good proportion is a 5-in. riser with 14-in. treads.

For formal steps every tread must be dead level, and should preferably have a formal balustrade, the severity of which can be relieved by stone figures, or plant tubs. If the tread overhangs the riser an inch or two the effect is good, whether the steps are formal or informal. The treads and risers can be made directly where they are to remain, of cement, or they can be pieced together from natural or artificial stone.

Very decorative steps of circular or semicircular type can be built of stone or cement, or even more easily by careful arrangement of bricks, which should be set into cement for security.

It is not necessary to excavate deeply in making the foundations for steps. The soil is roughly fashioned first to the required contours, and some attention should be given to drainage at the foot of the steps, since heavy rains will run there, and if allowed to collect they might easily cause a subsidence that would undermine the steps. The insertion of a quantity of hard core under the top spit of soil is probably sufficient in the little garden.

If the risers are stone slabs set nearly vertical (they should always slope up at the back just a little), great care must be taken to see that they are secure. Cement joints would be wise in such a case. The easiest and most decorative kind of steps for the amateur gardener to build himself would be made of a number of stone slabs set horizontally and partly overlapping, penetrating the soil bank, and packed with soil wherever there are crevices. These crevices can be set with small rock plants of the kind used for retaining walls and crazy paving, and the result is delightful. There is no need for an elaborate finish to the sides of such steps, for the soil bank can be planted with such plants as catmint, periwinkle, ivy, pinks or ferns (according to aspect), and these will bind the soil and also create an informal balustrade.

Just one other point. Not more than ten steps should ever be built without a landing. It really pays the garden maker to provide a landing, and if possible a bend in the stairway after six steps. In fact by such introductions, by the curving of the lowest steps, or by twisting the stairway to lead to an unexpected corner,

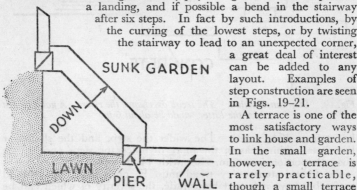

Fig. 20. Steps from lawn to sunk garden. At a corner in the angle of two balustrades, they give a good perspective.

a great deal of interest can be added to any layout. Examples of step construction are seen in Figs. 19–21.

A terrace is one of the most satisfactory ways to link house and garden. In the small garden, however, a terrace is rarely practicable, though a small terrace may sometimes be suitable if there is a big drop in level from front to back of the house. Another position for a terrace in the small garden is the artificial one produced by the excavation of the main portion as a sunk garden, with terraces at each end formed from the excavated soil. In certain cases too a portion of the garden near the house is treated terrace fashion, though no actual difference in levels exists. The paved or grassed area by the house is partially enclosed by a low hedge or balustrade of stone or low brick wall, leaving one or more openings on to the main garden. Such a terrace is illustrated in Fig. 22.

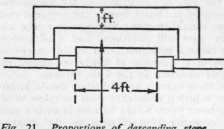

Fig. 21. Proportions of descending steps.

When a terrace proper is to be included in the design there are several items of importance to consider. First the proportion between width and length, and between house and terrace should be good. Usually from 10 to 20 ft. width is desirable. This elevated strip of soil must be dead level, rather formal in character, surrounded by some form of balustrade, living or non-living according to taste, and more or less linked with the house by a wise choice of material, colour and so on.

A terrace is designed primarily for residents in the house to walk there either in the day-time or night-time, in order to see the garden and possibly the view beyond, but without actually descending to walk over damp grass. The terrace therefore should be paved, or gravelled, or in some way surfaced so that it will be dry in most weathers. A part of the terrace can be roofed, but this is not essential. It must in any case be open to the winds—if it is furnished with glass windows it becomes a garden room or loggia, not a terrace.

With these facts in mind it will be seen that the treatment of the terrace must be on formal lines, an example of which is seen in Fig. 23, with paving or gravel, and that any flowers introduced should be in small formal beds, or in stone vases or tubs, or other formal containers. A

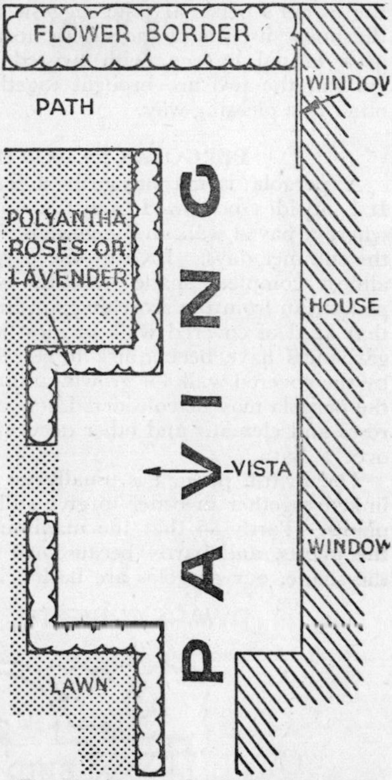

Fig. 22. *Terrace level with the garden.*

terrace can be supported by any kind of retaining wall, formal or informal according to the style of the garden—the wall itself is not seen until one reaches the garden. Stone piers, a pergola running the length of the terrace, fountains proportionate to the size of the terrace and garden—all these are features which can be introduced occasionally, but it is advisable to avoid overcrowding the terrace.

In construction these terrace features are in no way different from such features in other parts of the garden, and need not be elaborated here. The garden maker should merely bear in mind that the terrace is the link between house and garden, and that nothing should be allowed on the terrace that will create a feeling of disharmony. As a matter of fact harmony is frequently created in a difficult garden by the terrace treatment, as for example, where the owner's personal taste suggests an informal rock garden, while the house itself is of the strictly formal type. By the introduction of a formal terrace, with twisted stairways leading to the rock garden, the two are brought together and harmonized with each other in a pleasing way.

PERGOLAS IN NORTHERN CLIMATES

A pergola is not primarily a feature of British garden design. It is an idea borrowed from the sunny countries of South Europe, where a paved walk in the garden would be unbearably hot during the summer days. In Italy the pergola would be intended to give almost complete shade over the walk, in order to shelter the pedestrian from the scorching sunshine. We certainly do not want that kind of covered walk in most summers. Nevertheless, British gardeners have been quick to seize on the opportunities afforded by the covered walk for growing numerous climbers. Consequently the pergola may be considered here as chiefly a support for climbing roses and clematis and other decorative plants, and not as a screen over a path.

The British pergola is usually an affair of widely spaced arches, linked together in order to give still more support to the climbing plants. Partly so that the maximum of light and air may reach the plants, and partly because we need the sunshine rather than the shade, our pergolas are built with uprights not closer together

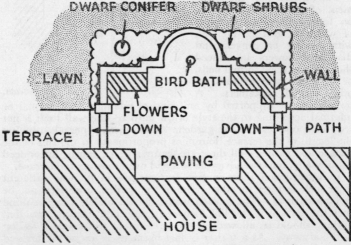

Fig. 23. *Small formal terrace, raised from the garden.*

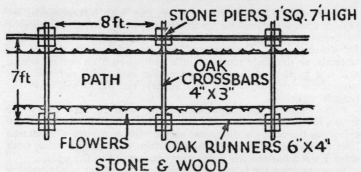

Fig. 24. *Suggested measurements for stone and wood pergola.*

than 8 ft. Quite a good proportion is a pergola built with upright pillars in pairs 8 ft. apart with 10 or 12 ft. between the pairs. Bricks or breeze blocks built into square pillars are very popular, and these should be linked with stout oak runners. Or the pergola can be entirely of wood, or of any other materials available and in harmony with the remainder of the lay-out (Figs. 24–25).

If wood is used throughout for a pergola, the uprights should be set in cement to a depth of 2 ft. Posts 6 in. square should be regarded as a minimum : thinner wood is scarcely worth the trouble of construction, and will perish before the full beauty of the pergola has matured.

Crossbars and runners should be fixed with stout bolts, and the height of these should be not less than 7 ft. from the ground. If oak can be used, and allowed to weather naturally, the result will be particularly pleasing. Owners who object to the appearance of untreated oak can treat it with lime, or with creosote.

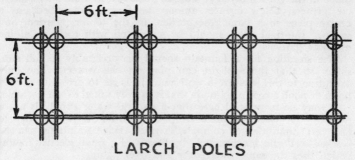

Fig. 25. *Simple all wood pergola design.*

In planting a pergola two climbers can with advantage be set to each upright, at least for the first year or two. After that it might be best to remove one, so that the remaining one has full room for development. These plants can be set by the side of the uprights, so that they receive a little protection from cutting winds, and if a good-sized hole is prepared for each, with rich soil substituted for any that is poor and hungry, the plants will cover the pergola rapidly.

Some pergolas are made with a low wall running the whole length on each side, the uprights being built into the wall. Where this is not the case, planting some such subject as groups of Madonna lilies alternated with delphiniums between the uprights along both sides, gives a particularly decorative appearance to the walk.

In considering the layout of the garden, the maker might remember the many original types of pergola that are seen at flower shows, such as the Chelsea and Southport shows—pergolas of semicircular pattern, often combined with a kind of rose temple or arbour, or other ornamental feature. These are variations on the same theme, but strike a somewhat different note, and are more acceptable on that account.

Just one other reminder—if a pergola is well constructed, and beautiful in itself, remember not to allow the plants that clothe it to smother its beauty. A slender trail of clematis over good stone pillars is more pleasing than a heavy smother growth of roses tied clumsily into position.

GARDEN POOLS AND FOUNTAINS

Certain items concerning the inclusion of pools and fountains must be considered at this stage, though the construction of water gardens will be fully dealt with later. First there are two distinct types of water features—formal and informal. Both have their place in the garden layout. Formal pools are suitable for inclusion on terraces, below terraces among the formal flower-beds, as a centre piece to a large rose garden, in the topiary garden, and so on. Informal pools should be associated with rocks or alpine meadow gardens.

The situation for a fountain should be preferably in full sunshine, so that the sunlight can play on the waters. The only exception to this is where a wall fountain is set to drip into a deep basin or pool, a type of fountain that is equally suited to sun or shade.

It may be mentioned here that a natural water supply is not a necessity for either fountain or pool. Neither is it necessary to use vast quantities of company's water, since fountains can be worked well and inexpensively by means of a small electric motor, which uses the same water over and over again.

It is probable that most garden owners would prefer to pay a contractor to carry out the far from easy construction of ponds and fountains for them. Wall fountains are often fashioned in lead, and may be extremely costly. So of course may fountains of other types. The same thing applies to pond construction, whether formal or informal. It is work that entails some amount of patience and hard labour.

Nevertheless even those who will call in the contractor to help ought to know a little of the essentials in this connection.

With regard to the position of a water garden, this should be in full sunshine if possible, so that plants and fish may be reared to perfection. At the same time it does not matter if a part of the pond is shaded, and this allows the lover of the informal to plan picturesque waterside planting. Water should find a place in the lowest part of a garden, not on a hill-top, since water gardens look best seen from above.

Then there is the question of water supply. If company's water is used, it can be taken to any part of the grounds, but it is not always so easy to dispose of the surplus water;

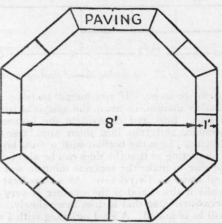

Fig. 26. A circular pool with paved edging.

the same problem also occurs if rain-water is collected and used. This problem in a small garden can be solved by the formation of a sump. This is a deep hole, lying lower than the water garden, and filled with very porous material, such as coarse clinker. A hole dug to a depth of 5 ft., refilled to within 18 in. of the surface with coarse clinker, and then covered entirely to the original level with soil and turf is quite a good sump, and this can be accommodated under a lawn, where its presence would be unsuspected. It would be necessary for a pipe to lead from the water garden to this sump in order to dispose of the surplus water.

A simple method of pool construction will be described here for the benefit of those who wish to carry out the work unaided, but naturally this will be adapted as needed according to the site and to what may happen to be the owner's individual requirements.

The first step is to excavate the site for the pool to a depth of

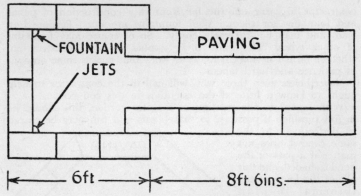

Fig. 27.   *A double-shaped pool equipped with fountain jets.*

18 in. or more.   If you intend to have a deep central part and shallow margin, excavate the marginal trench to a depth of nearly a foot.   Beat and consolidate the bottom and sides as much as possible, and ram into them any large stones discovered while digging.   Line the bottom with a 4-in. layer of concrete, and erect a shuttering so that the sides can be also lined with 4 in. of concrete. Be sure to make the concrete mixture wet enough to fill the cavity and leave no air pockets.   Also keep frost away from the concrete while it dries, and if the weather is very hot, water the concrete occasionally, so that it dries more slowly.   In this way a harder set will be obtained.   A final surfacing with Pudlo cement gives a good waterproof finish to the concrete.

A pond will be far more satisfactory if all this part of the work is done at one time, as joins in cement work are apt to crack easily.

MAKING A BOG GARDEN

To make a marginal bog garden you can either build a double wall to the pond, i.e., a wall to the deeper portion that will come an inch or so below the water surface, leaving an outer concreted trench that has a wall a few inches higher, the trench being filled with prepared loam, or you can make the complete pool first all the same depth, and then build with bricks an inner wall, coming nearly to the water surface.   The space between this inner wall and the outside can then be filled with soil for the reception of bog plants. Two simple pools are illustrated in Figs. 26 and 27.

If a fountain is to be included in the feature, it will be set in position first, and the concrete laid round the pipes.   Similarly, if a waste pipe for emptying the pool is desired, this will be set in position

of opposite characteristics mixed together give the ideal condition spoken of by professional gardeners as " medium loam."

However, roughly speaking, most gardens will have soil that falls into one of two categories, i.e., light or heavy, or if you prefer, sandy or clayey. Light soil is soil of the kind that does not readily stick in lumps on the spade, and does not hold much water, so that its weight is light (not its colour, which has nothing to do with this matter). Heavy soil clings together in sticky lumps, or sets into " concrete " in dry weather and then cracks. As it holds moisture, it weighs heavily on the spade. Generally, it is impossible to dig this type of soil with a spade until it has been first broken with a digging fork.

WHAT ARE CLAY AND SAND?

The actual difference between these two types is not so much a matter of chemical content as of the size of the particles which make up the soil. The soil that you will find in a garden consists of weathered rock, which has gradually been broken down through the centuries into small grains or particles, varying from about 0.002 mm. in diameter to 2 mm., the smaller particles being those of clay soils and the larger particles those of coarse sand. In addition to these there are, of course, larger stones, such as those that are found in gravel, and the large flints found in chalk, etc.

There is also, in many soils, a good proportion of lime, and humus. Humus is the decaying animal or vegetable matter in the soil. Water and various gases are present, too, and the mineral content of the soil is considerable and somewhat varied according to the type of rock from which the soil has been produced by weather action.

KEEPING SOIL IN GOOD CONDITION

What most new gardeners fail to appreciate is that the actual quantity of food taken by a plant from the soil (apart from water, which is considerable) is very small, and that in soil which contains humus the essential foods are generally present. Plants rarely need half the fertilizers that ambitious amateurs shower on the beds and borders. What they do need is soil in the right mechanical or physical condition to hold the essential foods in readiness for the roots when they need them. In other words, " tillage is manure " in its best form.

Even without digging a hole, the condition of the soil can be noted, especially if the weather is wet. Clay soil sticks to the shoes, while sandy soil does not cling much. In dry weather, sticky clay cracks badly, while sandy soil becomes powdery, and shifts under the feet. There are other differences, one being in the type of weeds that grow on the site; but unless the gardener is a botanist or

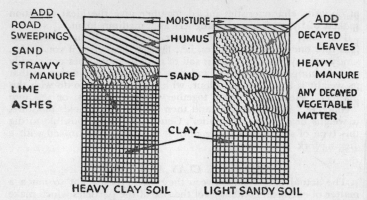

Fig. 1. *Composition and treatment of heavy and light soils. Note the varying proportions of humus and moisture.*

an experienced countryman it is not likely that a description of these will be of much assistance to him in determining his particular type of soil. Fig. 1 shows the usual composition of clayey and sandy soils, and the materials which should be added to each for normal purposes.

It must not be thought that every soil falls clearly into one of these two categories. There are intermediate types, and the ideal loam (existing where a garden has previously been under good cultivation) is about half-way between the two. But there are also other distinctions between soils of different districts. There is, for instance, the type of soil generally called chalky, where the soil lies over a subsoil of chalk or limestone, which is brought to the surface in small or large quantities whenever digging is done. Such soils are generally " hungry," that is, they have little food left in them, because plant food in solution can so quickly find its way through the limestone. The thinner the layer of dark soil over the chalk or limestone, the poorer it will be.

Then there is the soil known as peaty—the type that is found on moorland and bog. Bog peat is sour and unfriendly, but peat that is lying in such a position that it does not become constantly water-logged, such as the peat of the moors, is valuable garden soil, and particularly suited to certain plant families.

Alluvial soil or soil from river beds is another type—the richest and best type of all for garden making. Alluvial soil occurs all over the country, wherever old river beds have dried or been drained artificially. The reason for its fertility is that decaying organic matter has for many centuries been carried down stream, and gradually deposited in the river bed. This, combined with the breaking down of rock particles by the action of moving water, has produced a rich loam that holds plant food without waste (such as occurs on chalk) and that is comparatively easy to work.

Marl—the kind of soil which occurs in some of the midland counties—is really clay soil, but clay that contains a good deal of chalk or magnesium carbonate. It is in better condition for gardeners than simple clay, easier to work, and generally fertile.

Having noted the kind of soil that is available for you to use in making the garden, you might note also at this stage whether serious waterlogging is likely to occur on the site. In the foot-deep holes that you made in order to sample the soil, water will doubtless collect during rainy weather, especially if the soil is of the clay type. You can expect this, but you should also expect to find the water disappear from the hole after two or three days of dry weather. If it still remains, there is need for special drainage, and neglect on this point will lead to damp, sinking lawns, and unhealthy borders.

To drain a garden it is generally quite enough to take out a trench about 18 in. deep every 5 or 6 yards, and put 9 in. of coarse breeze or clinker, cinders from the house, or old tins, beaten flat, into the bottom as shown in Fig. 2. The soil can then be returned to the trench. This is a wise precaution on every garden where the

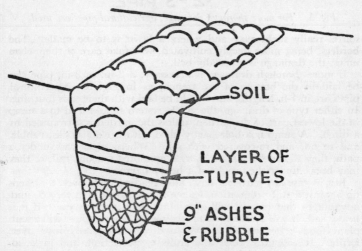

Fig. 2.   Cross-section of a simple garden drainage trench. These trenches should lead to a main trench and thence to the sump.

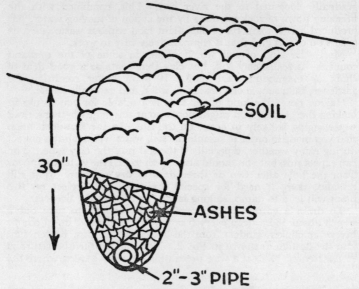

Fig. 3.   For more thorough drainage, agricultural pipes are used.

soil is really sticky clay and where a lawn is to be made. The borders, being more deeply cultivated, will take care of themselves unless the drainage is unusually bad.

If more thorough drainage is necessary, a 2-in. or 3-in. pipe can be laid in the bottom of the trench, as in Fig. 3. Agricultural pipes are in 1-ft. lengths, and should be laid with their ends touching. In either type of drainage, the whole system should lead to a sump in the lowest part of the garden, unless the garden is surrounded by a ditch. A sump is a hole partly filled with broken bricks, rubble, and so on, and re-covered with soil. Where pipes pass under a path, they should be supported by a creosoted wooden rail, or they may break under the weight of a heavy barrow.

Just in case any gardener feels, after reading these lines, that he is up against a stiff proposition, let me assure him of the very definite advantages that his soil will give him—whatever its type. If it is heavy soil, it will retain moisture better in hot weather, will retain plant food better at all seasons, and will therefore prove more fertile. It will grow roses and fruits to perfection, and make an excellent vegetable plot when it gets going.

If it is light soil, it will be very easy to turn frequently, and delightful for seed raising, for flower growing and for many of the most charming flowering shrubs. It will make a good winter garden, since light soil is generally warmer than clay; and crops of the vegetable plot, if not quite so heavy, will be much earlier than those on clay soils. In fact, every soil has its advantages.

To a great extent, the work done on the garden site is similar whatever the kind of soil, but it would be a mistake to begin without some appreciation of the soil type, and in outlining the methods to be adopted, constant reference will be made to the two extreme types. But whatever the soil, the first task is to dig it thoroughly.

HOW VIRGIN SOIL IS TREATED

Virgin soil, the kind of soil that has been idle for a year or two since it was bought for the garden enclosure, is generally old pasture land, or is covered with a kind of weedy pasture that has grown up during its idleness. A great many garden owners think that the right way to tackle this virgin soil is to take off the existing turf and burn it, but this is a great mistake. The argument used by old-fashioned gardeners is that wireworms are present in old turf, and that weed seeds will be destroyed by the burning. Actually the wireworms are as likely to be present in the soil just under the turf as in the turf itself, and weed seeds will probably in any case fall into the under layer as the turf is lifted. On the other hand, the turf and weeds, if buried under the top soil during digging, will gradually decay and form humus, which will add considerably to the soil fertility.

PREPARED AND HOME-MADE FUMIGANTS

Should it be desired to crop the garden with various vegetables the first season, it would be as well to use soil fumigant while preparing it. Soil fumigants are sold in prepared form. They consist of naphthalene with other ingredients, and this material when dug into the soil so that it lies below the top spit (spade-depth of earth) sends its fumes through the soil, and insect pests are gassed as they hatch from the eggs. It is obviously waste of fumigant to use it, as some beginners have done, as a top dressing, for the fumes then merely rise into the air.

A home-made fumigant consists of half naphthalene and half powdered lime, mixed and used at the rate of one or two ounces to each yard of open trench during digging. Horticultural naphthalene should be specified when ordering this material.

It has already been stated that soils in good mechanical condition, i.e., broken to a crumbly texture, so that air and moisture can both find their way through and be constantly available to plant roots are generally well enough supplied with plant food. This does not mean that all soil is equally fertile, nor that soil will grow any and every crop without ever needing additions of any kind. Soil fertility is apt to deteriorate unless care is taken, and to maintain it one should first understand what soil fertility is and what it implies.

To begin with, consider the plant roots and their requirements. They need two things—air and moisture; without air they begin to decay instead of carrying on their proper function, and without moisture the plant will die, since plant food can only be taken in by the roots in solution. Air and moisture depend on the ability of the soil to hold moisture during dry spells, and to allow for quick drainage of surplus moisture (and the inlet of air) during rainy spells.

BACTERIA AND SOIL FERTILITY

It has been found that an intermediate soil or loam, partly clay and partly sand, is best in this respect. It is also found, by practical experience, that soil rich in humus will retain moisture longer than a poor soil, and that well-broken soil, that is soil that has been dug over to a depth of nearly 2 ft., holds air and moisture better than soil that is never turned over. Further, it is found that soil dug over in early winter is better in this respect than soil turned over in late spring just before the crops are sown and planted.

The reasons for the greater fertility of soil dug in early winter have only been appreciated with increased knowledge of soil bacteria. These bacteria are living organisms, and depend for their health on congenial soil conditions, such as exist in well dug soil. If the soil is newly turned in early winter, the bacteria are active below the surface all winter, building up a reserve of plant food, and increasing in numbers so that they can be still more active when the growing season commences.

The bacteria are present, not in the gravel or sand which forms the bulk of the soil, but in the decaying humus. This explains why the addition of humus to the soil improves its fertility. Other uses of humus in the soil are that it darkens the colour of the soil, and the darker the soil the more solar heat it conserves, so that humus actually raises the soil temperature; further, in the process of decay, humus ferments, making the soil more porous. That is why humus in clay soils will make them seem lighter. In sandy soils the humus makes the texture heavier by holding moisture.

VALUE OF PLANT FOODS IN THE SOIL

Apart from texture and bacteria, fertility depends on the presence in the soil of plant foods. Of these there are three of supreme importance to the amateur gardener. One is nitrogen, a food that encourages the development of leaf and stem; another is phosphorus, which hastens flower production (and therefore fruit production); and another is potash, which is a kind of tonic and maintains the health of the plant. For most plants lime is also an essential, but there are certain plants that grow naturally in lime-free soils.

Lime in itself should not be regarded as a food. Its function is to prepare the other foods for the plants, to break down lumps of clay and make sandy soil more retentive of moisture, and in various ways to assist the plants to take their food supplies from the soil. It is often spoken of as the key to the soil, while the three plant foods—nitrates, phosphates and potash—are spoken of as the golden tripod.

In addition to these there are a number of other chemicals of which minute quantities are absorbed by the plants, and, in fact, chemists are constantly discovering that microscopic quantities of certain substances are absolutely essential to plant health. As, however, these substances are usually present in all well dug and manured soils, there is no need for the amateur gardener to consider them.

ROTATION OF CROPS

The golden tripod is therefore still of first importance in maintaining soil fertility, and appreciation of the various functions of the three classes of soil food helps the gardener to control his plants. It helps him in another way, too. As has been said, nitrates (substances containing nitrogen) are responsible for the development of leaf and stem. They are specially called for by such plants as lettuces and cabbages, and it is pretty obvious that after cabbages have been grown on a plot of land for one season, the soil will be less rich in nitrates than before.

The same sort of thing happens with the other plant foods. Certain plants take more than others, and the gardener's task in keeping up the standard of fertility is simplified if he remembers these points. After a cabbage crop, for instance, he will either need to use more nitrogenous fertilizer for the next crop, or he must change over to a crop that does not need so much nitrogen, but requires more potash or more phosphates. This principle of changing over the crops is generally called " rotation of crops."

It will be gathered from all these remarks concerning plant nourishment, that the methods of increasing and maintaining soil fertility are these :—

1. Regular digging, forking, hoeing, etc., so as to aerate the soil.
2. Keeping up the supply of humus in the soil.
3. Restoring the essential plant foods when soil has been impoverished by cropping.
5. Using of lime where necessary.

The word manure is synonymous in the mind of many an amateur gardener with stable or farmyard manure. The reason is that stable manure is so generally effective that when it was available in quantities, every gardener used it and found it good. Stable manure contains a little of each of the three plant foods, and in addition it improves the texture of both heavy and light soils.

Where animal manure of any kind is available, it should be either dug immediately into the ground, being mixed with soil of the top spit (if used in early winter), or buried in the lower part of the top spit of dry sandy soil (in early spring), or distributed on the soil surface in late spring, after planting is complete, where it helps to conserve moisture. Animal manure should never be stacked in the open without a soil covering, partly because it is offensive, but more because it loses half its value when exposed to air and rains.

ANIMAL MANURES

Where there is any choice, it may be noted that strawy horse manure and sheep manure are best on heavy land, while cow and pig manure are better on light sandy land. Chicken manure is best stored dry for a time before use. It is then used in place of stable manure, but less freely, being much richer in plant food. From one to two pounds to a square yard is a good dressing of poultry droppings. Of ordinary stable manure no exact quantities are reliable, since the quality is so variable; its chief value lies in its bulk of humus. Generally a rough layer of, say, 3 in. all along an open trench when digging, is sufficient for the annual dressing.

Pigeon manure is similar to poultry manure, but even more valuable, and one half the quantity, i.e., from half a pound to a pound to the square yard, is enough.

Any of these animal and bird droppings can be made into liquid manure by suspending a quantity in water. The usual way is to put the manure into a sack, together with soot, if this is available, and after tying the neck, to drop the sack into a rain tub. When required for use, the liquid manure is diluted to the colour of straw. Liquid manure used too strong is liable to injure plant roots, but this can be avoided by adding to the rain tub four ounces of gypsum to every gallon of liquid.

ARTIFICIAL FERTILIZERS

Artificial fertilizers are generally not much needed in the new garden, but after a season of cropping some additional feeding may be wanted for the second year. The chief artificial fertilizers in general use can be grouped under three heads, corresponding to the golden tripod, according to their purpose.

1. Leaf-forming or nitrogenous fertilizers. Nitrate of soda is one of the quickest in action, so quick, in fact, that it can be used while the plants are actively growing. It is so soluble that it should never be used at any other time, or it merely seeps through the soil and is wasted. An ounce of nitrate is sufficient for two or three square

yards of soil at one dressing, but this is best applied in liquid form, or dusted on the soil during showery weather. It is used on light soils, and is usually applied in the spring.

Sulphate of ammonia, a spring and summer fertilizer, is similar in action to nitrate, but as it can be mixed with other artificial fertilizers to make a complete all-round manure, it is perhaps more widely used. (It can be mixed with superphosphate and with sulphate of potash, but not with basic slag or lime.) It does not wash through the soil quite so rapidly as nitrate of soda, and is therefore better in wet seasons. Some lime must be present in the soil for sulphate of ammonia to be fully effective as a fertilizer.

Nitrate of potash (saltpetre) is somewhat similar in action to nitrate of soda, but includes the tonic potash, and so can also be classed under the third head. It is rather more costly than the sodium nitrate, and is generally used in greenhouses and on exhibition plants, such as roses and chrysanthemums. It suits all soils, and should be used at the rate of one ounce to one or two square yards.

Other nitrogenous fertilizers are nitro chalk, for heavy and acid soils, applied in the spring and summer, about two ounces to the square yard; soot, for all soils, which deters slugs, and celery, carrot, and onion fly; and calcium cyanamide, used on vacant lots of lime-free soil, seven days before cropping. Calcium cyanamide is toxic to plants.

2. Flower and fruit-forming or phosphatic fertilizers. Superphosphate of lime is one of the most widely used of this group. This is quick acting, and is generally used in the spring, and chiefly on light soils. Two ounces to a square yard is an average dressing.

THE USE OF BASIC SLAG

Basic slag, an insoluble fertilizer, is applied in autumn or winter, and is phosphatic. It can only become active in soils where there is plenty of humus, not in poor light soils, or chalky soils that have no humus. In a chalky soil, however, where plenty of decaying vegetation is dug into the ground during digging, basic slag would be good. It can be used at the rate of six or eight ounces to the square yard, and as it contains some lime, the proportion of lime used on the same plot can be decreased.

Phosphate of potash (see also under the third heading) is quicker in action than basic slag, soluble in water, and therefore very suitable as a quick stimulant on pot plants. Its price prohibits its general use in the garden. When used under glass, about half an ounce of phosphate of potash and half an ounce of nitrate of potash (see above) can be dissolved together in a gallon of water. (Warm water will dissolve them more readily.)

Bones are also phosphatic in various forms, as coarse bonemeal or boneflour. They are useful for light soils too dry for basic slag and too poor in lime for superphosphate. Bonemeal is generally used in all parts of the flower garden. It is slow acting, and a heavy dressing can be given whenever borders are being renovated—up to a pound per square yard without harm.

3. Tonic, i.e., disease resisting or potash fertilizers. These are often omitted by the amateur gardener because he does not realize their importance. Lack of potash is the cause of frequent failure with apples, with potatoes, and in fact with many flowering and fruiting plants in the garden. Potash can be applied to growing crops, but the pure form of sulphate of potash should be used for this purpose. Not more than an ounce to the square yard should be needed at one dressing. Sulphate of potash is best applied in spring and autumn, and is suitable for heavy soils, and also for indoor use.

Kainit is sulphate of potash with many impurities present. It can be used in autumn and winter, but not on actively growing crops. By the spring, when the plant roots become active, the impurities will have been washed away. Kainit checks pests and fungoid diseases, and is useful for asparagus and potatoes. Two ounces to the square yard is a normal dressing.

Muriate or chloride of potash is also unsafe to use in the active growing season, but in some districts this form of potash is preferred to kainit.

Phosphate of potash, mentioned on previous page, has only one fault, its comparative costliness.

Other sources of potash salts are wood ash and coal ash. Wood ash, if available, can be freely used anywhere in the garden. Coal ash, even when finely sifted, has a limited use, and in some parts of the garden is positively dangerous. Perhaps the best use for coal ash is on the lawn, or to serve as a foundation for a cold frame.

LIME—" THE KEY TO THE SOIL "

Lime, we have said already, is the key to the soil. It is not so important to know in what form lime can be applied, for almost any form of lime will do, and the cheapest local supply is generally the best to buy. Finely ground lime is ideal, since it quickly mixes with and sweetens the soil. Ordinary slaked lime from the nearest builder's yard is good, especially for heavy and acid soils. It should never be mixed with other fertilizers. Quicklime, when spread over vacant ground, is excellent, because it acts as an insecticide as well as a fertilizer.

As a rule a small application of lime annually—from two to four ounces per square yard—is better than a large dose every three years; but a neglected garden, where the soil has become sour, needs an extra large dose, and half a pound to the square yard can be given in such cases. The best time to apply lime is immediately after digging in the winter. Rains will gradually wash it down into the soil where it will do its work.

Chalk is a form of lime, and can be used with special advantage on sandy soils, where it assists in retaining moisture. Chalk should be used at twice the rate of lime, and as it has no burning action, it can be used at any season, and hoed or forked into the soil.

Chalk is valueless as an insecticide, but for other purposes may be regarded as a substitute for lime.

Gas lime when fresh is an efficient insecticide for vacant ground; it should be used not later than November, at a rate of not more than four ounces to the square yard, if planting is intended the following spring.

A useful all-round mixed fertilizer can be made up of one part each of sulphate of ammonia and sulphate of potash, and three parts of superphosphate. It can also be made up into liquid form, with a pound of mixture to twelve gallons of water; apply at the rate of about three gallons to a square yard.

HUMUS AND ITS SUBSTITUTES

As has been said, probably the most valuable part of stable manure is the decaying humus in it. Now that the time has passed when every gardener could have his share of stable manure, not only are chemical preparations being made as substitutes for the foodstuffs contained therein, but many firms are offering substitutes, based on some sort of organic waste material, with chemicals added, for the humus content. These are generally good, and can be used freely in the small garden.

They are, however, not so good as a form of humus which every gardener has to hand and which many gardeners waste. I refer to the accumulations of grass clippings, fallen leaves, weeds, cabbage stumps, dead tops of perennial flowers, old stems and leaves of annuals, and so on. Then there are wasted organic materials from the kitchen—parings, tea leaves, bones, and the tops and outer leaves of carrots and cabbages. The bulk of humus which an average small family might accumulate if all these were stored for a year, is very considerable.

An objection is sometimes made to the storing of waste matter, on account of its possible odour, or its unsightliness. There is no need for either. Even the smallest garden ought to be able to spare a small corner for a compost heap. The easy way to make it is to dig out a deep hole, say 4 ft. square and 2 ft. deep, piling the soil excavated round the edge of the hole. This leaves you with about a 4-ft. pit, and this will be enough for a little garden and household.

All the waste material available that will decay is thrown in from time to time, and over each layer a light dusting of lime or soil. So treated, the heap will decompose gradually without being offensive. Then, when winter digging (or any mid-season digging) is in progress, the contents of the pit will be wheeled to the plot, and buried under the top spit of soil.

A compost pit can be fenced in by a few yards of trellis, which will be covered with some climbing fruits, or in the larger garden the compost pit can be a bricked enclosure in some out-of-the-way part of the grounds, but preferably near to the kitchen garden, where it will be most in demand (*see* Figs. 4 and 5).

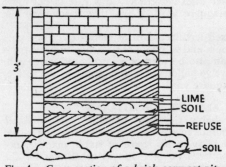

Fig. 4. Cross-section of a brick compost pit.

One point concerning the compost pit might be mentioned. A heap of decaying or fermenting vegetation of this kind will lose a good deal of the ammonia by drainings, which seep into the soil. This loss could be prevented by cementing the floor of the pit; but a simpler way, and one which is fairly satisfactory on clay soils, is to puddle the bottom before any rubbish is thrown in. That is, the clay is moistened, and then beaten and pounded to form a solid surface. Clay in a wet state puddles easily and solidly—that, of course, is the reason why clay soils should not be worked much in rainy weather.

OTHER SOURCES OF HUMUS

Other substitutes for stable manure are to be found in various waste materials such as shoddy from mills, spent hops from breweries, and so on. Fish manure is also organic in nature and an adequate substitute for stable manure. Seaweed is still another form of organic manure, which can be used by those who can get it at cheap rates. In all these matters the amateur gardener will be ruled largely by local supplies.

In some districts the corporation collects the contents of dustbins, and converts what is suitable into fertilizer, which is sold at reasonable rates.

A yet further source of humus is to be found in green manure. This method means that the land must lie idle for a part of the year. Rye, mustard, winter spinach, and annual lupins are among the plants grown as green manures. The principle is this. At any time

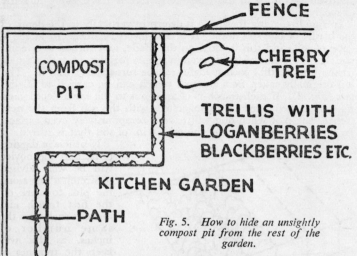

Fig. 5. *How to hide an unsightly compost pit from the rest of the garden.*

when the ground can lie idle for a while, between crops, seeds are sown and allowed to develop as much as they will, provided they do not actually reach flowering stage. They are dug in, usually when just ready to flower, and decay in the soil to enrich it with humus. A good time to practise green manuring is after an early crop has been gathered, when the seedlings will grow rapidly through the summer and be dug in during winter. Land that becomes vacant in September can be dug over and sown with rye, which will grow large enough to be usefully dug in by March.

So far we have been talking mainly about the principles underlying cultivation. Now for real action on the plot.

When a new garden is taken over, the question sometimes asked is : " When is the best time to dig it ? " The general answer is : " As soon as you can "; but if the garden is not wanted in a great hurry, digging might conveniently wait until autumn. This would be for the very good reason that winter will help with the work. The action of frost and rain on large lumps of soil breaks down the texture, and prepares the beds and borders for later surface cultivation with rake and hoe.

However, at any time when digging is to be done, it will be done in one of these ways.

Simple digging is quite satisfactory where you are preparing a lawn on a site that is already level. It is not necessary for the soil to be broken to a great depth; in fact, deep digging may easily be a disadvantage, since in this case the surface is more likely to settle unevenly.

In simple digging the spade is driven in vertically to the depth of the blade, or one spit deep. It is then levered a little, to loosen a cube of soil, and this is lifted on the spade, and turned over completely. It is an assistance, even in simple digging, to open a small trench first, so that each spadeful can be turned over into it. The soil originally taken from the first trench can be carried to fill the last (Fig. 6). If each trench is cleaned out to the same depth each time, and then filled up as suggested, with the soil from the next trench, the plot when dug will have a comparatively even surface. In simple digging it is only the top 10 in. of soil that is stirred.

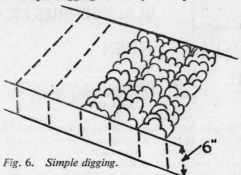

Fig. 6.   *Simple digging.*

Neatness in digging pays, and the novice will be well advised to stretch a line along the plot to mark off the first trench and move it each time the same number of inches, as this will keep the trenches of even size, and result in an even patch of dug soil.

The way a spade is held is responsible for success or failure. The grip on the handle at the top with the right hand, and half-way down it with the left, is correct. The spade should be raised before it is driven into the soil, and a push with the foot should drive it the full length of the blade. Should virgin soil be too stony or too solid for the spade to be used in this way, a large digging fork can be used. A spade should be handy, too, so that the trench can be cleared each time, otherwise the worker will very soon " lose his trench."

Since double digging, known as bastard trenching, is the most common form of digging adopted in the new garden, let me describe this process as applied to some old pasture which is to become flower or vegetable borders.

The first thing to do is to take the line of string, and stretch it where the edge of the border is to come. Then cut, with the spade, or with a turf cutter if you have one, along the line of the string, penetrating to about 3 or 4 in., i.e., through the turf. For a curved outline to a bed you cannot use the string but must use the spade or turf cutter as described in the first chapter.

Now, assuming that you have outlined, by cutting through the turf, a rectangular patch of soil that is to be dug, take the line again and stretch it across the plot at one end, 15 in. from the cut edge. Cut along this line, and with the spade cut also across the 15-in. strip, so that the turf is in squares. This turf, and the soil beneath it to a depth of 10 in. (i.e., one spit), you can move to some point near the far end of the plot : you will need it to refill your last trench.

Stand in the open, straight-sided trench that you have made, and with the largest digging fork break up the bottom soil. It need not be lifted and turned : breaking it is sufficient.

Move the line of string a further 15 in., and cut a second line of turves as before. Strip off each one with the spade or fork, and as you lift it, turn it over face downwards in the open trench. If you have plenty of time to do the work, you can, with advantage, break or chop the turf a little; but if time presses, leave it upside down as it is.

Turn over the soil from under this second line of turves, into the open trench, thus filling it, and leaving the second trench open. This you will treat like the first, and so on all down the plot until the last open trench is filled with the turf and soil taken from the first.

The plot will then have been double-dug, that is, the top spit of soil will have been turned over but kept in place at the top, while the undersoil will have been broken up, so that air and moisture can penetrate it.

This form of digging, which is shown diagrammatically in Fig. 7, is the most common, and generally the best. The top spit of

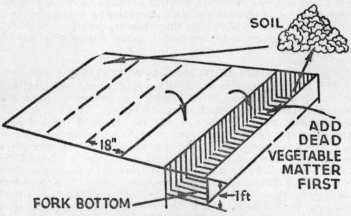

Fig. 7. Double digging or bastard trenching.

soil is the most fertile, the reason being that the active soil bacteria already referred to live in the top layer, and only where they live, and where air freely penetrates, can soil remain fertile. To turn in the top spit, and bring the infertile subsoil to the top, as is sometimes done, is asking for trouble.

Double digging is generally adopted in renovating herbaceous or mixed flower borders, in preparing ground for rose beds and for shrubs, and in all parts of the vegetable garden, at least once a year (with the exception of permanent beds of asparagus, etc.). In place of the layer of turf as described, any available organic

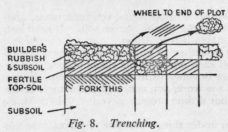

Fig. 8. Trenching.

manure, the contents of the compost pit, or other matter is thrown into the open trench, and preferably, in this case, forked into the subsoil. This gradually has the effect of deepening the fertile layer, with advantage to the plants.

Digging should everywhere finish with a dusting of lime over the surface. Lime is needed as well as manure—not instead of it, as many gardeners seem to think. Soil dug over in autumn and dressed with lime will, without attention during the winter, gradually break down to a crumbly surface that can easily be raked to make a good seed bed. All the same, soil that has been double-dug on the vegetable plot in October can with advantage be forked over once or twice during the winter, since this allows frost greater action in it, and also brings grubs to the surface to be devoured by winter-hungry birds.

WHEN TRENCHING IS NECESSARY

The difference between double digging, or bastard trenching, and trenching proper is that in the double digging just described, the top layer of soil only is turned over and it remains at the top, whereas in trenching (shown in Fig. 8), the two layers of soil are both turned right over and their relative positions are reversed. There are occasions when this practice is necessary. One is when, in a new garden, the owner discovers that the builder has buried the original top soil under a layer of soil taken from the foundations. This will be discovered when the foot-deep hole is first opened to discover the type of soil. Fertile top soil, with decaying humus (and bacteria) present in it, is of a darker colour, and more fibrous in texture than the subsoil. It has decaying or active weed roots present in it, and it is these that make the difference in colour by which it can be identified.

If, then, the top soil has been buried, and trenching becomes a necessity, this is how to proceed. First, mark out and open a trench as for double digging, but go further. Excavate the subsoil or second spit as well as the first spit, and take it to the other end of the plot. Next, mark out a second strip, turn the top spit over into the open trench, and turn the subsoil from the same width over on to the inverted top spit. Continue as before all down the plot, and fill in the top spit from the first trench in the bottom of the last trench, and the subsoil at the top. This method will have brought to the top the lower spit, which was actually the fertile soil.

Without actually bringing all the lower spit to the surface, an intermediate form of digging is sometimes adopted, if the old top soil of a garden seems to be impoverished and stale. A little of the subsoil brought up on the spade and left on the surface will improve such a garden plot. This method is useful in old town gardens where soot has soured the surface.

Reference to soil cultivation would be incomplete without descriptions of various lighter tasks that serve to keep soil healthy. One is hoeing. It is found that soil which is hoed regularly is warmer in winter and cooler and moister in summer than soil left unhoed. Hoeing means chipping through the top crust of soil, breaking down the sunbaked surface to a crumbly texture, and destroying small weeds in the process. Breaking the hard pan that quickly forms in hot weather after rain ceases allows air to enter the soil, and prevents cracks forming. Soil with a loose crumbly surface, and no deep cracks, is capable of drawing moisture from a considerable depth by capillary attraction— the way in which, for instance, the wick of an oil lamp draws up oil by providing a porous substance. Where deep cracks form, the soil dries into hard lumps, and moisture does not rise.

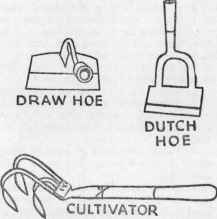

Fig. 9.   The three most common types of hoe for use in gardens.

Hoes are of various types, in two distinct groups (*see* Fig. 9). One is the type of hoe that is used with a pushing motion, the user working backwards along the rows of growing crops as he works. This is called a push hoe, or thrust hoe, of which the best known kind is called the Dutch. The other group comprises the drag or draw hoe, used with a downward and drawing motion, the user working forwards between the rows. In both cases the weeds are cut through just below the surface, and the soil is left broken and crumbly. There are hoes, such as the cultivator hoe, that combine both possibilities; and there are hoes of various sizes, for use between rows of large vegetables, and for use between rows of small seedlings in the nursery plot.

Hand forks and weeding forks are used for a similar purpose in flower beds where a hoe cannot be used.

RAKING AND FORKING

Raking is too well known to need description. Constant raking will break down the surface of almost any kind of dug soil in time. The novice should beware of the temptation to rake off all soil lumps, instead of knocking them to pieces with the rake. This is a tiresome job, but only large stones and loose weeds should be raked off and taken away.

Forking, or pointing as it is sometimes called, consists in turning over just a few inches of soil between established plants, being careful not to let the fork penetrate so deeply that it disturbs the roots unduly. The object is chiefly to remove weeds, aerate the soil, and generally to give a clean, well-cared-for look to the beds and borders. When manure is needed in the borders, and plants cannot be lifted for thorough digging, it is generally distributed on the surface, and lightly buried with the fork, the prongs of the fork penetrating only about 4 in.

I will end this chapter with just a few hints to new gardeners concerning these primary operations.

1. Never dig when the soil is very wet.

2. Never wheel a heavy barrow, filled with manure, soil, or sand over a lawn area, even if the lawn is not yet made. Use one or two planks to take the weight: it will save you lots of trouble later.

3. Never have sand or manure dumped where you intend to make a gravel path. Its weight will make the ground sink unevenly.

4. Never leave your tools outside after use. Keep them under cover, and always clean them before they are put away. Stainless steel tools need only a wash, but other tools should be wiped with an oily rag each time.

5. Don't tackle too much heavy work at once if you are not

used to manual labour. Try it little and often for a time, until you " get the knack."

6. Don't let the garden be a worry to you; let it be a pleasure. Don't talk of garden *work*; call it play. You probably worked far harder at football when you were at school.

CHAPTER III

PLANT PROPAGATION

PLANT propagation is one of the most exciting of all forms of garden activity. To the pleasure of planning and planting—the arrangement of beauty—can be added the thrill of raising fresh plants from seed and multiplying cuttings; and, when we become experienced gardeners, of raising new varieties by cross-breeding.

Before describing details of the various methods of plant propagation, I should like to stress the importance of careful selection of plants to breed from. Animal breeders take particular care of their stock, and in no circumstances would they attempt to breed from sickly parents. Yet I have seen runners taken from sickly strawberries, and seed potatoes from a diseased crop, and then have even heard the propagator complain in surprise that the new plants were no better than the old ones.

Almost as foolish is the practice of freely rooting cuttings of common shrubs, when there are others of better type available; or of propagating from inferior varieties of border plants. Plant increase is, in the majority of cases, quite easy if the known rules are obeyed, and the gardener who learns to buy a little of the best and make the most of it is being more economical than the man who buys quantities of cheaper material.

There are a great many different ways of effecting plant increase, but each falls into one of two groups. These can be illustrated very easily by describing the simplest form of life known—the single living cell—and the way in which it reproduces itself, or " grows."

WHAT IS AN AMŒBA ?

The single cell, consisting of a sort of globule of liquid, enclosed in a thin wall, with a slight thickening at the centre which we call the nucleus, grows by the simple process of splitting into two, or sometimes into four, parts, each having exactly the same characteristics as the original cell. Fig. 1 shows an amœba, one of the simplest of the unicellular creatures which multiply in this way. They swell as they absorb nourishment, and when large enough, they divide again. So the process is repeated, and the group of cells becomes larger and larger. The cells may separate, and if they are in water some may float a considerable distance and meet with other cells.

Then it may happen that two separate cells touch each other and begin to join forces. The cell wall between them breaks down, and the cells fuse into one. A little later the first process recommences, the cell splits up again and again as before and so makes a number of new cells. But, it will be noted, these second generation cells are not exactly like those of the first generation : they are a little like each of the two cells that joined together. They have, in fact, inherited some characteristics from each of the two parent cells, just as plants and animals inherit different characteristics from their forbears.

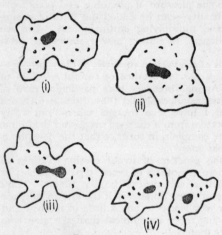

Fig. 1. *Reproduction by division. An amœba multiplies by splitting up into separate units, each with its own nucleus. The nucleus gradually changes its shape preparatory to splitting.*

What happens in the case of these simple cells happens also in all plant life. We can separate a part of a plant, and from it grow a new plant. We do this when we take off a cutting, and the new plant thus raised will be like its parent in all its characteristics. But if we let a plant ripen its seed, we have allowed the second process—cell fusion—to take place. Pollen from one flower has fertilized the seed ovaries of another flower, and so the seed has ripened or " set." The seed therefore, is a child of two parents, and its characteristics may have been inherited from both, or from either, parent.

This form of increase—sexual increase—does not give us new plants of fixed or known habit. In many cases the plants may appear very much the same as the old ones, and the grower then declares that the seed " breeds true to type." In other cases, the variations are so marked that the new plants are given special names, i.e., they become " new varieties." Sexual increase, therefore, is always more or less a gamble, while vegetative increase (the simple division type) is a safe and certain way to reproduce plants of particular colours or habits.

Recognition of these facts explains many things which sometimes puzzle the unscientific gardener. It explains why gardeners go to much trouble to reproduce some new plants by cuttings when there is plenty of seed available and seed raising is comparatively easy. It explains, too, why the price of good seed is high, and why seed that has been tested is better than home-saved seed.

FERTILIZATION BY POLLEN

In the home garden only one parent of the seed is known : the pollen that fertilized the seed ovaries may have come from any of the garden plants or from the hedgerow or field beyond. In the seed grounds special precautions are taken to exclude other types of the same flower, or to prevent insects from carrying pollen from one type to another; and so the resulting seedlings are uniform in colour and habit. Plants raised from home-saved seed often vary to a remarkable degree, and seedlings so raised may be nearly worthless.

It has already been suggested that seed raising is easy. This is true, since seeds have a wonderful vitality and Nature is very resourceful. Extremely interesting photographs have been taken which illustrate how obstacles are overcome by seeds that do not happen to fall in with ideal conditions. Some of these show how a seed will turn itself over completely as it grows, if it has started upside down. Some show how a rootlet will gradually draw the seed under the soil as it grows. Some illustrate how a growing seedling will move out of its way quite a large stone or other obstruction.

Seedlings will, in fact, win through and become mature plants, even when badly treated. But with seeds, as with human beings, it does not make for good health to be constantly fighting against adversity, nor does it make for health to be too much coddled. The gardener's business is to see that the conditions are somewhere between these two extremes.

COMPOST FOR SEED RAISING

After a large number of experiments with all kinds of seeds, the John Innes Horticultural Institute has reported that the ideal seed-raising compost is this mixture, which is right for practically every kind of seed raised in gardens :—

  2 parts good garden loam, sterilized.
  1 part clean sand.
  1 part good moss peat (or sterilized leaf-mould, if peat is difficult to obtain).

This compost is, of course, for seeds raised under glass. It provides a medium free from pests and diseases, able to hold moisture, and at the same time to hold air, and friable enough (i.e., it crumbles easily enough) to offer no serious obstruction to the growing seedling.

These conditions allow for free and even germination. A seed, to begin growth, must have three things. First moisture, the immediate action of which is probably purely mechanical. Water is absorbed by the seed, which swells, and bursts its hard outer covering. This allows moisture and the second essential, air, to be received by the tiny root, formerly dormant inside the seed.

SEEDS NEED WARMTH

In addition to moisture and air, warmth is necessary for proper development. The amount of warmth varies according to the kind of seed—tropical plants frequently need a very high temperature to start them on their way, while some plants seem to need a temperature but little above freezing point. Watch how weeds germinate and grow in winter. What concerns the gardener in this connection is that a temperature too low is likely to retard growth for so long that the seed decays instead of germinating properly. It is because temperature is so important that gardeners usually prefer to raise expensive seeds under glass, where conditions can be better controlled than in the open.

Seed raising is a simple operation, but failures are frequent, and their cause is often to be found in small items that have escaped the raiser's notice. To prepare a box of compost, and scatter seeds over it, finishing with a dusting of fine soil, is the ordinary procedure. Water is given, usually overhead from a fine rose can, and sometimes shading is also provided.

Probably seventy-five per cent of the seeds sown in this rough general way will germinate and produce a sufficient number of seedlings to satisfy the ordinary gardener. Any that do not are forgotten, or the seedsman is blamed. However, with the object of lessening the proportion of failures, the following summarized hints are given, under separate headings for easy reference.

SOWING IN THE OPEN

We will take first open ground sowing. To raise seeds in the open the soil *must* be well dug, well drained, and raked until there is a fine surface tilth, i.e., a surface 2-in. layer of fine crumbly soil free from large stones.

Seeds can be sown broadcast, i.e., scattered freely over the soil surface, or in drills, i.e., in shallow depressions drawn with a pointed stick, hoe or rake, and running parallel to each other, as shown in Fig. 2.

Seeds to be transplanted early can be broadcast, but seedlings that remain for some time in the seed bed should always be in

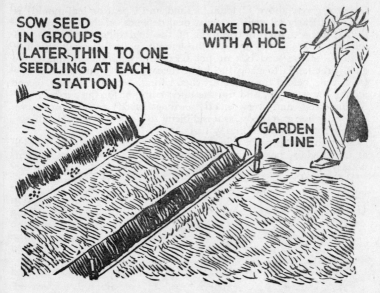

SOW SEED
IN GROUPS
(LATER, THIN TO ONE
SEEDLING AT EACH
STATION)

MAKE DRILLS
WITH A HOE

GARDEN
LINE

Fig. 2. *Open ground sowing in drills made in prepared soil.*

drills, so that a hoe can be used to keep down weeds and aerate the
soil.

A light dust covering, or no covering at all, is the rule for fine
seed. Larger seeds can have twice their own thickness of soil over
them.

A row of small twigs pushed in on either side of the seed rows
protects young seedlings. Portable cloches are an even better
protection. A cloche is a small "tent" of glass, easily taken to
pieces and packed away flat in winter months.

Avoid watering immediately after the seed is sown; it is far
better to sow the day after the top spit has been well soaked with
rain or hose water. Overhead watering may cake the surface and
seal the seeds in, so that they do not germinate freely.

Always thin out ruthlessly, but preferably in several stages,
removing the weaker seedlings if they are to be discarded. Particularly
in the case of autumn sowings, leave the seedlings comparatively
thick in the rows, and only remove them when they appear to
crowd. They give each other a little protection, if they are not too
drastically thinned at first.

Let us now deal with seeds raised under glass. Although the
SSG—C*

compost given above (2 loam, 1 sand and 1 peat or leaf-mould) is good for nearly all seeds, a great deal depends on the texture, that is the fineness and distribution of the ingredients. A common mistake is to use too fine soil throughout, with the result that the contents of the seed box or pot become a consolidated mass. A good practice is to chop the loam (decayed turf) and store it dry for a time before use. Then, when sifting, keep the lumpy pieces for the lowest layer, and use the finest compost for the surface.

Fine seed and very small seedlings need a compost more uniformly fine and sandy, as it is difficult to transplant small seedlings if their roots penetrate lumpy turf.

Seed boxes and pans, which are of course used in the open as well as under glass, need drainage holes. A layer of pieces of broken pottery or other material at the bottom of the box prevents the soil from clogging these holes. Boxes with loose-fitting sides, however, do not often need special holes for drainage holes.

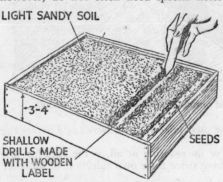

LIGHT SANDY SOIL

3"-4"

SHALLOW DRILLS MADE WITH WOODEN LABEL

SEEDS

Fig. 3. Seed sowing in boxes under glass.

Charcoal and sphagnum moss are both useful over the bottom of pans where seeds that germinate slowly are to be raised. They prevent souring of the soil. Decayed leaves or spent hops can also be used; both hold moisture and also feed the roots of the young plants. Too much leaf-mould is undesirable when raising seedlings that tend to damp off.

Seed boxes should be filled to the rim *loosely* with prepared compost, after the moss, or leaf-mould, has been laid in position. Light even pressure over the whole surface, from a flat board, should then be used to prepare a flat level seed bed. The seeds are sown in very shallow depressions, about $\frac{1}{4}$-in. deep, made in parallel lines across the box with a point such as a wooden label (*see* Fig. 3).

The finest possible dusting of soil over this, followed by a thorough moistening of the soil, if necessary by partial immersion, completes the operation.

A sheet of glass over each seed box, with brown paper over that, to exclude light until such time as the seeds have germinated, is generally advisable. Seeds raised in a cold frame do not need this extra sheet of glass if the frame is filled with one kind of seed, as the light can be excluded by shading over the whole frame; but different seeds need different amounts of shading.

Seed boxes are best stood in moist ash, or moist coconut fibre, either of which will keep the temperature more even than if the boxes are surrounded by air.

When germination has taken place, the maximum amount of light is needed, and as much ventilation as the plants can stand, according to the weather. On no account should seedlings be exposed to full sunshine in a closed frame—they will almost certainly scorch. Moreover, the hardier the plants are encouraged to be, the better they will succeed when at last they reach the open ground. Seedlings that have been kept too

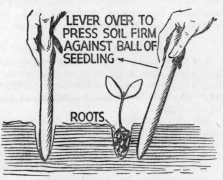

Fig. 4. Pricking out a seedling

close become tall, thin, pale in colour, and generally weak. Seedlings that are grown in cool, well-ventilated frames are short jointed, thick, and dark green in colour.

The first leaves to appear are generally the seed leaves—that is, they are the leaves that actually existed inside the seed, packed with food, and they merely grow by raising themselves on stalks through the soil that covers the seed. Almost at once other leaves begin to appear, and when two or three of these " true " leaves have developed, the seedlings can be pricked out. Pricking out, by the way, is the same thing as transplanting, but applied to tiny seedlings that are sometimes too small to be actually handled. The seedling is lifted in a cleft stick from its bed of fine, crumbly soil and held in position in a prepared hole, while soil is levered against it (Fig. 4).

The greatest care should be given to the work of pricking out; for a seedling carelessly handled, and bruised, will not only fail to grow well, but will often become diseased, and may even be a source of danger to other seedlings.

Tender plants are generally pricked out either into other boxes of similar compost to that of the seed box, or into separate pots, which are then placed under glass. Hardy plants raised from seed are sometimes set out direct in the open ground from the seed box.

The general management of a greenhouse will be dealt with in a later chapter, but it may be remarked here that seeds germinate most freely when raised over heat of some kind. It is common to stand the seed boxes over hot pipes, since bottom heat is so generally acceptable, moving them to shelves near the glass roof as soon as the seedlings are through the soil.

A great many of the plants we loosely call " alpines " are merely dwarf herbaceous or annual plants that do not require any special treatment when raised from seed. Others, such as a number of the saxifrages, androsaces, ramondias, etc., need special compost, and special precautions concerning drainage.

DRAINAGE PRECAUTIONS IN COMPOST

For these plants the ordinary seed compost can be made to serve by adding to it a quantity of old mortar rubble, well crushed, so that it will pass through a fine sieve. If mortar rubble is unobtainable some crushed flower pot, burnt soil, or even crushed sandstone can be substituted.

Sift this material, and use the coarse siftings to fill 5-in. pots two-thirds of the way up. Special alpine pans can be obtained which are provided with rather more drainage holes than are in the ordinary pot or box; use these only half filled with coarse siftings.

The surface should be specially fine and porous, and all watering should be done by partial immersion, holding each pan in the water until the moisture rises to damp the surface.

Early pricking out is desirable, specially with seedlings that seem slow to germinate, as the removal to fresh soil acts as a stimulant.

If only one or two seeds seem to have germinated, do not throw away the seed pan. Remove the germinated seedlings carefully, fill their places with sand, and replace the pan in the frame or alpine house. Other seedlings will often appear even months later.

Never use much, if any, heat to raise alpines; in fact, the better way to encourage germination is to pile snow over the pans during the winter months. The action of the snow has been proved to speed up germination among " difficult " subjects.

WHEN TO SOW PERENNIALS

Perennials may be sown under glass in the early months of the year, or later in the summer either in the open or under glass as preferred. Many of them if sown early will flower a little the same season, and this allows the gardener to discard the worthless seedlings the first season, and to propagate by cuttings only from the best plants.

Summer sowing results in sturdy plants that winter well and should flower well the following season, or as soon as they have made sufficient growth. (Some perennials, such as irises, may take more than one year to reach the flowering stage.)

Most bulbous plants of a hardy nature, and many that are grown in the greenhouse, can be raised from seed. These often take some years to reach flowering stage, and for that reason bulbous plants are more frequently introduced to the garden in the form of dormant bulbs.

If seeds are sown, they should be sown as soon as they are fully ripe. They are best placed in pots, sown thinly, so that transplanting is not needed for some time. It should be possible to leave the plant undisturbed until a bulb has been formed, when any desired transplanting can take place during the dormant season.

Bulbs generally appear first as small " grass-blades," and the novice should remember this. I have heard of cases where bulb seedlings (iris, narcissus, etc.) were all pulled out, under the impression that they were weeds !

FERNS FROM SEED

Comparatively few gardeners raise ferns from seed, though the operation is really quite simple, and can be carried through successfully even in a living room. The seeds or spores, to be strictly accurate, are to be found on the underside of the frond. The spores are too minute to be visible individually to the naked eye, but can be seen as brown dust.

They must be sown when fully ripe, and the best way to do this is to wait until the " dust " is ready to drop when the frond is touched, and then to take pieces of the frond and lay them, right side up, on prepared seed pans.

Use deep pans or pots, half full of drainage material, and then fill with the ordinary seed sowing compost, with perhaps rather more sand than usual, and made very fine on the surface. If brick or flower-pot, broken to pea size or smaller, can be used as drainage material, the pan can stand in an inch of water until the spores germinate. After this there is no difficulty in potting out and growing the young plants, provided a compost similar to that needed for adult plants is used, with a little emphasis on the amount of sand in it.

The question of heat depends of course on the ferns to be raised; hardy ferns need no artificial heat, while most of the ferns usually grown in rooms need a little bottom heat to start them on their way.

THE FUNCTION OF BERRIES

A great many plants, particularly shrubs and trees, grow their seeds in the form of berries. Shrub berries generally present little difficulty in raising, but they cannot be hurried too much. The natural way with such seeds is for the berry to be carried some distance by birds. It may then be dropped, or the seeds may be discarded, or they may pass through the bird undigested, and so be sown surrounded by "hot" manure. In any case, the seed covering of fleshy pulp and skin is disposed of before the seed germinates.

The best way to deal with berries is to pack them into sand, after gathering them fully ripe, and to leave them for a twelve-month. Then the sand and berry together are sown in the ordinary way, and germination is generally satisfactory.

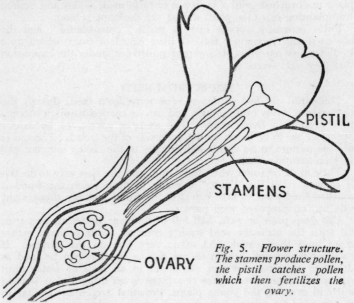

Fig. 5. Flower structure. The stamens produce pollen, the pistil catches pollen which then fertilizes the ovary.

Hybridizing is a special branch of horticulture, and many long treatises have been written on it. Perhaps a few words will be of interest here.

The hybridizer must first understand a little of the structure of a flower. There are two important parts, the pistil and the stamen (or stamens, for they are usually present in numbers). Fig. 5 shows how these parts are constructed.

The pistil includes the ovary, or seed vessel. If you look at a daffodil you can see the ovary as a small green swollen part just where the flower and stem meet.

The stamens hold the pollen dust. You can see several of them in the daffodil, and as the flower grows older, the heads of the stamens send out golden pollen dust when the flowers are shaken.

Until the dust from daffodil stamens (not necessarily the same daffodil's stamens) has fallen on the moist tip of the pistil, and found its way down to the seed ovaries to effect fertilization, the seeds cannot ripen. When fertilization has taken place, the seed becomes a new plant though still in embryo, carrying the inherited characteristics of the plant that produced the pollen, as well as those of the plant that produced the seeds.

All other parts of the flower have an incidental purpose; the brightly coloured petals, or sepals, or bracts, of flowers take no real part in reproduction, except that they attract insects who pass the pollen from flower to flower, and so effect pollination between different flowers, or, as we generally call it, "cross pollination."

The business of the hybridist is to take the place of the visiting insect, and to pass, deliberately, pollen from one flower to another. This he must do at the right time, i.e., when the pistil is in the right condition to receive the pollen, and when the pollen is in the right condition for the purpose too. The precise effect of such cross-fertilization it is not possible to forecast; but some rules affecting this branch of horticulture have already been discovered, and a study of them makes fascinating reading.

HOW TO HYBRIDIZE

For the would-be hybridizer, here is a brief description of the operation, which can be adapted as required to most flowering plants. The plant which is to carry the seeds is first isolated from others by some kind of screen, made of gauze or muslin. This is erected so that fertilization by bees or other insects is impossible. As soon as possible, and well before they have started to discharge their dust, the stamens on the flowers of this plant must be removed.

When the pistil is in the right condition for receiving the pollen, generally when it is quite sticky and moist, stamens are carried from the other chosen parent, and their dust shaken or brushed on to the waiting pistil or pistils. Any blooms on the plant that are not needed for seed-bearing should be cut away, otherwise there is a danger of self-pollination, which would, of course, upset the plans of the hybridist. The fertilized flowers are kept protected until the seed has set.

It is important to keep strict records of experiments of this nature, and also important to gather the seed immediately it is ripe, and to store it carefully, if it is not sown at once.

Just one more point : on no account throw away the first generation of seedlings when you begin your experiments in hybridizing, even if they appear worthless. Mate them among themselves, and watch for the results of second and third generations, for startling new colours and forms may not appear until then. For fuller particulars of this interesting subject, books in local libraries might be consulted.

Of all the various forms of vegetative plant increase, root division is probably the simplest and most common. Everyone who has ever had charge of a garden has been asked for a " bit of that when it grows," or has been given " bits " to start the new border on its way. Root division is generally practised during the resting months, or when the stems and leaves are inactive, that is, during winter. The ordinary herbaceous plant almost disappears from view during the winter, and at that time it does not so much resent being lifted from its soil bed.

Any plant that can, after lifting, be easily divided into portions, each of which will have some of the fine root hairs that are present on all roots, is suitable for division. Plants that are difficult to divide in this way are plants like lupins, which have often just one long tap root, which does not easily recover if it is roughly torn apart.

PLANT PROPAGATION BY DIVISION

Plants like Michaelmas daisies make large quantities of spreading roots each season. From these rise numerous new stems, and if not checked, the group quickly becomes overcrowded, and flowers become starved and small in consequence. Such plants are best divided annually, and then the newest, plumpest pieces of root only should be retained.

A sharp, clean knife is the best tool for root division (Fig. 6),

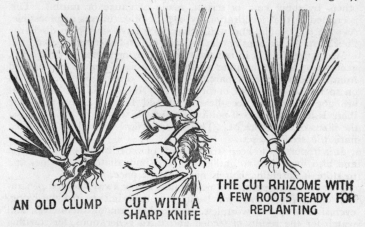

AN OLD CLUMP CUT WITH A SHARP KNIFE THE CUT RHIZOME WITH A FEW ROOTS READY FOR REPLANTING

Fig. 6. The stages of root division with a knife.

but at times a large old clump of roots can be broken by pushing into it two handforks back to back, and levering them apart. Fig. 7 shows how this is done.

Plants with fleshy roots, such as the June irises, should be divided with a clean cut, and only fresh, new healthy portions should be kept for replanting.

Plants that resent disturbance, such as pæonies, are best not lifted at all, the root division being made in the following way. About September, when the foliage has withered, some of the soil should be gently removed from the side of the pæony root, and then one or two small pieces, each with an " eye " or two, can be slipped off with a sharp knife, together with a few rootlets. Soil can then be replaced, and the old crown will generally not suffer at all, while the new pieces, planted in congenial soil, will grow on to make large flowering plants.

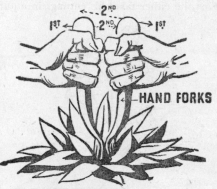

Some plants, such as chrysanthemums, which send up dozens of new growths from the old stools, can be treated like the pæonies in early spring, when the first

Fig. 7. Root division by forking. Inserted in the plant's centre, the forks lever the root into two parts.

green growths appear. If no rootlets can easily be taken off with the young shoots, it is generally possible to grow them on just the same, so long as the young growths are potted up in a sandy compost and kept moist.

WHAT IS A CUTTING?

The difference between cuttings and root division is that cuttings are pieces taken from one part of the plant only, whereas root division generally implies the division of a root with some active or dormant stems and leaves attached to each portion. In effect it is the whole plant that is divided. In the case of a cutting, more after-care is generally needed, until the missing parts of the plant have developed. Cuttings can be grouped under various headings, which will be described below.

Stem cuttings are the most common. The idea underlying these is that any part of a plant severed from the remainder will, in time, grow to a complete new plant if (*a*) it does not dry out and die,

(b) the necessary food supply can be maintained, and (c) it does not decay through lack of air. To take a portion of stem and keep it under water would prevent drying, but lack of air would cause decay. To set the base in water and leave the top exposed to the air sometimes means that evaporation takes place rapidly from the leaf surfaces while the amount of water that can be absorbed through a cut stem is insufficient to make good the loss by evaporation. Thus it can be seen that a middle course must be steered between these two extremes.

The gardener solves the various difficulties in these ways : First, he either takes his cuttings in autumn, when he inserts them in the open and knows that there will be no lack of moisture during the winter, or he takes them at other seasons and keeps them under glass, where the air is kept moist and also warm. (A bell glass, or a closed frame, serves to keep the air warm.) He takes cuttings in the open air at a season when plants are taking in little or no food, so that the question of food supply does not arise. Under glass he watches the cuttings carefully, and as soon as roots develop, he allows them a slightly richer compost in which to find their food supply. Finally —though he keeps his cuttings and the air moist—he uses either pure sand or a very sandy compost, which allows air to filter through to the roots and stems that are under-ground. The use of sand is necessary for cuttings both in the open and under glass, and is perhaps the most important point in connection with them.

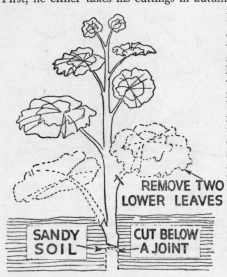

Fig. 8. Taking a cutting of a soft plant.

REMOVE TWO LOWER LEAVES

SANDY SOIL

CUT BELOW A JOINT

Soft cuttings root fairly easily so long as they can be kept sufficiently close and warm. Pure sand is probably the safest medium, and a propagating frame is advisable. Such cuttings are generally small side growths, taken off as soon as they have made perhaps three or four pairs of leaves. The lowest leaves are removed, to allow a clean piece of stem to enter the sand (Fig. 8). The actual cut is made just below a joint, or, if convenient, the cutting may be pulled from the parent plant with a downward jerk, so that it comes away with a " heel."

The cuttings can be inserted close together, made as firm as possible, and watered lightly overhead before the glass is set over them. Shading from brilliant sunshine is necessary, and the cuttings should be examined daily and surplus water that collects on the glass should be wiped away. Immediately new growth is apparent, the cuttings may be potted up singly in thumb pots, and grown normally.

Soft cuttings can be rooted in summer in a shady part of the open garden, if they are kept moist overhead; but there is always some risk in this if the summer is dry, and it is really safer to use glass.

TAKING CUTTINGS OF HARD WOOD PLANTS

Hard wood cuttings, that is, cuttings of shrubs and trees, are generally taken in the autumn, and when hardy subjects are being increased, these cuttings are usually inserted in the open ground. Preparation of the nursery bed for them consists in thorough digging and cleaning, and the use of sufficient sand to make an open porous compost all over the bed.   In the case of a bed on stiff clay, a 2-in. dressing of sand over the whole surface before any cuttings are inserted is useful. Some of this will trickle into the holes made for the cuttings, and will help to avoid decay.

Wood most suitable for cuttings is that of one season's growth, but well ripened in the sun, not soft and sappy. Pieces vary in length according to the kind of plant, but generally a piece with half a dozen joints to it is good enough. The cut is made just below a joint, and the bottom leaves (if present) are removed to allow a clean stem to enter the soil. From one-third to one-half should enter the soil, which must be made quite firm. An old garden rule is to " lay the cuttings over towards the north "; but it is not certain that this method is any better than leaving the cuttings in an upright position.

There are a few plants which require special treatment, but these the gardener will quickly discover for himself. Cuttings of clematis, for instance, root most readily if cuts are made midway between the joints or " nodes," and there are a few other shrubs that favour inter-nodal cuttings.

Some shrubs have, in the past, been particularly difficult to root from cuttings, but a modern discovery has made success with these much more certain. This discovery is commercialized in the form of " Hortomone A," a substance which can be bought from any horticultural sundriesman. Cuttings are soaked in a solution of the chemical, and after such treatment they root more rapidly, and make stronger root systems.

It is not a practical proposition to use this treatment for all cuttings, but when " shy " rooters are being inserted, even the amateur gardener might be well advised to use Hortomone A.

There is no essential difference in method between a leaf cutting

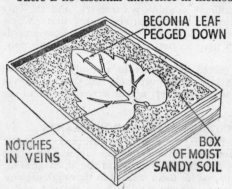

and a stem cutting. Both need warmth, moisture, air and a clean, gritty rooting medium. To make leaf cuttings a suitable leaf is scored across in several places on the underside, the cuts being made part way through a vein. The leaf is then laid flat on some sand or very sandy soil, as shown in Fig. 9; pegs are generally needed to ensure contact between the cut portions and the

Fig. 9. The method of taking leaf cuttings.

compost. As soon as roots form, the portions are severed and potted up separately. Similar conditions are needed for leaf as for stem cuttings. Begonia *rex* and gloxinias can be propagated in this way.

Any plant that makes suitable fleshy roots, such as the roots of the oriental poppy, can usually be successfully propagated by root cuttings. These are almost the same as root division, but no obviously growing stem or dormant " eye " is required on each portion. All that is done is to cut pieces of the thick fleshy root about the length and thickness of a man's little finger, making a clean cut across both top and bottom. These pieces are planted in open gritty soil, the top being covered with perhaps 1 to 2 in. of the soil. Anchusa *italica* is a border plant that responds particularly to this form of increase, and as young plants are the showiest, it pays to treat a number of the roots in this way annually.

Offsets are another form of root division. Bulbs of all kinds when they reach their maximum size begin to split up, or send out small side bulbs or offsets. These can be taken off at any time during the dormant season, and if planted in congenial soil, they will eventually grow to full sized, flowering bulbs. The advantage of this method of bulb increase over the raising of seeds is, of course, that the young plants bear an exact resemblance to their parents.

It is worth noting that a bulb which is growing offsets in this way must have them removed, or serious overcrowding will soon result.

Layering is one of Nature's own methods of plant reproduction. In a natural state, shrubs that grow long arching stems, such as those of the blackberry family, layer themselves. Where the tip of the long arching stem touches the ground, as it does always when allowed to grow unchecked and unsupported, roots form, and these gradually set up a fresh " stool," from which new stems rise.

In the same way, some herbaceous plants, such as the strawberry, send out " runners," and at the tip of these runners roots also form, and establish themselves as new plants.

In each case the roots form while the stem is still attached to the old plant; therefore each young plant can draw for a time on the food supply of the old plant.

When gardeners wish to root cuttings that are " shy rooters," they frequently adopt variations of this method. Side stems of carnations, and long stems of various shrubs such as rhododendrons and forsythia, are deliberately bent down to the soil level (or, if more convenient, a pot of soil is raised to the level of the stem), and a slight incision is made in the stem. This cut portion is then bent down under the soil surface, and fastened into position with a peg. When the roots have formed, the stem dividing the two plants is cut through, and as soon as convenient the new plant is moved to a permanent position elsewhere. Fig. 10 shows how a carnation is layered.

This method of propagation can be adapted by the individual gardener to varying conditions. In the case of a plant of

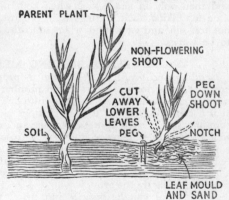

Fig. 10. *Layering a carnation.*

border carnations, for instance, the procedure is this. About the end of July, when the plant has a number of strong side growths round the flowering stem, a little fresh sandy compost is prepared, and strewn thickly round the carnation. Some crushed mortar rubble or lime should be added to the compost. Each side growth is taken in turn, stripped of one or two of the lower leaves, cut half through with a slanting upward cut, and then pegged down so that the cut is open under the gritty compost, while the tip is held firmly in a normal position.

It takes usually about three weeks for roots to form, and then the new plant may be severed from the old one. It is generally advisable to leave it where it is for a further three weeks, so that it becomes firmly established on its own roots before it has to stand up to the shock of transplanting.

One or two indications of the times suitable for each operation so far described have been given, but it is not possible to give any absolutely constant rule. The gardener must learn by experience.

A rough guide, however, is this. Hard wood cuttings are best taken in the open in autumn, when rains are probable, and no leaf growth is expected for some time. This allows the cutting to make roots during the dormant season.

Soft cuttings, of new growth, can be taken under glass at any season when such growths are available on the plant in question. They are generally available towards the end of the flowering season, or at the beginning of a new season of growth; but much depends on the individual plant.

Soft cuttings will root in the open only during warm weather, and then only in shade and when kept moist. The best general time for taking such cuttings is in August, when the growths are not too soft and new, and when soil, air, and rains are all likely to be warm.

WHAT BUDDING MEANS

Budding and grafting are a form of propagation. By budding, however, you do not increase the number of plants; you merely transform a plant of inferior variety into one of some desired variety. It is a common practice to take cuttings of some easily propagated common shrub, such as a briar rose, and when these cuttings are well rooted, to bud on to them some rose novelty, or buds from a rose that is a particular favourite.

Rose budding is more widely practised than any other kind, though a great many shrubs can be budded successfully. All shrubs are budded in exactly the same way.

A rose briar can be budded just below the soil level to form a bush rose, or at some height from the ground to form a standard. If a standard is desired, it is usual to insert three or four buds, on the side stems, close to the main stem, as these more quickly produce a shapely head.

June and July are good months for budding, for the briar stock is then in full growth, the bark ripened sufficiently to lift easily, and the " bud " on the scion (i.e., the rose from which the briar is to be budded) is then well formed.

A sharp knife with a blunt " paper-knife " end is needed. Special budding knives are so made. Some soft tying material such as raffia is also required.

The best way is to cut a stem with several buds on it from the scion and take it to the stock. " Buds " in this case do not mean flower buds, but the tiny, dormant leaf buds that lie in the angle between the leaf and the stem. Make a T-shaped cut on the bark of the briar, where the bud is to be inserted. Do not cut too deeply, but always cut deep enough for the bark to be easily lifted at the edges.

Make a curved cut behind a bud, thus cutting out a leaf with a dormant bud and a small portion of the stem. From behind the

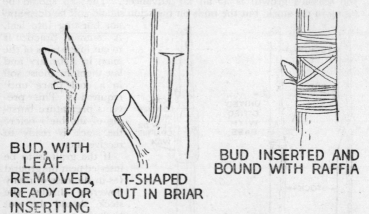

BUD, WITH LEAF REMOVED, READY FOR INSERTING

T-SHAPED CUT IN BRIAR

BUD INSERTED AND BOUND WITH RAFFIA

Fig. 11. *Propagation by budding. The stalk to which the leaf bud is attached, is slipped into the cut and bound as shown.*

bud, remove the woody portion of the stem, leaving only bark and bud, and at the same time trim away the leaf, leaving only a tiny portion of stalk, with which to handle the bud. Raise the corners of bark where the T-shaped cut was made on the stock, and slip the bark of the bud under, so that this bark lies flat against the woody part of the stock, and the bud tip protrudes. Bind raffia round above and below the bud to hold the bark and bud all firmly in position, still leaving the bud tip visible. Fig. 11 shows the whole process.

If the operation has been done swiftly and neatly, and is successful, the bud will begin to swell very shortly, and as it swells, the raffia can be loosened a little, but not removed. Nothing further need be done until spring, when the whole of the stock above the budding point should be cut back, and only the new bud allowed to grow. Henceforward, only stems that come from the new bud (or buds) must be allowed to develop, otherwise the rose will gradually revert to the common briar.

Should budding be done in early June, and prove unsuccessful, the bud withering and falling out, a second attempt, a little lower on the same stem, can be made in July, often with good results.

Grafting differs but little from budding. In both cases a part of one plant is taken and inserted into another; but in the case of a graft the new piece is larger, and grafting therefore gives quicker results. Grafting is commonly practised on old fruit trees.

The usual time for grafting is in late spring, but not so late that the season's growth is at all far advanced. The sap should be rising in the stock, but the buds on the scion should still be dormant, not bursting into leaf.

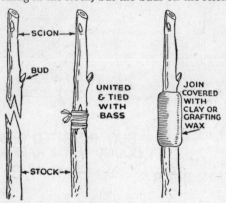

A common practice is to cut long stems of the scion in February and lay them in moist soil in a cool place until required. This prevents premature bursting of the buds before the stock is ready to receive them.

If the graft is to be inserted near the ground (as in the case of many flowering shrubs) the stock should be cut back to within about 6 or 8 in. of the ground in January. Assuming

Fig. 12. Three stages of whip-grafting.

that the thickness of the stock and scion stems are much about the same, a cut should be made 3 or 4 in. from the ground in the stock, and one at the base of the scion (which may be a shoot say 6 or 8 in. in length, taken from a favourite shrub) which will allow for the two to be fitted exactly together (*see* Fig. 12). A cut shaped like one half of a pot hook is a good shape, and allows for a close fit. If there is a difference in size, the fit must be as good as possible, and the shape of the two cuts can be varied as convenient. The important thing is that the cut surface of the inner bark of each should meet.

The cut suggested above is called " tongue, or whip grafting." If the stock is cut to a point, and the scion cut notch shaped, to fit over it, that is called " saddle " grafting; if a cut is made in the side of the main stem, and a graft inserted rather as described for rose budding, that is called "rind" grafting. If the scion is cut to a point, and the stock is notched so that the point slips exactly into position, the process is called "slit" grafting.

When the graft is in position, the next step is to bind the join with raffia, so that it is quite firm. It is sometimes desirable to use an additional small stake to which both stock and scion can be tied, so that it is not possible for the graft to be moved by winds.

Finally, the point of union is covered entirely with grafting wax, to exclude air and rainwater. Grafting wax is sold by all horticultural sundriesmen ready for use, and it is not worth while for the amateur gardener to make it for himself.

After-treatment is much the same as with buds. When the graft grows, it must not be allowed to become choked, and the grafting wax generally has to be removed, while the raffia that binds the graft has to be loosened. And, of course, no other parts of the shrub or tree must be allowed to grow and oust the scion.

Grafting practices vary considerably. When old trees are grafted several scions are usually inserted; but these are matters which the experimenting gardener will discover for himself.

OTHER METHODS OF GRAFTING

A form of grafting known as inarching is sometimes practised with grape vines. Two adjacent vines are chosen, and one stem of each is cut. These two stems are brought into contact with each other so that they join. When the union has established itself, the parent root of the scion is severed well below the join. The upper growth of both stems thus become dependent on the one root.

Ringing is a method of making a new plant of the whole of the top of a plant which is too "leggy." It is practised with room and greenhouse specimens which have grown too tall for convenient management. A small portion of bark is taken from the stem all round in the form of a ring, and by any suitable means this bared part is kept covered with moist soil. A split flower-pot of soil held in position round the stem is a common way. When the roots have formed, as they quickly do, the lower part of the plant is cut away, and the top with its new roots is potted up to be grown as before. Aralias are suitable subjects for this treatment, as they generally become inconveniently leggy after some years' growth.

Grafting, as far as the amateur is concerned, has two main purposes—to save time and to revitalize a weak plant which is worth keeping on account of its colour or for some similar reason. Experiments with grafting are interesting, but the results are very uncertain without a wide knowledge of the characteristics of both stock and scion; some stocks have more influence on the resulting growth than others, and plants grafted by amateurs often tend to revert to the stock.

PLANT PROPAGATION

ROCK PLANTS AND HERBACEOUS PERENNIALS

Cuttings	Seed	Division
(Early Autumn)	*(Spring)*	*(Spring or Autumn)*
Stem	Alyssum	Achillea
Anthemis	Aquilegia	Aconitum
Dianthus	Delphinium	Anemone japonica
Nepeta	Digitalis	Aster
Pentstemon	Gaillardia	Campanula
Violas	Gypsophila	Chrysanthemum
	Hollyhock	Echinacea
Root	Linum	Helenium
Anchusa	Lupin	Iris
Oriental Poppy	Verbascum	Kniphofia
		Lychnis
Offsets	**Layering**	Phlox
(Spring)	*(Early Spring or*	Pyrethrum
Sempervivum	*Summer)*	Rudbeckia
Bulbs (Lilies, Gladi-	Androsace	Solidago
oli, etc.)	Carnation	Thalictrum
	Pink	Veronica
	Strawberry	

SHRUBS

Cuttings	Seed	Division
(Late Summer or	*(Spring or Autumn)*	*(Spring or Autumn)*
Autumn)	Berberis	Bamboo
Aucuba	Colutea	Kerria
Berberis	Cotoneaster	Ruscus
Buddleia	Cytisus	Spiræa
Buxus (Box)	Escallonia	
Caryopteris	Hypericum	**Grafting**
Ceanothus	Pernettya	Cratægus
Choisya	Spartium	Cydonia
Cistus	Tree Lupin	Golden Holly
Clematis		Hamamelis
Deutzia	**Layering**	Hibiscus
Diervilla	Chimonanthus	Laburnum
Forsythia	Lilac	Prunus
Fuchsia	Pernettya	Pyrus
Jasmine	Rhododendron	Syringa (Lilac)
Lavender	Rubus (Raspberry,	
Olearia	Loganberry, etc.)	
Philadelphus	Syringa (Lilac)	**Budding**
Ribes	Wistaria	Roses
Spiræa		

CHAPTER IV

ANNUALS, BIENNIALS, BULBS AND BEDDING PLANTS

LOOKING at the title of this chapter, the reader may wonder why this particular assortment of flowers has been grouped together. The reason is that, whereas flowering shrubs, including roses and the herbaceous perennials, generally live on undisturbed for a few years, the remainder—the annuals, biennials, bulbs and bedding plants of our title—occupy the attention of the gardener afresh each season. They are, so to speak, only temporary inhabitants of the garden, and fresh quarters have to be found for them, fresh supplies bought or raised annually. From a garden maker's point of view these flowers may therefore well be considered together.

I suppose only those of us who have experimented know how extremely difficult it is to produce a definite colour scheme in a perennial border. We can plan a blue and orange display with delphiniums and poppies, only to find that the poppies have faded before the delphiniums opened, or that the rain has beaten down the poppy stems so that they are almost useless. And so it is with a dozen other schemes; the weather affects the date of flowering, the sun fades the brilliant colours, the colours that the catalogue called red turn out to be orange or bronze, and those the catalogue called crimson turn out to be maroon. In fact, colour schemes in the herbaceous border are a matter for planning over many years, and I doubt if anyone has yet felt that perfection was in sight.

COLOUR IN THE BORDER

When we come to the temporary guests, however, the tale is different. We do not have to wait long for the display to appear, and mistakes, if they occur, are not carried over from year to year. We can choose our seed, and sow it, with at least a reasonable certainty that the plants will be what we intend, and we can plan next year's picture while this season's flowers are still in bloom, so that we can be sure of harmony. We can, in fact, be sure of seasonal colour of the right kind when we use spring bulbs, annuals, biennials and bedding plants. Bedding plants and bulbs, in particular, are safety-first investments, of which the colour and variety is known in advance. A typical annual border arrangement is shown in Fig. 1.

In discussing ways to raise and use these various types of flowers we will begin with annuals, because they are the simplest of all.

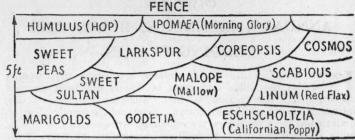

Fig. 1.   *Suggested arrangement of an annual border.*

Annuals are plants that grow from seed, flower, and die in the space of twelve months.

Annuals themselves are of different types. There are hardy annuals, which can be grown in the open, without glass protection, all the year round. With few exceptions they do not flower in the coldest weather, but the plants will live through the winter if the seed germinates before the frosts come.

Hardy annuals can be sown for garden decoration either in spring or in autumn. The spring-sown annuals do not all begin to flower until rather late in the summer, though some will flower and fade before midsummer. Autumn-sown annuals will begin to flower rather early : they may or may not continue for a long time, according to the kind. Most annuals will flower over a longer period if the dying blooms are regularly cut away so that no seeds form. Since it is Nature's desire that seed should form, so long as the plant has strength it will continue to produce blooms in the hope of setting seed.

When seeds are allowed to form, the plant ceases to bloom, and uses its remaining strength to swell the seed. This explains why some gardeners have flowers of annuals in bloom for a much longer period than others.

WHEN AND HOW TO SOW ANNUALS

The method of sowing hardy annuals is simple. It may be assumed that the beds to receive them have been well dug, and that the soil is in good heart, i.e., sufficiently supplied with humus, and broken to a considerable depth. Very rich soil, however, is not desirable; annuals flower better in soil with not too much humus. Bonemeal is an excellent fertilizer for annual flower-beds or borders.

Seed sowing days should be chosen with care. March and late August are good times to sow; but it is wiser to wait a few extra

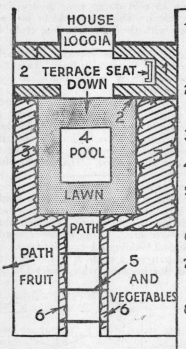

1. POLYANTHA ROSES OR BEDDING AND EARLY DWARF BULBS

2. DWARF ALPINES IN PAVING & WALL

3. PERENNIALS

4. WATER LILIES

5. CLIMBERS ON PERGOLA

6. ANNUALS

7. EVERGREEN FLOWERING SHRUBS

8. SCENTED FLOWERING SHRUBS

9. ALPINES & DWARF BULBS IN ROCKWORK

10. SCENTED CLIMBERS

11. NATURALIZED BULBS

12. STD. FLOWERING TREE

USE OF PLANT MATERIAL IN A SMALL GARDEN

days rather than to try sowing in cold damp soil. A dry day, during showery weather, is the ideal. The soil should be at least dry enough to be easily broken with the rake to a fine crumbly and stone-free surface.

The seed can be sown broadcast, that is, just scattered irregularly over the prepared seed bed, or it can be sown in lines. In either case the rule with most hardy annuals is to sow thinly, so that the young plants are not damaged by thinning out. This thinning out process is always necessary, except with a few edging annuals such as virginia stock, flax (scarlet), nemophila and others. A few annuals will allow themselves to be transplanted while they are still small seedlings, so that there is little waste; but the majority prefer not to be moved, and surplus seedlings that crowd have to be either pinched off or pulled out and wasted. That is why thin sowing is so important.

Beyond watching to prevent crowding, keeping weeds pulled out, and, in the case of large plants, staking when necessary, hardy annuals need little further attention after sowing. They are extremely showy as a class, making bright masses of colour that are particularly useful in garden designs, and no gardener would care to be without them. If formal bedding schemes are favoured, hardy annuals can be sown to a pattern; a circle of white virginian stock round the edge of a bed, for instance, with scarlet flax for

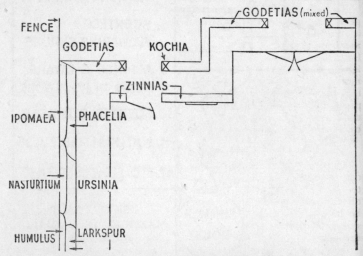

Fig. 2. Narrow border of annuals to follow spring bulbs

an inner ring and tall white candytuft in the centre would make a pretty formal planting scheme in a little circular bed, and would cost only a few pence.

A suggestion for a display of annuals to follow your bulb season in narrow borders is illustrated in Fig. 2, and Fig. 3 shows an attractive layout in blue and yellow for the small front garden.

HALF-HARDY ANNUALS

Annuals of the half-hardy kinds are those which are hardy enough to be grown in the open garden during summer, where they flower just as well as, and often for a longer period than, the hardy annuals, but which will not stand winter days in the open. Some of these half-hardy annuals can be sown in late spring in the garden, in the same way as hardy annuals are sown, but waiting until there is no danger of frost. Others of the half-hardy class are better sown in pots or boxes, in a cold frame or greenhouse, early in the year, and grown under glass until frosts are past, when they are planted out in the beds and borders to flower.

The reason for this method of growing is that many of these plants if sown late in the spring would not reach flowering stage until so late in the autumn that they would be worthless in the garden. Early sowing under glass allows them a longer season of growth, and the plants are then often just ready to flower when they are set out in the open garden.

To raise half-hardy annuals under glass is simple. The seed is generally sown in shallow boxes filled with prepared compost. As a rule the box sides are ill-fitting, so that no extra drainage holes are needed. The compost used is a mixture of about half loam from the garden borders (or chopped turf that has been stacked for a time) one-quarter leaf-mould and one-quarter sand. Less leaf-mould can be used when dealing with the more delicate plants that show a tendency to damp off under glass; but an even better precaution against this trouble is to drench the soil with Cheshunt compound before any sowing is done. Cheshunt compound is sold by all stores and florists.

SOIL FOR SEED BOXES

The soil, when mixed, should be sieved, and the coarser parts can be put at the bottom of the box, while the remainder is used to fill the box loosely. A piece of board can be used to smooth off the surface level with the rim. Afterwards the board should be laid flat on the soil surface and pressed lightly, so that the soil surface is flattened and comes $\frac{1}{2}$ in. or so lower than the rim of the box.

Seed can be broadcast over the box, or sown in parallel lines 2 or 3 in. apart. The thinner it is sown the better, as transplanting will be simplified. A piece of glass over each box is always advisable, as this allows the gardener to air the frame for the benefit of other plants, while the seeds are not harmed. Shade from brilliant sunshine is desirable at first, and watering should be done very carefully—preferably by partial immersion of the seed box, if fine seed is sown, as it can so easily be washed away by the use of the can. The sheet of glass should be turned over each day to remove condensed moisture.

IMPORTANCE OF LIGHT AND AIR

Bottom heat—standing the seed boxes over the hot pipes in the greenhouse—speeds up seed germination, but is not necessary with half-hardy annuals. As soon as the seedlings can be seen above the soil, they should be allowed all the light and air possible —frost being strictly excluded of course. When the second pair of leaves has formed, look over the boxes, and if there is the least tendency for the seedlings to crowd, prick them off at once into other boxes, filled with similar compost. Pricking off has been described in the previous chapter, where further advice on the planting of seeds has also been given.

Seedlings pricked off into boxes for market are usually set 2 in. apart over the box. Those grown for home consumption may be allowed more room if it can be spared. They may even, in some cases, be best set separately in small pots, so that they can be planted out with a minimum of root disturbance. Cosmeas are a case of this kind. They prefer to be set in small thumb pots and left there, even though their roots fill the pots, until planting-out time. In fact, if the first flowers are visible on the seedlings when they are planted in the open garden, the plants will flower continuously until the frosts.

As soon as the weather permits, half-hardy annuals raised in this way are hardened off by gradual stages. First they are left in the frame at night with the glass lights half open. Then the lights are left off entirely, unless there are hard frosts. Then the boxes may stand on the path for a few days, and finally the plants are hardened sufficiently to be set out in the open border.

WHEN TO PLANT OUT

The time at which planting out can occur varies according to the tenderness of the plants in question. Annual carnations, for instance, can be set out as soon as they are large enough. They are not really tender, except perhaps in the baby stage, but are grown under glass because they need a long season of growth before they begin to flower. Zinnias would not be safe to transplant until the end of May, as a late frost would kill them.

Throughout the world of horticulture and botany the work of

plant classification goes on year after year, never ceasing. The reason for this is two-fold. It is partly because new plants are constantly appearing, as a result of cross-breeding; and partly because there are seldom any hard and fast dividing lines. Most sections of the plant world are so closely related to one another that the groups tend to merge, and hence a plant of one species is sometimes re-classified and grouped with a nearly related species.

So we find a close relationship between the plants we classify as annuals, biennials, and perennials. An annual is a plant that lives its allotted span within a twelvemonth—yet some of the plants we know as annuals occasionally live longer. You may, for instance, often find an old root of the common pot marigold flowering into the second and even third year.

Biennials are only different from annuals in that they generally take two seasons to complete the cycle of life, one season to grow to strong healthy plants, and a second season in which to send up flower stems and carry seed. A great many of the plants commonly

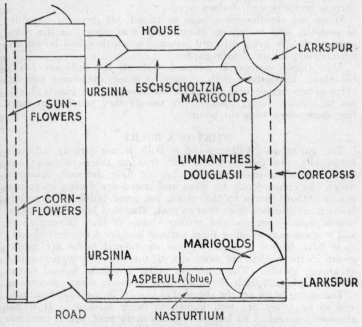

Fig. 3. A blue and yellow scheme for annuals.

SSG—D

called biennials can be grown and flowered in a single season if the seed is sown under glass in the early months of the year. And further, as this method is a very convenient one for amateur gardeners, seedsmen are gradually obtaining by selection what are known as " annual " varieties of such biennials as Canterbury bells and anchusa.

The hardy biennials of the old type are such favourites that it is not likely they will be ousted altogether. Wallflowers, for instance, are easily raised in the vegetable garden, and planted out after the summer flowers are over; they furnish the garden in midwinter with their evergreen foliage, and break into a blaze of colour at the first sign of spring.

To raise hardy biennials, glass is not necessary; though it is sometimes convenient to sow costly seed in a frame, where it can be safely guarded from birds and other troubles.

Wallflowers can be sown in lines in the vegetable garden, or in a nursery plot. About 8 in. should be left between the rows, and during the early stages a hoe should be run through the soil, to keep it crumbly and destroy weeds.

When the wallflowers appear to crowd, lift them as carefully as possible, and transplant them about 6 in. apart, in the same nursery plot, to grow on until autumn, when they will be set out permanently in the flower garden.

This simple method is adopted with all the ordinary hardy biennials. Canterbury bells, it may be noted, sometimes take an extra season before they are ready to flower. Late plants should not be thrown away, however, for usually they provide an extra fine show when they do bloom.

WHAT IS A BULB?

The gardeners' definition of a bulb is not strictly accurate botanically. In the garden a bulb may be taken to mean any kind of swollen underground tuber or fully dormant rootstock which can conveniently be lifted and stored dry during its resting season without harm to the plant, but some bulbs are certainly best left undisturbed from year to year, Madonna lilies for example; this is mainly because the resting season of lilies is very short, and it is not easy to move them without damage if the new season's roots have begun to form. These exceptional bulbs are mostly grown in the herbaceous border, with the other hardy perennials, or among shrubs. The common bulbs, grown in formal flower beds and planted fresh seasonally are, however, what concern us.

The spring bulbs are the showiest of all—tulips, narcissi, hyacinths and so on; they are well known to every gardener. It is not absolutely necessary to buy fresh bulbs every year, but it certainly pays to buy fresh ones for formal bedding schemes where strict uniformity of size, and in the date of flowering, are important.

The cultivation of bulbs is simplicity itself. When the natural soil of the garden is sandy, it is sufficient preparation to dig over the beds, and incorporate any available old decayed manure, leaves, etc. On heavy soils, however, bulbs may be inclined to decay if care is not taken. The soil should be dug well, to improve the drainage, and dressed with lime after digging to assist in breaking down the sticky lumps.

When the bulbs are planted a trowel should be used to open a hole for each, and a little sand should be kept handy, so that a small handful can be dropped into the prepared hole before the bulb is set in place. This prevents the accumulation of water at the base of the bulb, and so minimizes the danger of decay.

The depth and distance apart of bulbs used for formal bedding can be roughly estimated by the planter. About twice the bulb's own depth of soil should be over it, and the distance apart should be roughly about the same number of inches; e.g., assuming that a tulip bulb measures 2 in. from tip to base, it can be planted in a hole made 6 in. deep, and from 4 to 6 in. can be left between the bulbs. (*See* Fig. 4 for the planting depths of various bulbs.) Remember, when planting in heavy soil that the holes

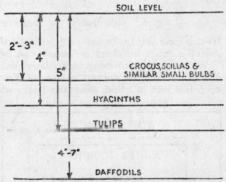

Fig. 4.   Depths at which bulbs are planted.

must be a little deeper to allow for the handful of sand referred to above.

This is merely a rough guide, and some bulbs, particularly those that are to remain and naturalize themselves in the less formal parts of the garden, can do with deeper planting.

BULB PLANTING METHODS

In planting large quantities of bulbs, an easy plan is to spread a layer of sand all over the beds first : then as each hole is made some of the sand falls in, the bulb is dropped in, and rests on the sandy base. All the holes can be filled in at one operation with the rake, leaving the bed neat and tidy. If other plants are set out from the nursery, with the bulbs, the planting is done alternately (as shown in Fig. 5), and the bulbs covered as the planting proceeds.

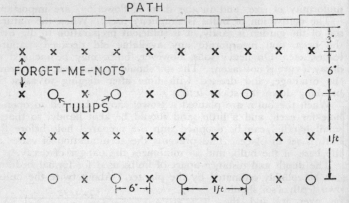

Fig. 5. *Bulb spacing for tulips and forget-me-nots.*

In this case the bulbs are best laid out on the soil surface first, so that the exact numbers necessary can be calculated.

When spring flowering bulbs have finished blooming they have not finished their normal season of growth. It is important to keep this fact in mind, since the bulbs will be useless another year

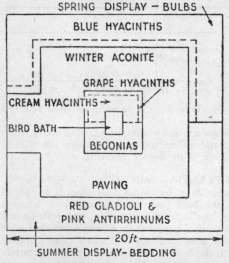

Fig. 6. *Formal layout for spring and summer.*

if they cannot grow on through the early part of the summer, developing more foliage, and by this means also making a fresh store of plant food in the bulb. However, since the appearance of gradually dying foliage is not pleasant in formal beds, the bulbs can be lifted, as carefully as possible, with soil round the roots, and these roots can be replanted in the nursery plot, or some part of the garden where they are not on view. They can then, if space is precious, be packed into deep boxes of soil and left there to

finish their season of growth.   Only when the foliage has completely
turned colour should the bulbs be dried off, in the open air, and
then stored until the autumn planting season.

Apart from the use of bulbs in the formal beds (Fig. 6) they are
valued by gardeners for the patches of colour they give in the spring
in all other parts of the garden—e.g., in groups in the mixed borders,
in the rock garden, in the shrubbery, and under trees, where they
can naturalize themselves in the grass (Figs. 7 and 8).

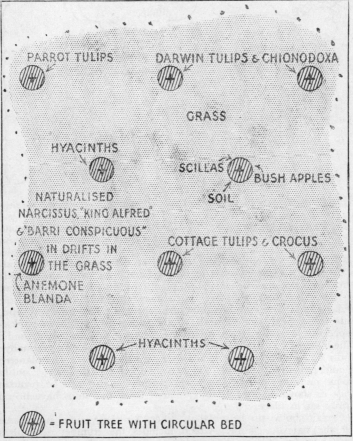

Fig. 7. Bulb planting round trees in a small orchard.

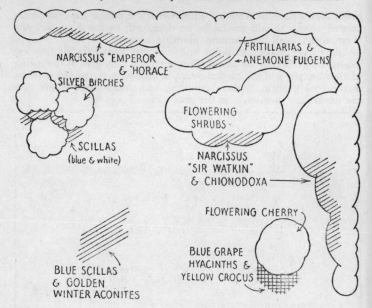

Fig. 8.   *Bulbs in the informal garden in relation to flowering shrubs.*

A good practice is to buy fresh bulbs each season for the formal beds, and to use those from the store shed for informal groups, in the mixed borders, or for naturalizing.

To plant for naturalizing (a subject discussed more fully in Chapter X) a good way is to take a handful of bulbs and scatter them over the grass or woodland, planting them where they happen to rest.   Irregular drifts are much more attractive than circles of bulbs round trees—an irregular drift spreading out widely to one side will appear very natural.   Bulbs naturalize happily in banks, especially in grassy banks where the mower is seldom if ever used. The foliage of naturalized bulbs must, of course, die down gradually if the bulbs are to remain healthy season after season.   The planter should remember that this will prevent the use of the mower until about midsummer.   In the lawn, portions of turf can be turned back as shown in Fig. 9, and replaced when the bulbs have been firmly set in place.

Certain bulbs do better than others for the various purposes. All the narcissus family—which includes the trumpet daffodils, short cup daffodils, poet's narcissus and many other types, all of which are fully described in catalogues—prefer early planting, and like if possible to grow on year after year without disturbance. They gradually increase in number and beauty in gardens where they can be left alone in this fashion.   August is not too early to plant, if the bulbs are obtainable then.

Hyacinths are best planted in late September or October, and are fine for formal beds.   The bedding size hyacinths should be used; they are less expensive than " top size " and generally more uniform.   Hyacinths invariably deteriorate in gardens as the seasons pass, and old bulbs are only fit for woodland and orchard planting.

Tulips are the bedding bulbs that deservedly take pride of place in popular favour.   They are uniform, brilliant, neat and reliable. Tulips should not be planted until November, for if they are too far forward in the early days of the year, and are subjected to too many hard frosts while the flower-bud is unprotected, they will fail to flower.   Certain tulip types—the May flowering tulips for instance, and a number of the tulip species—will grow well if left undisturbed, but the main plantings of florists' tulips should be regarded as bedding subjects, and lifted and dried for storing when the foliage yellows.   Do not dry tulips in scorching sunshine, or the bulbs may be damaged; but see that they are thoroughly dried off before storing, or they may become mouldy.

BULBS FOR THE SUMMER GARDEN

Summer flowering bulbs are also suitable for more or less formal bedding schemes.   The gladiolus is one of the most useful of bulbs for this purpose.

Gladioli are planted from February onwards. If some are planted every three weeks, there will be a continuous supply of flowers for cutting over several months. About mid-May the last batch should be set in the ground, and these will flower in late autumn.

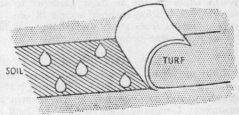

Fig. 9.   *How to roll back a square of turf and insert bulbs underneath.*

Gladioli and other summer bulbs are planted in exactly the same way as spring bulbs, and like them can be used formally or informally.   Some of the summer bulbs are quite hardy and can remain in the ground for many years; others are only hardy enough to remain in the open in the warmer parts of the country.   Soil conditions make all the difference in this respect, and a garden on naturally sandy soil is always warmer than one on clay. Lilies, for instance, can be grown quite well for many years without being moved, and will gain in beauty as the years pass, if the soil is sandy and leafy, as where a woodland exists on a sandy hill-side. But if grown in heavy loam, they will only do well if lifted at the end of each summer, stored in dry sand, and replanted in early spring.

Whenever a doubt exists about the hardiness of the summer bulbs, they can be lifted as the foliage turns colour, and hung in bunches in a shed until they are dry. Then the bulbs (or corms) should be rubbed clean, carefully inspected in case any disease is present, and finally stored in boxes of dry sand. Sawdust and cork chippings are other materials good for bulb storage.

ALWAYS DESTROY DISEASED BULBS

Diseases affect most plants, and a diseased tuber of any kind should never be either stored or replanted, since the spores of the disease will quickly travel to others. The safest way in a little garden is to burn all diseased specimens, and buy fresh ones. Some diseases can be controlled, but I doubt if it ever pays the small garden owner to fight diseases among bulbs that are reasonably cheap to buy.

A question often asked is whether bulbs can be raised from seed. Obviously they can, since seed is the natural method of increase; or perhaps one should say it is one natural method, for bulbs would also increase by division, in their natural state. With most bulbs, however, the waiting period is rather considerable, and it is not worth while for the amateur gardener to sow seeds and wait for several years before raising a first bloom. New varieties are, of course, raised from seed; and those who like to experiment can do so with some prospect of success.

HOW TO RAISE BULBS FROM SEED

Bulb seeds are generally sown in an ordinary seed mixture of sandy loam with leaf-mould. The first leaves are usually fine and grasslike, and many a novice has thrown away his seedlings by mistake. Generally they should be kept in the pot in which they were sown until the end of the second year, when they can be planted out to grow on in a nursery plot.

Some of the lilies offered in modern seed catalogues grow to flowering stage in a year—Lilium *regale* will do this in favourable conditions. These are among the more rewarding bulb plants as subjects for the seed boxes.

Any plant which is propagated afresh each season in large quantities, used for seasonal bedding, and then discarded, is properly called a bedding plant. The term therefore includes annuals, biennials and bulbs, such as have already been mentioned in this chapter. It may also include certain herbaceous perennials, and certain shrubs, hardy and tender.

Bedding plants are increased in any of the ways possible in gardening—by seed raising, cuttings, root division and so on—as described in Chapter III. The majority of them are used for only one season after being propagated; but there are exceptions. Some of the taller, shrubby kinds, for instance standard fuchsias, are used year after year. They may be kept in their pots and the pots sunk just below the soil surface for the duration of the summer only; or they may be knocked out of their pots when they are put in the garden, and potted up afresh in the autumn.

As the average novice finds it difficult to distinguish between annuals, perennials, shrubs and so on, and as to some extent the method of treating plants may be different, even though they belong to the same class, we will describe in detail an all-the-year-round treatment for various bedding plants that are fairly typical of a large group.

Ageratum. This is a half-hardy annual, used freely for edging summer beds. It is sometimes raised from seed in the way usual for half-hardy annuals; but frequently old plants are kept in pots, through the winter, at a temperature of 50 degrees, as stock plants. Cuttings of the young growths can be taken in March at the same time as seed sowing is done, and grown for use in the summer beds. Stock plants are not allowed to flower—they are pinched back periodically to encourage the production of plenty of young side growths. Pinching is the term used for nipping off the tiny growing tip of the central stem, or of the side stems.

Antirrhinums are the kings of the formal flower beds. Nothing makes a brighter or more compact mass of uniform colour. There are various types; the dwarfs for edgings, intermediates for main bedding displays, and tall varieties for the mixed flower border. Antirrhinums are actually perennials, but the first season produces the best blooms. Moreover, uniformity is only obtained among the young plants. They can be raised from seed, and many varieties of the seed now breed almost entirely true to type. Odd " rogues " in a formal bed should be taken out immediately they show their flower, and to replace them it is well to have growing on in pots one or two extra plants from the same packet of seed, which can be used if needed.

Antirrhinums, like ageratums, can also be increased by cuttings; but the usual method with antirrhinums is to take them from the plants in the beds, in autumn. Side growths that have no flowers are selected, and pulled from the old plant with a downward jerk.

SSG—D*

The lowest pair of leaves is stripped off, and the cuttings inserted about 1 in. apart over a bed of sandy soil in the cold frame, or, if more convenient, in boxes of prepared sandy soil. They are kept close for a few weeks, but are later ventilated whenever possible, though frosts must be excluded.

By about April the plants should be ready to leave the shelter of the frame. If they show a tendency before then to run up into tall, " leggy " plants, the tips should be pinched out. This will result in short, bushy plants of even appearance when planted out in the beds.

Antirrhinums are very easy plants to fit into a general scheme such as the one sketched in Fig. 10; they blend well with most kinds of flowers, as both their colour and their shape can be chosen with reasonable certainty of attaining the effect you desire.

Begonias are fine bedding plants for beds where the soil is moist. They prefer a full sun, but will also do reasonably well in partial shade. There are two groups — the fibrous-rooted, which are usually raised from seed sown in a warm greenhouse in the early months of the year, or from leaf cuttings (*see* Chapter III); and the tuberous-rooted group, which can be bought as tubers, if preferred, though it is also possible to raise these from seed.

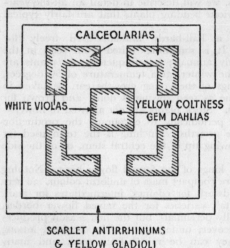

CALCEOLARIAS

WHITE VIOLAS

YELLOW COLTNESS GEM DAHLIAS

SCARLET ANTIRRHINUMS & YELLOW GLADIOLI

Fig. 10. *Formal parti-coloured design to include various bedding plants.*

If tubers are bought, they should be set to sprout in moist coconut fibre or leaf-mould, in a warm greenhouse. As soon as the young shoots are visible, the roots can be potted up into sandy, leafy soil, and grown on until the end of May, when it is safe to use them in the garden beds. About mid-September the plants should be lifted, packed into pots or boxes, and gradually allowed to dry off under cover. It will then be possible to use the tubers again.

Calceolaria is an example of a shrub which is only rarely recognized as such by the amateur gardener. There are herbaceous calceolarias; but these are the large flowered type that are grown under glass all the time. Bedding calceolarias are shrubby, and given a warm enough climate would make larger, more shrubby growths than they are, in fact, allowed to make in our gardens. The usual practice with these is to take cuttings in mid-September or soon after, i.e., before the frosts ruin the plants in the beds, and to keep them through the winter like antirrhinums. As a matter of fact calceolarias propagate very easily in this way; without a cold frame and using only one or two small sheets of glass, the amateur can supply himself with sufficient bedding plants from these very useful flowers. All that is necessary is to dig out a deep hole, just a little smaller at the top than the piece of glass, and see that there is a depth of at least 4 in. of good, sandy soil in the bottom, leaving 6 or 7 in. of space above. The cuttings are taken (as for antirrhinums) and inserted close together in the prepared soil, and a sheet of glass is then laid over and pressed down on to the surrounding soil. It need not be moved to give ventilation during the winter—the plants will keep quite well unattended in most seasons. In spring the glass can be propped up at the return of bright sunshine, and if it is convenient, the plants can be potted up separately and given a few weeks of steady growth in a frame before planting out in mid-May. Even this is not imperative, however, and plants can often remain where they are until needed for the beds.

Cannas are fleshy, tuberous-rooted perennials of somewhat tender nature, similar to dahlias, and requiring much the same treatment. (*See* below.)

Cineraria maritima is the grey foliaged plant that is often used for summer bedding. This is best raised from seed sown in heat in the spring.

Dahlias are tuberous-rooted perennials; because they are somewhat tender, they must be either raised from seed in the manner of half-hardy annuals, or stored as tubers during the winter and re-started into growth in the spring. Seeds of many modern strains give a fine selection of colours, and are a cheap and easy way to grow dahlias for general decoration in the garden, or for cut flowers in the house. Named varieties of dahlia must, however, be grown from the stored tubers.

Dahlia tubers are lifted in the autumn, before the first frosts, or immediately the frost blackens the leaves, and after being dried a little they are either hung in bunches in a frost-proof shed or cellar, or stored in boxes of dry sand or sawdust, whichever is the more convenient.

Very early in the year—usually about February—the tubers are taken from store, and separated, since they are usually in bunches. They are then laid on trays of moist leafy soil, standing in the warm

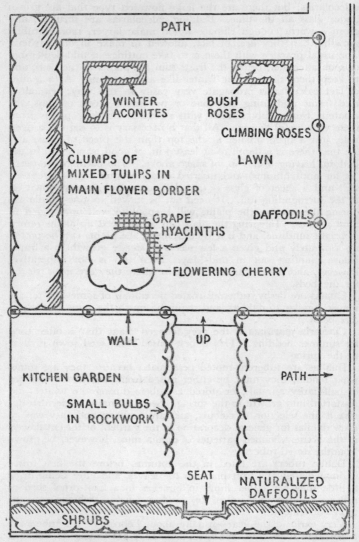

Fig. 11. How bulbs can be used in the garden layout.

greenhouse, preferably over bottom heat. This induces young shoots to develop from the dormant eyes of the tubers. These young shoots are cut off with a sharp knife when they are 2 in. long, if possible with a portion of the tuber attached, though this is not essential. They are inserted at once in pots of sandy soil, and kept in a propagating frame, or in a close atmosphere, for two or three weeks, until they have well rooted. The pots are then put on the light shelves of the greenhouse, or into the cold frame, and grown on until the end of May, when they are wanted for the summer beds.

Dahlias are hungry plants; even in the small pots they should be kept well supplied with water, and in the later stages, with occasional doses of liquid manure. When they have grown to a height of about 9 in., the tips are pinched out, so that a bushy growth results. Feeding is also important when the plants reach the border, and soil preparation for dahlias should always be on generous lines. A spadeful of old stable manure, or some sub-stitute, worked into the subsoil is a help, since it retains moisture during dry weather. Dahlias rarely grow successfully without some artificial watering, and a pailful of water every other night in hot weather, followed occasionally by a dose of liquid manure, is the best way to ensure healthy strong plants and a fine crop of flowers. Dahlias are sun-lovers, too, and can be grown to perfection only in full sunshine.

One other point concerning dahlia culture : there are, as every catalogue will show, many types of dahlias, from dwarfs to giants. All except the small bedding types need stakes, and the tall kinds need very stout stakes. These should be set out when the plants are first put into the open, and ties should be made frequently, for dahlia foliage and stems are very heavy, and wind damage cannot be repaired.

Eucalyptus is an example of a tender greenhouse shrub which must also be included in summer bedding types. Eucalyptus is actually a large tree, but rather tender. E. *citriodora*, or the " lemon-scented gum," is the species generally grown in pots. E. *globulus* is used often for summer bedding. Eucalyptus is propagated by seed sown in pots of sandy soil in a temperature of 60 to 65 degrees, and later grown in a compost of loam (two parts) leaf-mould and sand (one part each) and some charcoal. The plants are generally re-potted in March, and are planted out for summer bedding from June to September. They can be kept in the pots, which may be sunk below the soil surface for the summer, and brought indoors again for the winter. If con-venient, cuttings can be rooted under glass in June.

Fuchsia is another type of shrub which is very suitable as a bedding plant. The fuchsias of the greenhouse are often grown to a very large size, either in hanging baskets, or as standards, according to type. Standard fuchsias are frequently taken into the open in the summer, and often sunk in their pots in the formal beds, to give them height. Fuchsias are also raised annually from cuttings, taken in spring, to provide small plants for formal bedding. Ordinary bush types of fuchsia are cut back about February, so that they make strong new growths and become bushy plants.

If young bedding plants are desired, these new growths are taken off and inserted in sandy soil in a propagating frame. They are then potted up in a compost half of loam, and a quarter each of sand and of leaf-mould. In this they are grown on until May, when they can be set out in the beds. Fuchsias are useful for formal beds in partial shade, and mix well with calceolarias and violas.

Geraniums can be treated like the fuchsias for bedding, but the best way is to take cuttings in late autumn, before the old plants are lifted from the borders. Geraniums used for bedding are botanically known as Pelargonium *zonale*, and are not true geraniums. Cuttings struck in spring often fail to flower until rather late in the year, while autumn-rooted cuttings, inserted close together in boxes, and wintered in a cool greenhouse, and then potted up separately in spring, usually flower freely all the summer.

Heliotropium, the favourite " cherry pie," is a shrub, and can be treated like the geraniums, i.e., raised from autumn cuttings and wintered under glass. It is also possible to obtain strains of seed that will produce good flowering plants the first season, if treated as half-hardy annuals, and this method sometimes has advantages.

Salvias used for bedding are of varied types. The scarlet S. *splendens* is best treated as a half-hardy annual. The vivid blue S. *patens* is tuberous-rooted, and can be treated in the same way as a dahlia.

Arabis is one of the many useful early flowering plants that are used for spring bedding. There are two good ways to increase arabis—root division and cuttings. When the arabis in the spring beds has served its turn, it can either be cut back hard and left where it is to form a green edging to the summer border, or lifted for increase. If lifted, the roots can be torn apart into as many pieces as convenient, and set out in a nursery bed to grow on until autumn, when they will again be wanted to associate with spring bulbs. Alternatively, cuttings of pieces 2 or 3 in. long, pulled off without much ceremony, can be inserted in sandy soil, in a shady nursery bed. Arabis, aubrietia, cerastium—this last used sometimes for summer beds, but inclined to become untidy—and many other such " carpet " plants, root quite easily, and masses can be raised annually for distribution where needed in the garden picture.

Violas can, just like pansies, be raised from seed, which can be sown towards the end of summer, in late August, so that plants are well grown for spring planting, and provide plenty of early flowers. Violas raised from seed can be set out as edgings to the bulb beds in autumn, but preferably cuttings should be taken, and a fresh supply of young plants obtained by that means. Cuttings will root easily if taken in autumn or spring, or at any time when suitable side growths are available. They need to be put into sandy soil, and kept close in a cold frame until rooted. Cuttings taken in late autumn should remain in the frame all the winter, but should be allowed plenty of ventilation after the first three weeks. Golden alyssum and many similar bedding plants can also be raised from seed or cuttings.

The above selections are by no means all the valuable and easily raised bedding plants, as the attached lists will show. They are merely typical of the kind of plants that are so used, and of the ways in which the plants are produced.

HINTS FOR BEGINNERS

Generally speaking, the beginner in garden matters will buy most of his bedding plants as he buys his bulbs, probably from a local nursery or market. As he may wonder how to buy to best advantage, and what to look for in buying, the following general hints may prove useful.

First of all, it does pay to order in good time. If you have no glass at all, and cannot give temporary shelter to tender plants, tell the nurseryman this, and refuse to accept delivery of the summer bedding plants until the last week in May. It will then be too late for severe frosts, and you are not likely to suffer big losses.

It pays to order in good time for another reason. If the bedding scheme is to be successful, you must be able to pick and choose colours and varieties. This you may be able to do, if your nursery is large, at any time up to the date of delivery. It is sometimes best, however, if you can call at the nursery even as early as January with a list of possible requirements, especially if you want a particular variety. The nurseryman will be only too glad to sow varieties for a certain market, and will choose his seed accordingly.

In buying, make sure that you obtain plants that are short jointed and thick in the stem, with foliage of rather dark colour, according to variety, of course (some antirrhinums have naturally darker foliage than others). If the stems are thin and drawn, with long spaces between the leaves on the stem, the plants have been weakened by too much heat, or by lack of sunshine. Moreover, if you are to put the plants straight into the garden, they should have been hardened off by standing in the open for a time; this would have caused the foliage to be darker.

If you have to accept plants that are inclined to be " leggy," pinch out the growing tips, so that side shoots are encouraged. It is

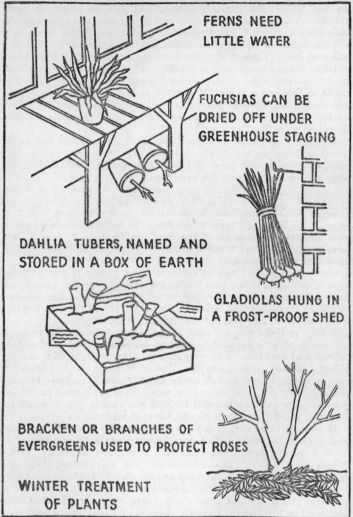

FERNS NEED LITTLE WATER

FUCHSIAS CAN BE DRIED OFF UNDER GREENHOUSE STAGING

DAHLIA TUBERS, NAMED AND STORED IN A BOX OF EARTH

GLADIOLAS HUNG IN A FROST-PROOF SHED

BRACKEN OR BRANCHES OF EVERGREENS USED TO PROTECT ROSES

WINTER TREATMENT OF PLANTS

HOW TO STORE PLANTS UNDER GLASS.

safe to do this on most bedding plants of the antirrhinum type, and on dahlias. Pinching back actually results in more flowers, though it may possibly delay the arrival of the first blooms a little.

When unpacking the plants from the usual market box used for seedlings and cuttings, break off one side of the box first. If the soil is dry, water the plants well, and leave them to soak for an hour or two.

In planting, first make a hole with a trowel, then take the plant from its box or pot with as little disturbance as possible of the soil round the root, hold it in position, and press moist (but not too wet) soil round it. If the weather is very dry, you may be well advised to water the bed or border an hour or two before starting to plant out.

THE BEST TIME FOR PLANTING

Plant out in the evening or late afternoon if you can conveniently arrange it, and water the plants overhead immediately after planting. They will then have time to settle in during the night, and will suffer less from the sun the following day.

Plant very firmly, pressing the soil well against the plant roots. More fatalities occur through loose planting than from any other cause.

And, by the way, whatever plants or bulbs you use for spring or summer bedding, do make a note of the name and variety. You may prefer not to use labels in the beds; if so, make a note in a garden note book. This is very important, not only because friends will ask you what the name of the variety is, but also because you yourself will be wondering, at the end of the season, whether you will be able to repeat your successes in the formal beds, or to avoid your failures, another season. The note book habit really is worth a little trouble to cultivate.

Here is a sowing table for annuals and biennials. This is followed by tables classifying the various types of bulbs and a full planting table for bulbs. Finally you will find a full classification of the various varieties of annuals and biennials.

BIENNIALS

Sow outside May to July. Transplant in autumn (or spring).

ANNUALS

Sow half-hardy annuals under glass—January to April.
Sow half-hardy annuals outside—May.
Sow hardy annuals outside—March to May, and September.
Plant out annuals sown under glass at the end of April and May after hardening them off a few days prior to the planting out.

BULBS

Suitable for Naturalizing in Grass

Crocus	Fritillaria meleagris
Daffodils (all kinds)	Snowdrops

Suitable for Use in Wild Garden

Anemones	Dog's Tooth Violets	Squill
Chionodoxa	Grape Hyacinths	Snowflakes
Corydalis	Hyacinths	Winter Aconite
Daffodils	Lilies (dwarf ones)	

Suitable for Use in Rock Garden

Anemone	Grape Hyacinths	Narcissus triandrus
Chionodoxa	Iris reticulata	Snowdrops
Crocus		

Suitable for the Waterside

Daffodils	Tulips	Iris

Suitable at different Seasons

Spring

Anemones	Hyacinths	Narcissus
Crocus	Muscari	Tulips
Fritillary		

Summer

Begonias	Gladiolus	Iris	Lilies

Autumn

Colchicum	Gladiolus	Montbretia

Winter

Iris reticulata	Snowdrops
Iris stylosa	Winter Aconites

PLANTING TABLE FOR BULBS

	Best month to plant	Depth of top of bulb below surface in inches	Distance apart in inches
Allium	October	4	4
Anemone fulgens	October	2	4
„ (St. Brigid) ..	October	2	5
Chionodoxa	August	3	3
Colchicum	August	6	3 to 6
Crocus	August	3	3
Fritillaria (Crown Imperial)	August	4	4 to 9
„ (Snake's Head) ..	August	3	3
Galanthus (Snowdrop) ..	August	3 to 4	3
Galtonia	March	4	9
Gladiolus	April	4	9
Hyacinths	October	4	8
Iris, English	September	5	4 to 6
„ Dutch	October	5	4 to 6
„ Spanish	October	4	4
„ reticulata	September	4	3
Ixia	October	3	4
Leucojum	August	3	4
Lily of the Valley	November	2	4
Lilium auratum	October	6 to 8	12
„ Henryi	October	6 to 8	12
„ speciosum	October	6 to 8	12
„ pardalinum	October	4	12
„ tigrinum	October	8	12
Muscari	October	3	3
Narcissus	September	6	6
„ (dwarf)	September	4	4
Scilla sibirica	August	3	3
Tulips, long-stemmed ..	November	4	6
„ short-stemmed ..	November	4	6
Winter Aconite	August	2 to 3	3 to 4

ANNUALS AND BIENNIALS

R. = Suitable for Rock Garden.

Name	Colour	Height in fee.	Seed Sowing When	Seed Sowing Where	Hardy or Half-hardy	Remarks
Acroclinium	Pink	1	March	Open	H.	Everlasting
Ageratum	Mauve	¼	„	Inside	H.H.	R. Edging
Alonsoa	Scarlet, pink	1	„	„	H.H.	R. Edging, carpeting
Alyssum maritimum	White	⅜	Sept.	Open	H.	—
Ammobium alatum	White	2½	Spring	Inside	H.H.	Everlasting
Antirrhinum	Various	¾–3	Feb.	„	H.H.	Bedding
Arctotis	Orange	2	„	„	H.H.	—
Aster	Various	1–3	May	Open	H.H.	Bedding
Bartonia aurea	Yellow	1½	Spring	Inside	H.	—
Cacalia coccinea	Scarlet	1½	„	Inside	H.H.	—
Calendula	Yellow, orange	1½	Sept.	Open	H.	—
Candytuft	Various	1	„	„	H.	—
Canterbury Bell	Blue, white, pink	3	April–July	„	—	Biennial
Cheiranthus allioni	Orange	½–1	August	„	H.	Bedding
Chrysanthemum	Yellow	1–3	March	„	H.H.	—
Clarkia	Various	1	Spring	„	H.	—
Collomia coccinea	Red	¾	„	Inside	H.H.	Bedding
Coreopsis	Yellow, bronze	3	„	Open	H.	—
Cornflower	Pink, blue white	3	Sept.	„	H.	—
Cosmea	Various	4	Spring	Inside	H.H.	—
Dianthus	Various	1	„	„	H.H.	Bedding
Dimorphotheca	Orange	1½	„	„	H.H.	„
Dimorphotheca	Orange	1½	May	Open	H.H.	„

Name	Colour	Height	Month of sowing	Where sown	Hardiness	Remarks
Erysimum	Mauve	1½	Spring	Open	H.H.	R.
Eschscholtzia	Various	1	,,	,,	H.	R.
Felicia	Blue	½	May	,,	H.H.	Bedding
Godetia	Various	2	Spring	,,	H.	Excellent for cutting
Gypsophila elegans	White	1	,,	,,	H.	Everlasting
Gypsophila muralis	Rose	⅜	,,	Inside	H.	,,
Helichrysum	Bronze	3	,,	,,	H.	
Hollyhock	Various	3	May	Open	H.H.	R.
Ionopsidium acaule	Mauve	¼	,,	,,	H.H.	—
Ipomœa	Blue, white	Climbing	Spring	,,	H.H.	—
Jacobea	Various	1½	,,	,,	H.	Bedding
Larkspur	Blue, pink	2½-3	,,	,,	H.	Excellent for cutting
Lavatera	Pink, white	—	,,	,,	H.H.	R.
Leptosiphon	Various	¼	May	,,	H.	R. Very early spring flowering
Limnanthes Douglasii	Yellow	½	Sept.	,,	H.	R. Sow where to flower
Linaria	Various	1	Spring	,,	H.	
Lobelia	Blue	¼-½	,,	Inside	H.H.	R. Edging or massing
Mignonette	White, red yellow	1	,,	,,	H.H.	Scented
Nasturtium	Various	Climbing	May	Open	H.H.	—
Nemesia	,,	1	Spring	Inside	H.H.	Raise singly in pots for best results
Nemophila insignis	Blue	½	,,	Open	H.	Edging
Nicotiana	White, crimson	3	,,	Inside	H.H.	Sweet scented
Nigella	Blue, white	1½	Sept.	Open	H.	
Papaver	Various	2	Spring	,,	H.	Sow where to flower
Petunia	,,	1½	,,	Inside	H.H.	
Phacelia	Blue	1	,,	Open	H.H.	
Phlox Drummondi	Various	1	,,	Inside	H.H.	Bedding
Rhodanthe	Pink	¾-1	,,	,,	H.H.	Everlasting

ANNUALS AND BIENNIALS—Continued

R. = Suitable for Rock Garden.

Name	Colour	Height in feet	Seed Sowing			Hardy or Half-hardy	Remarks
			When	Where			
Rudbeckia (Autumn Glow)	Yellow	1½	Spring	Outside	H.H.	Sept.–Oct. flowering
Salpiglossis	Various	3	,,	Inside	H.H.	—
Scabious	,,	3	,,	,,	H.H.	—
Silene	Pink	⅛–1	,,	Open	H.	—
Statice	White, pink purple	1½	,,	Inside	H.H.	Everlasting
Stock (Ten Week)	Various	1½	,,	,,	H.H.	Bedding
,, (Brompton)	,,	1½	July	Open	H.	—
,, (Inter)	,,	1½	Spring	Inside	H.H.	—
,, (Virginian)	Mixed	⅛	,,	Open	H.	R. Edging
Sunflower	Yellow	3–10	,,	Inside	H.	—
Sweet Pea	Various	Climbing	,,	Open	H.H.	Set outside or inside in pots or boxes
Sweet William	Yellow, orange	1½	May–July	Open	—	Bedding; biennial
Tagetes	Yellow	1½–2	Spring	Inside	H.H.	Bedding
Tropæolum canariensis	Orange	Climbing	,,	,,	H.H.	—
Ursinia	,,	1	,,	,,	H.H.	Bedding
Venidium fastuosum	,,	2–3	,,	,,	H.H.	—
Verbena	Various	1	,,	,,	H.H.	—
Viscaria	,,	1	,,	,,	H.H.	—
Wallflower	,,	2	July	Open	H.	Bedding; biennial
Xeranthemum	Purple	2	March	Inside	H.H.	Biennial; bedding; everlasting
Zinnia	Various	1½–2½	,,	,,	H.H.	Bedding

CHAPTER V

HARDY PERENNIALS

A ROUGH classification of plants has already been made in the previous chapter. There a variety of plants were dealt with, all of them being more or less temporary inhabitants of their garden positions, either because they are short-lived and unable to stand the winter in the open, or because the gardener desires to use the plants in his garden composition only during their brief season of spectacular beauty.

We now come to the kind of plants that are a little more permanent. That is to say, they are allowed to remain for several seasons in the borders where they were first planted, and though they die back during a part of the year, their roots remain alive to send up fresh stems annually. These plants we call perennials—hardy perennials, for the most part, since any of tender type would have to be lifted and stored during the winter. It is, however, invariably difficult to draw a hard and fast line between hardy and tender plants, though equally difficult to classify garden plants in any other way.

To take an obvious instance : the early flowering types of Japanese chrysanthemums are, in fairly warm gardens and congenial soil, justly regarded as hardy herbaceous perennials, and can be treated in the same way as Michaelmas daisies. That is, they can be left outdoors all winter, and merely divided and replanted whenever the border is renovated. But in a great many colder gardens they cannot be safely left in this way; they must be lifted and wintered in a cold frame.

Such border-line cases will be included here as hardy perennials, though individual treatment in differing soils will be indicated where necessary.

MERITS OF THE HERBACEOUS BORDER

The herbaceous border, that is the border where most of the inhabitants are perennials of herbaceous habit, is a common feature of most gardens, large or small, but do not forget that perennials can often be used with effect in formal beds (Fig. 1). From many viewpoints it is the most satisfactory of the garden features. Its inhabitants do not have to be constantly replaced; indeed the opposite is the case, for unless plants are regularly divided, and the major portion scrapped, the border quickly becomes overcrowded. The herbaceous border does not ask for so much attention as the seasonal beds; lifting and replanting are only necessary on an average about once in three years. Some plants, of course, are divided more often, some less.

But the care of the herbaceous border must not be neglected.

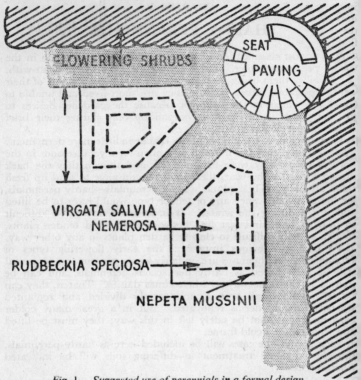

Fig. 1. Suggested use of perennials in a formal design.

Although not much planting and replanting is required, some cultivation of the surface soil is needed for good results. Staking, thinning and other work is also required from time to time, and the war against soil pests and flies must be waged. Further—and this is a point which is frequently overlooked—the border at its best should be a pleasant and colourful picture throughout most of the year. Only the experienced gardener knows how difficult this is.

Properly planted, with due regard to the seasons of bloom of each subject, to their disposal in the border, to their height and habit of growth, the value of their foliage and so on, the border will be never less than pleasant to look at, and in the height of its glory it will be a feature of real beauty.

I do not know whether to regard herbaceous borders as more

important to the large garden or to the small. Possibly their importance is equal; but if there is any difference, I should say that the mixed border is more vital in the small garden. Collections of flowering shrubs, seasonal beds, rose, iris, or other special flower gardens carry a continuity of interest in the layout of a large garden, whereas in a small space seasonal bedding not only limits the

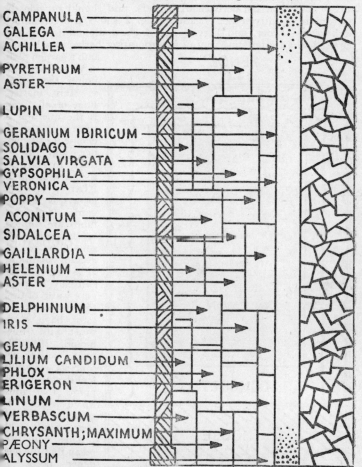

CAMPANULA
GALEGA
ACHILLEA
PYRETHRUM
ASTER
LUPIN
GERANIUM IBIRICUM
SOLIDAGO
SALVIA VIRGATA
GYPSOPHILA
VERONICA
POPPY
ACONITUM
SIDALCEA
GAILLARDIA
HELENIUM
ASTER
DELPHINIUM
IRIS
GEUM
LILIUM CANDIDUM
PHLOX
ERIGERON
LINUM
VERBASCUM
CHRYSANTH; MAXIMUM
PÆONY
ALYSSUM

Fig. 2. A planting scheme for a sunny herbaceous border.

selection of flowers to the point of dullness but also results in long flowerless periods between the seasons.

In the small garden, the herbaceous borders are usually the main feature, apart from grass and shrubs. For that reason it becomes a matter of supreme importance that these borders should be well planned, with regard to other garden features as well as to the actual flowers in the herbaceous borders, and should provide the maximum of interest and beauty. Fig. 2 shows a well-planned herbaceous border, and Figs. 3 and 4 show an uninteresting as opposed to an interesting way of incorporating herbaceous borders into a garden plan.

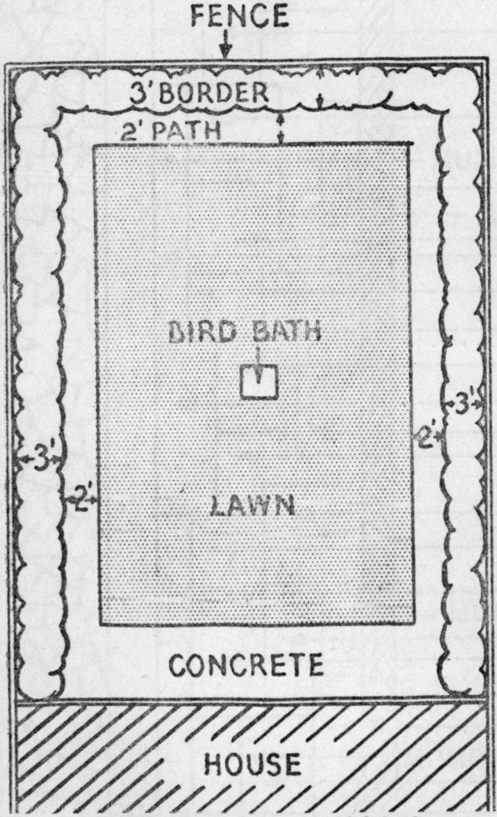

What are the points that count in this matter? First of all, there is the question of what plants to choose for the border, and this at once introduces the question of soil. Plants should always, in a little garden, and when funds are limited, be chosen for their suitability to the existing conditions. If a garden has stiff clay, it would be a waste of time to grow plants that must have sandy peat and leaf-mould. If it has light, sandy, dry soil, it would be foolish to grow plants that must have plenty of moisture all the year round.

This does not mean that the gardener needs to limit his choice too

Fig. 3. *An unimaginative way in which herbaceous borders should not be arranged.*

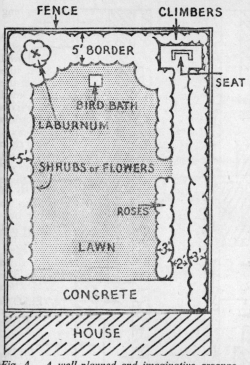

FENCE   CLIMBERS

5' BORDER

SEAT

BIRD BATH

LABURNUM

5'

SHRUBS or FLOWERS

ROSES

LAWN   3'

2' 3'

CONCRETE

HOUSE

Fig. 4.   A well-planned and imaginative arrangement of herbaceous borders.

strictly. All soils, as already explained, can be improved, and the texture altered from hard, sticky clay or light, open sand to the ideal medium loam that will suit the majority of garden plants. It is also possible to take out entirely a cubic foot or so of soil here and there, and substitute more congenial compost. This is frequently done where lilies are wanted and the natural soil is uncongenial. But generally speaking, and certainly for the main spectacle of colour, it is wise to keep to the kind of plants likely to thrive in the type of soil that is natural to the border ; for only plants that really make themselves at home will flower continuously over a long period. Others will flower, but their beauty will rapidly pass.

Another point in plant selection is to have plants of various heights and various habits. Tall plants for the back of the border, bushy, spreading or medium-height plants for the middle distance, and rather dwarf, or even " carpeting," plants for the front edges, suggest themselves as a matter of course. In a border of any considerable length there should be an uneven slope from front to back; you do not want a border to resemble a market flower stall. Occasional broad bushy plants, such as tree lupins or white moon-daisies brought to the front of the border, make a welcome break.

Colour grouping is important, but not, I think, so important as it may seem at first sight. The mixed border can be well varied

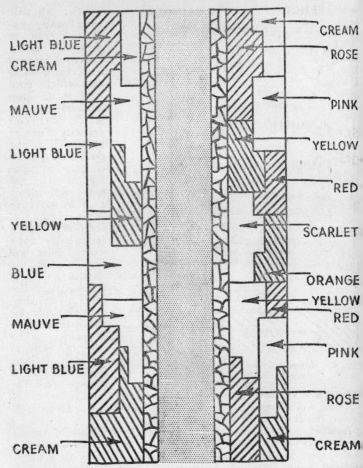

LIGHT BLUE
CREAM

MAUVE

LIGHT BLUE

YELLOW

BLUE

MAUVE

LIGHT BLUE

CREAM

CREAM
ROSE

PINK

YELLOW

RED

SCARLET

ORANGE
YELLOW
RED

PINK

ROSE

CREAM

Fig. 5. Herbaceous borders arranged in an unclashing but brilliant colour scheme. These borders would be effective in a small garden.

without any harm, and it is only in the larger garden, where a particular colour value is desirable in a border, that much limitation need be placed on the colours used. There are some obvious precautions, of course. Scarlet should not be used against magenta or rose pink, nor orange against cherry red. Yet in both cases it would need only a small group of grey foliage or white flowers separating the colours to avoid discordant effects. Suggested colour schemes for double borders are shown in Figs. 5 and 6.

Then there is the question of how many plants to use in a group. Here the width and length of a border must be taken into account. In the narrow 3 or 4-ft. border that is common in tiny villa gardens, I should prefer to use three plants of most kinds together—three geums, for instance, or three root portions of Michaelmas daisy.

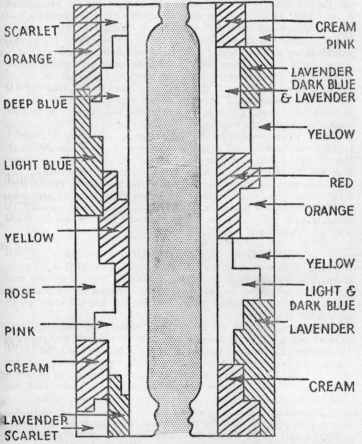

SCARLET
ORANGE
DEEP BLUE
LIGHT BLUE
YELLOW
ROSE
PINK
CREAM
LAVENDER
SCARLET

CREAM
PINK
LAVENDER
DARK BLUE
& LAVENDER
YELLOW
RED
ORANGE
YELLOW
LIGHT &
DARK BLUE
LAVENDER
CREAM

Fig. 6.   An alternative arrangement to that shown in Fig. 5.

In the 12-ft. wide border, which is ideal, a constant succession of loveliness is really possible. Plants might be set in groups of five or seven. Very large plants would, of course, be satisfactory set singly; a large delphinium, well grown, occupies a square yard of space, and needs no companion.

It should be remembered that though " clumps " are the common sight in most gardens, a better floral display is always obtained where flowering stems are ruthlessly restricted to just enough to fill the allotted space. A single flowering stem of Michaelmas daisy might, for example, spread 2 ft. each way, and present a mass of flowers, poised symmetrically on the radiating side branches. If half a dozen stems were allowed to occupy the same space, each would have fewer flowers, and none of them would appear so symmetrical and decorative. It needs courage, when twenty flower stems are developing from one root stock, to pull out sixteen or eighteen of them, but it definitely pays, and to the amateur who doubts this statement, I recommend an experiment with one root out of his number. Limit it to one, or if it is a large root, to three stems; and watch the result.

Hardy plant catalogues of today nearly all offer a complete herbaceous border, and supply a planting plan. I should be the last to suggest that these plans are undesirable, except in one way— they are " ready made," and therefore have no individuality. My own suggestion to the novice in gardening is that he should study these trade plans, and the plans of borders given in these pages, and see from them how plants can be grouped, apparently casually, but actually with great care, so that colour and interest will be spread over the seasons and over the borders.

WORKING OUT A PLANTING SCHEME

I suggest then that he should make out, for himself, a list of the plants he specially likes in borders, choosing them from the most up-to-date catalogue he can find, since varieties of all plants are constantly being improved on by hybridizing and selection on the part of the nurseryman.

With the formidable list he probably selects, he can then begin to work out a border planting scheme that is original and personal. He can begin by noting against each plant of his choice the height season of flower, colour, and general habit, i.e., spreading, upright etc. For this he may have to consult both catalogue and gardening book, since new varieties of old plants may have different characteristics. At the same time, he may find it wise to strike out of his list certain plants not suitable for his type of soil, or which need so much extra care that, for the present, they must be excluded.

Next a plan of the border should be drawn, preferably on squared paper, so that each square can represent a square yard, or a squar

oot. This makes it much easier to allocate the various plants to
their positions.

Now comes the tricky part of the business—trickier than the most
involved crossword. The plants must be disposed along the border,
so that spring, summer and autumn each have a show in each part
of the border, and so that tall plants are not set in front of short
ones, unless the short ones are early flowering and will be fading
by the time the giants begin to run up. At the same time, colour of
flower and foliage, the delightful contrast of various leaf and flower
forms, and the relation of the colour effects to other parts of the
garden must all be kept in mind. Tricky? Yes ! So much so that a
good herbaceous border is the hall-mark of success in garden making,
and is, in fact, an ideal that few gardeners achieve. However, I
know of no task in the garden which is more fascinating; and I
should beg every gardener to make time to plan his own borders.

FORMAL BORDERS FOR SMALL GARDENS

On this subject of planning, let me make one other suggestion.
In the small garden, where formality reigns for the most part, and
where the herbaceous border is only a 3-ft. strip along the garden
boundary, there is, I think, a strong case for rather formal or limited
use of herbaceous plants. For example, in such a border one might
make a ribbon-edging of pinks, alternated with dwarf campanulas,
with groups of early bulbs, such as snowdrops or crocus or scillas
immediately behind the edging plants. The campanulas and
pinks keep their foliage all winter, the bulbs would flower in early
spring, and the others during the summer.

Behind this edging, doronicums for spring flowering could be
alternated with chrysanthemums for the autumn, with an occasional
standard rose for summer, and groups of gladioli, half a dozen in
each group. This limited planting scheme would give colour and
interest over twelve months, with a neatness that is impossible with
a well-mixed planting scheme.

A point often asked by novices is whether one can mix shrubs
such as roses with herbaceous perennials. As a general principle,
such mixed borders are best avoided, though there are times when
a skeleton of shrubs such as rosemary and lavender can well be
used, the groups of mixed herbaceous perennials being set between
the shrubs, so that in winter the border is partly furnished (Fig. 7).

Roses should generally not be set in a border with herbaceous
perennials, the exception being where a garden is too small to
allow for separate rose borders; the use of an occasional standard
rose, as suggested above, is then permissible. Bush roses should
never be jostled by herbaceous perennials.

Further mixing is done frequently where annuals are used in
groups among the herbaceous perennials. Bulbs also are used in

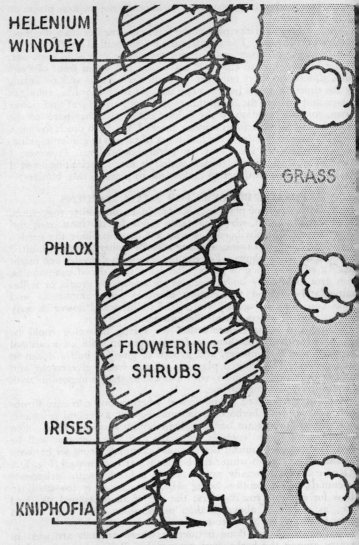

HELENIUM
WINDLEY

GRASS

PHLOX

FLOWERING
SHRUBS

IRISES

KNIPHOFIA

Fig. 7.   A good design for a mixed border.

this way. Such mixing, though it alters the character of the border a little, is a wise move in a small garden, for it makes it easier to keep up the colour interest all the year. A line of tulips behind the perennial edging flowers does not interfere much with the main occupants of the border, and when the tulips are lifted, the substitution of a line of quick-flowering annuals will make a welcome contribution to the colour in late summer.

The best place for the herbaceous border is in full sunshine; for where sun is plentiful, flowers will also be plentiful, whereas shade tends to encourage lanky growth with too much foliage and few flowers.

THE SHADED BORDER

Having recognized this fact, we turn our attention to those borders which are, through force of circumstances, set in partial or entire shade. Let us first be frank and admit that there will never be the continuous blaze of colour in the shady border that there is in the sunny one. That is a good reason for making the two opposite side borders in a long narrow garden, running from east to west, quite different in character. The border that faces south might well be made twice or three times the width of the other, and the garden design can be built up in recognition of this difference.

Where one of two borders suffers from partial shading only, as where a tree is the cause, the balance of colour can be kept up best by the use of pot plants, and by judicious removals from the nursery plot. For instance, phlox, and various other perennials, grown in a nursery plot until the flower buds are formed, will transplant remarkably well, if care is taken to keep soil round the roots, and to water overhead after the move. Japanese chrysanthemums grown in pots in the sun, and knocked out of the pots, or merely sunk into position in the border when nearly in bloom, are useful in the same way.

PLANTS FOR FULL SHADE

Then, of course, there are certain plants more suitable than others for permanent positions in full shade—lily of the valley, Solomon's seal, sweet rocket, Japanese anemones, heleniums, campanulas, primula *polyanthus*, violas, honesty, aconitum, foxgloves, funkia, pulmonaria, polemonium, spiraea *palmatum*, lilium *martagon*, and veronica *virginica*—all of these succeed pretty well without any sunshine.

As a shrubby skeleton for the border a few plants of mahonia, hypericum, and periwinkle would be extremely useful. It needs extra care over plant selection to achieve success in the shaded border, but it is by no means the hopeless task some gardeners are apt to think it. A suggested planning for such a border is seen in Fig. 8.

Extra care should also be taken in the preparation of the soil. Humus should be used sparingly, and bonemeal and lime freely. The surface soil should be kept open by constant hoeing or stirring

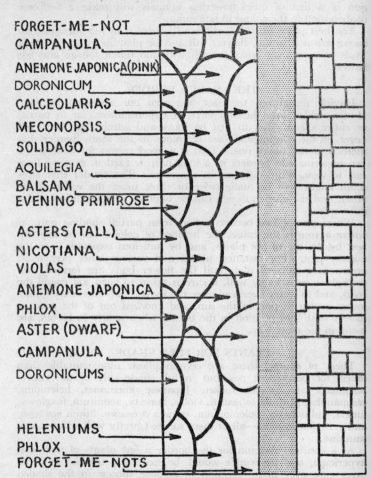

FORGET-ME-NOT
CAMPANULA
ANEMONE JAPONICA (PINK)
DORONICUM
CALCEOLARIAS
MECONOPSIS
SOLIDAGO
AQUILEGIA
BALSAM
EVENING PRIMROSE

ASTERS (TALL)
NICOTIANA
VIOLAS
ANEMONE JAPONICA
PHLOX
ASTER (DWARF)
CAMPANULA
DORONICUMS

HELENIUMS
PHLOX
FORGET-ME-NOTS

Fig. 8. Arrangement of plants suitable for shady borders.

with a hand fork; and frequent border renovation is recommended to prevent souring of the soil. Other problems that arise in connection with herbaceous borders are their backgrounds and edgings. The former may be in the form of hedging, a fence concealed by climbing plants or a wall (Fig. 9). Various types of edging—good and bad—are illustrated in Fig. 10.

Now for the actual methods of planting. The border will first be well dug, usually by means of the bastard trenching method (*see* Chapter II), unless trenching is necessary through the mistaken efforts of the builders. Whatever method of soil treatment is adopted it should result in an under-layer of well-broken soil, through which air and moisture will pass freely, with a surface-layer of at least 10 in. of good medium loam, porous, able to hold moisture, and at the same time well broken, so that it makes a congenial home for plant roots.

There should be lime enough in the soil, and a sufficiency of other plant foods.

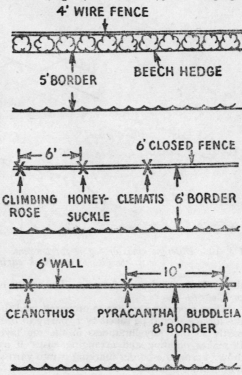

Fig. 9. Various backgrounds for herbaceous borders. These are chosen with regard to the width of the borders.

One of the most useful fertilizers for any herbaceous border is bonemeal, particularly, as already mentioned, for the border in partial shade. Bonemeal is phosphatic and encourages early flower production. Moreover, as it is only slightly soluble and is not wasted by seepage like the quick-acting fertilizers, its effect lasts for several years. I like myself to use half to a pound of bonemeal per square yard whenever

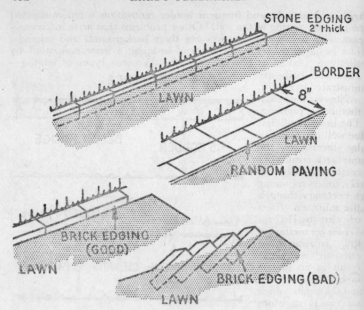

Fig. 10. *Different kinds of edging for borders. Note the right and the wrong way to use brick edging.*

the herbaceous border is remade. The results have always been most satisfactory.

When a border has been so prepared, and the plants have arrived, the surface should be raked over, partly to prepare a level bed, and partly so that any lumpiness in the top layer may be corrected. It makes planting and arranging easier if at this stage lines are drawn across the border marking it into yard squares or, on a small border, foot squares.

A further help is to prepare labels, each clearly marked with the name of the plant, and preferably also with the number in each group, date of planting, and any other useful details. White painted wooden labels, written with a garden pencil, or with any sharp tool while the paint is still wet, remain legible for a long time, and are generally satisfactory. There are a number of equally good or better labels on the market, but the ordinary wooden label lasts generally for as long as it will ever be needed in the border.

Set the labels out in the various positions where the plants are to go. Any necessary adjustments—for we all make mistakes, and errors in measurement are very common—can be made before planting is begun. Also, by setting out the labels first, you can plant each bundle as you open it, so that there is no opportunity for the plant roots to die through being left exposed to the air.

Always use either a spade or a trowel for planting. Make a hole large enough to take the plant roots comfortably, and if the roots are exposed and fibrous, spread them out well horizontally in all directions.

Of course, if a plant is sent out from the nursery with a good ball of soil round the roots, and this has been wrapped carefully in damp moss so that it arrives unbroken, take the tip from the grower, and plant with as little disturbance of the roots as possible. Press soil very carefully over and round the roots, but do not plant either too deep or too shallow. Try to plant at exactly the same level as the plant was in the nursery. The way to plant dwarf perennials is shown in Fig. 11.

Pæonies and similar plants with fleshy crowns resting just below

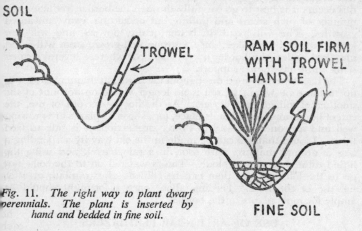

Fig. 11. *The right way to plant dwarf perennials. The plant is inserted by hand and bedded in fine soil.*

the surface of the soil, are planted with 1 or 2 in. of soil over the crown; but this soil should be of a very porous sandy nature, so that moisture will not collect and cause decay. A useful precaution here is to cover all such crowns with bonfire ash, or finely sifted coal ashes. The ash keeps away slugs, and prevents decay at the same time.

A further precaution when a border is planted in soil much troubled by slugs is to strew bran and Meta slug bait freely. This

slug bait is merely bran with which a quantity of crushed Meta, the
solid methylated spirit fuel for lamps, sold by all ironmongers, has
been mixed.   The Meta drugs the pests, which will be found in
hundreds on the border surface the next day.

The operation of planting should be done on a mild day, preferably
in autumn or spring, though many herbaceous perennials can be
safely moved at any time during the winter so long as there is no
frost in the soil.   If the soil is too dry, planting should be postponed,
or, if possible, a hose should be used to soak the border, and after
it has been left for several hours for draining, planting can be done.

Evening or late afternoon is the best time to plant, as the night
air is relatively damp, and there will be little evaporation from
leaves during the hours of darkness.   If warm dry weather follows,
an occasional overhead bath from the hose or water can will help;
but watering must not, of course, be done during frosty weather.

THINNING OUT THE STEMS

As soon as the warm days of spring arrive, most of the plants
will begin to throw up stems that are to carry the flowers.   When
this occurs it is best to go carefully through the border, reducing the
number of such stems and pulling out or cutting away unwanted
growths.   This will result in better quality flowers, and will also
lessen the need for stakes, since a strong well-grown stem will stand
unstaked, unless the border is very exposed; whereas several weaker
stems must have some support.

The hoe should be used throughout the border at frequent intervals,
up to the time when the soil is no longer visible on account of the
smother of foliage and flowers.   As the hoe passes out of use, the
can of liquid manure takes its place, for as soon as plants are growing
well and are on their way to flower production, it is safe to feed
them.   Liquid manure can be made in the old way by suspending a
bag of animal manure, with soot, in a rain barrel, and using the
liquid diluted to straw colour.   This is watered on to the soil—not
on to the foliage more than can be helped—after rainfall, or after
the use of the hose.   Feeding about once a fortnight should be
ample for most plants in the border.

USE OF ARTIFICIAL FERTILIZERS

If preferred, artificial fertilizers can be used.   The one-three-one
mixture—one part sulphate of ammonia, three parts superphosphate
of lime, one part sulphate of potash—recommended by the Ministry
of Agriculture for general garden use, is quite satisfactory; a little
can be scattered between the plants and watered well into the soil,
or any of the general fertilizers sold by sundriesmen can be used.
The rule of " little and often " should be kept, as plants can be
severely damaged by an overdose of any fertilizer.   Also, no

fertilizers should ever be used on dried-out soil, but only after rainfall or watering.

As soon as flower stems run up, staking (Fig. 12) should be attended to. Staking is an art, and an art that pays handsomely. It would surprise the novice to know how many stakes are used in a good herbaceous border. These stakes are of several kinds and sizes, from thin bamboo canes for such plants as carnations, where one cane is used to a flower stem, to thick 6 or 8-ft. dahlia stakes for the tall heavy plants.

In staking, the aim should be to use enough stakes to stake out each stem, so that its beauty is fully seen. The novice is generally prone to draw in his stems, so that when they are tied to a stake, they resemble a truss of straw. In the case of a group of say fifteen Michaelmas daisy stems, the method should be to set three or four stakes round the group and to tie one stem to each, in front of the stake, so that the stakes are, or will be, hidden. Then a string can be run round the whole group and passed round each stem of the outer ring, while other strings can, if needed, be taken across and across.

Some of the plants in the herbaceous

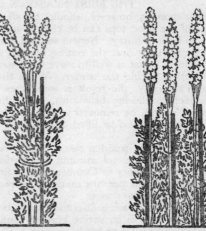

Fig. 12. Staking—good and bad. On the right the foliage and flowers are spaced attractively, while on the left they are bunched together in an ugly manner.

border are not amenable to this treatment.   Oriental poppies, for instance, are sometimes better staked merely by pushing in twiggy stems among the developing flower stems.   These twigs are completely hidden by the time the flowers open; but they serve their purpose, that of supporting the brittle growths of the poppy.

There are also numerous patent devices on the market for staking, mostly good and time saving, but these cost a little more.

Whatever staking methods are adopted, they should begin before the need seems apparent.   A summer storm may easily ruin a whole border through delay in this matter.

So far the creation of a border has been our subject.   Let us now turn to the general routine to be carried out by the amateur gardener in order to maintain the border over a period of years.

At the end of the first season, it may be apparent that certain alterations in the relative positions of different plants should be made. On the other hand it is likely that many of the subjects have done very little towards making a fine border display this first season. Such plants as pæonies, oriental poppies, and others with fleshy roots, resent a move so much that they frequently produce few and insignificant flowers the first season. It would be a mistake to lift such plants the first autumn.

THE FIRST SEASON'S CLEAN UP

The border, however, should be cleaned up generally. Some part of the dead tops can be cleared away; yet here, too, it is well not to be in a hurry. Nepeta *mussinii*, for instance, may have a fine tangle of stems over the resting crowns, and, especially in exposed gardens, it is just as well to leave these stems. They serve as a slight protection during the winter. When the over-tidy gardener takes them all away, the result is sometimes disastrous. Old stems of Michaelmas daisies, heleniums, and other coarse, strong growths, can, of course, be removed without harm, and vigorous growers of this kind may also be lifted and divided if the clumps have grown well.

A point that puzzles many beginners is that gardening books generally recommend autumn renovation of the border, to take place in September or October. They find, however, that Michaelmas daisies, and perhaps many other plants, are only just in their full beauty by this season.

This is where some discretion must be exercised. The practice in large estates is for spring borders, summer borders, and autumn borders to be more or less kept apart. The early herbaceous border, or one that has mainly lupins, irises, and oriental poppies in it, would naturally be renovated, and the plants lifted and divided when necessary, in the autumn. The late-flowering herbaceous plants would be left undisturbed until the spring.

LEAVE AUTUMN FLOWERING PLANTS

Where a single border includes plants of all seasons, the first year autumn clean up will be merely a matter of removing such plant tops as are completely dead, except for those retained for merely protective reasons, and of forking over the border surface to bury small weeds and rubbish. At the same time a few groups of spring flowering bulbs will be set in place of any annuals that have withered.

The herbaceous plants still in flower will be left until later. Michaelmas daisies can be attended to at any time during winter, so long as there is no frost in the soil. The roots will then be lifted out entirely, the best, outer pieces of new growth selected and replanted, and the remainder consigned to the bonfire. But for the majority of the border plants nothing apart from the forking of the soil is necessary.

In spring, a repetition of this treatment will be advisable, i.e., the forking of the soil surface between the plants—not too deep forking, but just sufficient to keep the surface open and friable. Opportunity will be taken of the forking to dress the soil with lime or some other fertilizer, according to its suitability to the nature of the soil in the garden.

THE THREE YEAR RENOVATION

Once every three years the border should be given a much more thorough renovation. The time for this operation may be decided by the owner, partly according to his own free time, partly according to the weather, and partly according to the type of plants that predominate in the border. It does no plants much harm to be lifted from the border if their roots are kept surrounded by soil, and even oriental poppies can be moved occasionally in this manner if necessary. A spade should be used for the task, so that the ball of soil is kept intact.

Any plants that can conveniently be left undisturbed, or that would be likely to resent disturbance, such as pæonies, may be dug round, but often it is convenient to move everything from the border at once. Plants so lifted should be set on to sacks or newspapers, not on to the lawn, where they leave dirt and stones. While they are out of the soil their roots must be kept moist and free from frost.

The border is then dug from end to end, and the plants reset in position, just as if it were a new border. Manuring, the use of lime and bonemeal, etc., must be carried out during these triennial renovations.

Borders treated in this way should gain in beauty from year to year, for every renovation means some improvement in the quality or arrangement of the plants.

THE VARIOUS PERENNIALS

Below will be found a list of the more common perennials found in herbaceous borders, together with their chief characteristics and how they should be treated. N.O. means the natural order of the plant, from which varieties are developed.

Achillea (Yarrow, Milfoil), N.O. Compositæ. Achilleas like full sun and good drainage. The flat heads of flowers are produced in July and August. Plant 1 to 2 ft. apart, according to the variety, and to increase divide in spring or autumn.

Varieties.—PTARMICA, the pearl, pure white double, 2 ft.;

EUPATORIUM, large, bright yellow, 4 ft.; MILLEFOLIUM, cerise queen, crimson, 3 ft.

Aconitum (Monkshood), N.O. Ranunculaceæ. For monkshoods full sun or partial shade in any ordinary soil is suitable, and they should be planted in bold groups 2 ft. apart. To increase, divide in spring or sow seed outside in April. As the roots are deadly poison care must be taken when handling them.

Varieties.—NAPELLUS SPARKS' VARIETY, deep blue, 5 ft., July to August; WILSONII BARKER'S VARIETY, deep blue, 6 ft., September to October; FISCHERI, clear blue, 3 ft., September.

Alstroemeria (Herb Lily), N.O. Amaryllidaceæ. Grow alstroemeria in a well drained, sandy soil and a sheltered position in full sun. They require little other treatment. Plant in large groups 18 in. apart. They take two or three years before a good display will be produced. To increase, divide or sow seed in spring.

Varieties.—AURANTIACA, orange, 2½ ft., July; CHILENSE, varies from pale pink to bright red, tender in exposed districts, 2 ft., July; LUTEA, yellow, 2½ ft., July; PSITTACINA, green and red, 1½ to 2 ft., September.

Althaea (Hollyhock), N.O. Malvaceæ. A light soil is most suitable, as on a heavy one they will die during the winter through excessive wet. In any soil they are best treated as biennials, as fresh stock can so easily be raised from seed each year. They grow 6 to 8 ft. high and bloom throughout the summer. To increase, sow seed outside in June in a well prepared seed bed and transplant in spring 1 ft. apart.

Varieties.—Good strains of double and single varieties are obtainable in white, cream, pink, apricot, salmon and similar shades.

Anchusa (Alkanet), N.O. Boraginaceæ. Given a sunny, well-drained soil with plenty of well-decayed manure, they require little other attention. If staking is found necessary, one stout support is sufficient. Plant in groups 1½ ft. apart. To increase, insert root cuttings in early spring.

Varieties.—ITALICA DROPMORE, gentian blue, June, 5 ft.; MORNING GLORY, deep rich blue, June to July, 5 ft.; ITALICA OPAL, pale sky blue, August, 5 ft.; ITALICA PRIDE OF DOVER, clear blue, June, 5 ft.

Anemone (Wind Flower), N.O. Ranunculaceæ. This class of anemone is suited to the wild garden and ideal for shady borders. The addition of a little manure is beneficial, otherwise ordinary garden soil is suitable. Japanese anemones should be moved as little as possible, but if necessary, planting is best carried out from October to November, or from February to March. Plant 1½ ft. apart. To increase, sow seed outside in June or divide at planting time.

Varieties.—JAPONICA ALBA, single, white, 3 ft.; JAPONICA HUPEHENSIS, single, rosy-crimson, 3 ft., August to September;

JAPONICA KRIEMHILDE, large semi-double, rich pink flowers, 3 ft.; JAPONICA MARGARETE, dark pink, double flowers, 2 ft., August; JAPONICA RICHARD AHRENDS, large single, white-tinged lilac.

Aquilegia (Columbine), N.O. Ranunculaceæ. Columbines grow best in a light, well-drained soil, in full sun, but they require plenty of moisture during the summer. Plant in groups 9 in. apart. To increase, sow seed outside in spring. The plants should flower the following year.

Varieties.—CRIMSON STAR, long crimson spurs and pure white corolla, 2½ ft., May to July; GLANDULOSA, pale blue with pure white corolla, 1 ft., May to July; HENSOL HAREBELL, pure sapphire-blue, 3 ft., June to July; LONGISSIMA, yellow with exceedingly long-spurs, 2 ft.; LONG-SPURRED HYBRIDS, a beautiful strain of delicate shades of pink, blue and yellow, 2 ft., May to July.

Artemisia (Wormwood; Southernwood), N.O. Compositæ. They are useful for their decorative foliage effects. Provided there is moisture at the roots, partial shade and any ordinary soil is suitable. To increase, divide in spring.

Varieties.—STELLARIANA DUSTY MILLER, ornamental grey foliage, 2 ft.; LACTIFLORA, creamy-white, fragrant, summer, 5 ft.

Aster (Michaelmas Daisy), N.O. Compositæ. A very large genus, the earliest of which commence flowering in August, and the latest flower in November.

Varieties.—Section 1. *Amellus.* In this section are dwarf-growing single flowered varieties : KING GEORGE, large, rich violet-blue flowers, 2 in. across, 2 ft., August to September; SONIA, the best pink, 2 ft., September to October; ULTRAMARINE, deep violet-blue, 2½ ft., September.

Section 2. *Novæ-Angliæ.* These come into flower a few weeks later than the Amellus section, commencing about mid-September and continuing well into autumn. All are tall growing and produce double flowers : BARR'S PINK, bright rose with a golden centre, 5 ft., October; RYCROFT PURPLE, purple-blue, 4 to 5 ft., October.

Section 3. *Novi-Belgii.* All flower freely on long, branching stems and are excellent border plants : BLUE EYES, deep violet buds opening to a rich lavender-blue, single, 3 ft., September to October; CHARLES WILSON, single, bright cerise-red flowers, 3½ ft., September to October; CLIMAX, single, clear lilac-blue flowers, 5 ft., October; LITTLE BOY BLUE, double, blue flowers, 3 ft., September, of stiff habit; LITTLE PINK LADY, semi-double, pink flowers, 3 ft., September to October; MOUNT EVEREST, large, semi-double, white flowers, 4 ft., October.

Section 4. *Cordifolius.* These grow in long arching sprays covered with innumerable small flowers : SILVER SPRAY, pale lilac, 4 to 5 ft., October; IDEAL, pale lavender, 2 ft., September to October.

Section 5. *Ericoides.* These also grow in long arching sprays and numerous small dainty flowers : CHASTITY, white, 4 ft., September to October; BLUE STAR, pale lilac, 2½ ft., October.

Section 6. *Dwarf Hybrids.* These are in habit similar to the novi-belgii section, but are less than a foot in height. They are useful in the rock garden as well as in front of the herbaceous border : NANCY, pale pink, 10 in., end of September; COUNTESS OF DUDLEY, Deep pink, 1 ft., October; VICTOR, dark mauve, 6 in., mid-September.

Section 7. The following are found growing wild in this country and abroad, and should find a place in the border : ACRIS, bright, lavender-blue flowers, useful for massing, 2½ ft., August to September; FRIKARTII, light blue flowers, 2½ ft., August to September; HYBRIDUS LUTEUS (syn. solidago missouriensis), the only yellow, 1½ ft., August; SUB-COERULEUS, lavender-blue flowers with a golden centre, 1 ft., July.

A deep, heavy, moist loam is best for all types of aster, with full sun. Plant in autumn or spring in clumps of three, five or more plants, according to the size of the border, with 1½ ft. between the plants. The amellus section should be planted in spring only. Every three or four years lift them, and replant small pieces from the outside of the clumps. To increase, divide in spring or autumn, using two forks. Cuttings taken in spring will root in gentle heat.

Astilbe (False Goat's Beard), N.O. Saxifragaceæ. ASTILBES are excellent plants for growing in woodland or alongside a stream, as well as in the herbaceous border. To increase, divide in early spring.

Varieties.—BETSY CUPERUS, white, 5 ft., July and August; CERES, pink, 3 ft., July to August; GERTRUDE BRIX, deep crimson, 2½ ft., June; GRANAT, crimson, 3 ft., June; W. REEVES, dark crimson and bronzy foliage, July and August; VENUS, silvery-pink, 4 ft., July to August.

Bocconia (Plume Poppy), N.O. Papaveraceæ. They like a rich soil that has plenty of stable manure incorporated, and good drainage is essential, also full sun. They are gross feeders and should be given weekly applications of liquid manure during the growing season. Plant 3 ft. apart. To increase, suckers can be taken and planted in spring or autumn.

Variety.—CORDATA, cream, 6 ft., June to September.

Campanula (Bellflower), N.O. Campanulaceæ. Campanulas grow quite well in partial shade, although full sun is best. They require a deeply dug rich soil and should be planted in spring or autumn 9 to 12 in. apart. To increase, divide in spring or autumn or sow seed outside in July, particularly for the species.

Varieties.—LACTIFLORA, pale blue, 4½ ft., July to August; PERSICIFOLIA, blue, 2 ft., June; LACTIFLORA ALBA, white, 4½ ft.; LACTIFLORA MOLYNEUX, deep blue, 2 ft., July to August; LACTIFLORA, violet-blue, 4 ft., June; PERSICIFOLIA PRIDE OF EXMOUTH, semi-double,

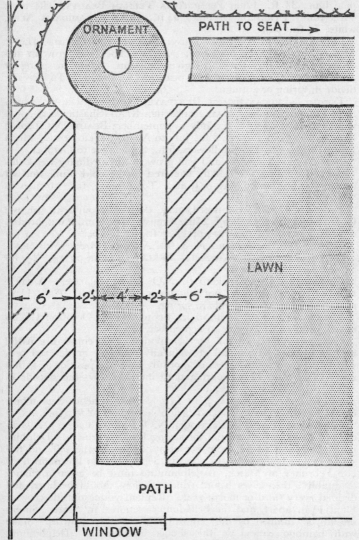

ORNAMENT

PATH TO SEAT——→

LAWN

←— 6' —→ ←—2'—→ ←— 4' —→ ←—2'—→ ←— 6' —→

PATH

WINDOW

HERBACEOUS BORDERS ARRANGED TO GIVE VISTA FROM HOUSE.

pale blue, 3½ ft., June; PERSICIFOLIA TELHAM BEAUTY, pale blue, 4 ft., June; PYRAMIDALIS, blue, 5½ ft., July; PYRAMIDALIS ALBA, white, 5½ ft., July.

Chrysanthemum (Ox-eye Daisy; Marguerite; Shasta Daisy; Moon Daisy), N.O. Compositæ. *Hardy.* They will grow in any ordinary well-cultivated soil if given full sun. Plant in spring or autumn about 2 ft. apart and use pea sticks for staking. To increase, divide in spring or autumn.

Varieties.—LEUCANTHEMUM RENTPAYER (Ox-eye Daisy), white, 3 ft., June to October; MAXIMUM ESTHER READ (Shasta Daisy), pure white, double, 1½ to 2 ft., July to September; BEAUTE NIVELLOISE, large frilled white flowers, 3 ft., July to August; ULIGINOSUM (Moon Daisy), large, single, white flowers, 5 ft., September to October.

Half Hardy. They like and will grow in any ordinary well-cultivated soil. Plants are usually wintered in the cold frame and set out in the border in May or June. To increase, take cuttings in September.

Varieties.—*Double.* CRIMSON CIRCLE, deep crimson, 3 ft., August; GOLDFINDER, bright yellow, 2½ft., August; MRS. PHIL PAGE, bronze, 4 ft., August; ROSE PRECOSE, pink, 2½ ft., September.

Single. WHITE BUTTERCUP, 3 ft., August; MARY McALPINE, creamy-white, 2½ ft., August; SHIRLEY TERRA-COTTA, 2½ ft., September.

Cimicifuga (Black Snakeroot), N.O. Ranunculaceæ. A fairly rich soil is most suitable, but full sun is not essential. Plant 1½ ft. apart and to increase, divide in spring.

Varieties.—SIMPLEX, white, 3 ft., September to October; CORDIFOLIA, white, 5 ft., August to September.

Coreopsis (Tickseed), N.O. Compositæ. Coreopsis are useful for cut flowers. They will grow in any ordinary garden soil provided there is not an excess of moisture and the position is in full sun. Plant 9 to 12 in. apart and to increase sow seed outside in April.

Varieties.—GRANDIFLORA, 2 to 3 ft., yellow, June to September; GRANDIFLORA PERRY'S VARIETY, double, yellow, 2 ft., July.

Delphinium (Perennial Larkspur), N.O. Ranunculaceæ. A well-drained, rich soil is essential for strong healthy growth. Delphiniums grow best where there is plenty of lime in the soil and full sun. If it is not possible to plant in September do not plant until late February or March, as delphiniums must be given a chance to establish themselves before winter. They should be lifted and divided every third or fourth year. Replant young outside crowns. Plant 1½ ft. apart, and the belladonna section 1 ft. apart. Shoots should be thinned by the removal of all weakly growths. Stake with bamboo canes, tie the shoots individually. Delphiniums should be planted in a well-manured soil. During the growing season use applications of liquid manure. Water regularly if the weather is dry. To increase, sow seed outside in June. Special varieties can be divided or cuttings taken in spring, potted and put in a cold frame. Keep seed heads removed.

Varieties.—BLUE GOWN, semi-double, ultramarine with black eye, 6 ft., June to July; CAMBRIA, Cambridge blue, overlaid mauve, 5 to 6 ft.; LADY ELEANOR, sky blue, suffused mauve, 6 ft., June to July; LORD DERBY, deep rosy mauve, white eye, 5 ft., June to July; MILLICENT BLACKMORE, blue and mauve, large black eye, 5 to 5½ ft., June to July; MRS. NEWTON LEES, mauve, suffused pale blue, 5 ft., June to July; MRS. PAUL NELKE, cornflower blue, small white eye, 4 to 5½ ft., June to July; MRS. TOWNLEY PARKER, sky blue, white eye, 5 to 5½ ft., June to July; NORAH FERGUSON, light blue, flushed mauve with white eye, 4 to 5 ft., June to July; REV. E. LASCELLES, royal blue, large white centre.

Dianthus (Pink), N.O. Caryophyllaceæ. Pinks are fine for edging the border, being neat and tidy the year round, and ever-green. The flowers, too, are excellent for cutting. For good blooms a full sun is necessary but pinks are very accommodating and succeed in the coldest of soils. Border carnations require more drainage as well as full sun and so on wet soils should be grown on raised beds. A deeply dug soil gives the best results, but it should not be rich, and do not use leaf-mould. Border carnations should not be stopped in their growth, but require staking, pre-ferably with short canes and metal rings. To increase, layer shoots in summer. Cuttings taken in September can be rooted in a cold frame and planted out in March.

Varieties.—*Pinks.* INCHMERY, lilac pink, 1 ft.; MRS. SINKINS, white, an old plant but still a favourite, 1 ft.

Border Carnations. COCKATOO, rose-pink, 1½ ft.; ELAINE, pure white, 1½ ft.; GORDON DOUGLAS, glowing crimson, 1½ ft.; MARY MURRAY, yellow, 1½ ft.; MISTY MORNING, grey-lavender, 1½ ft.; SCARLET CLARE, sweet scented, 1½ ft.

Dicentra or Dielytra (Bleeding Heart), N.O. Fumariaceæ. A plant of dainty growth that looks delightful in rockwork, or in the front of the mixed border. It can also be grown as a pot plant. A warm, light soil containing plenty of food is best, and a sheltered position is advisable to prevent the young growths from being cut by late frosts. Plant 1½ ft. apart. A top dressing of manure in spring is beneficial, and applications of liquid manure should be given during the growing season until the buds appear. To increase, root cuttings can be inserted in spring in gentle heat.

Varieties.—SPECTABILIS, May to July, 2 ft.; FORMOSA (syn. eximea), May to July, 1 ft.

Doronicum (Leopard's Bane), N.O. Compositæ. Full sun is not essential and any ordinary soil is suitable. Plant 1 ft. apart. If the plants are cut back immediately after flowering a second crop of flowers will be produced in late summer. To increase, divide in spring or autumn.

Varieties.—AUSTRIACUM, 1½ ft., yellow, April to May; HARPUR CREWE, 3 ft., yellow, April to June.

Echinacea (Purple Cone Flower), N.O. Compositæ. An ordinary soil suits these plants, but they need to be well fed. Plant 1½ ft. apart. To increase, divide in spring or autumn, or seed may be sown outside in April.

Variety.—PURPUREA, the king, 2 to 4 ft., purplish crimson, August to September.

Echinops (Globe Thistle), N.O. Compositæ. Any ordinary soil is suitable, in a sunny position. Plant 1½ ft. apart. Use stout stakes and twine to support them. To increase, divide in spring.

Variety.—RITRO, 3 to 5 ft., blue, August to September.

Erigeron (Fleabane), N.O. Compositæ. A moist soil in a sunny position is best and when staking pea sticks are most suitable. Plant 1 ft. apart. To increase, take cuttings in August and insert them in a cold frame for the winter months or divide the plants in spring.

Varieties.—B. LADHAMS, rose-pink, 1½ ft., May to August; MERSTHAM GLORY, violet-blue, 2 ft., May to August; QUAKERESS, lavender-pink, 2 ft., May to August.

Eryngium (Sea Holly), N.O. Umbelliferæ. A group of eryngiums gives a splash of unusual colour in the border. The entire plant is steel blue in colour. As cut flowers they are excellent, provided that the flower head is picked when fully open. A light, sandy soil in a sunny position is necessary. To increase, sow seed in cold frame in April or May. Plant 2 ft. apart.

Varieties.—AMETHYSTINUM, steel-blue flowers and stems, with marine-blue foliage, 3 ft., June to September; VIOLETTA, 3 ft., July to August.

Funkia (Plantain Lily), N.O. Liliaceæ. Valuable ornamental foliage plants and particularly useful for growing in shade. Its leaves are the main attraction and a rich soil will give the most luxuriant growth. Plant 2 to 3 ft. apart. To increase, divide in the spring.

Varieties.—FORTUNEI, lilac, 2 ft., July; FORTUNEI MAJOR, lilac, 3 ft., a larger form, July; LANCIFOLIA VARIEGATA, 9 in., leaves marked with cream, July.

Gaillardia (Blanket Flower), N.O. Compositæ. A light, well-drained soil is best, and to stake use pea sticks. Plant 9 to 12 in. apart. To increase, divide in early autumn or sow seed in early summer.

Varieties.—IPSWICH BEAUTY, crimson with golden edge, 3 ft., June to August; MRS. HAROLD LONGSTER, deep yellow with crimson centre,

3 ft., June to August; TANGERINE, orange, 2 ft., June to August.

Galega (Goat's Rue), N.O. Leguminosæ. They will grow any-where and should be planted 2 ft. apart. To increase, divide in spring or autumn.

Varieties.—DUCHESS OF BEDFORD, bright mauve, 3 ft., June to July; HARTLANDII, lilac, 5 ft., June to July; LADY WILSON, mauve and white, 3 ft., June to July.

Geranium (Cranesbill), N.O. Geraniaceæ. Their foliage is orna-mental during all the summer and autumn, and so they are excellent plants for the front of the border. They grow best in a well-drained soil, and should be planted 1 ft. apart. To increase, divide in spring or autumn. The common geranium has a red flower.

Varieties.—GRANDIFLORUM, blue with crimson veins, 1½ ft., June to July; GRANDIFLORUM GRAVETYE, deeper blue, 1½ ft., June to July; IBERICUM, violet-blue, 3 ft., June to July.

Geum (Avens), N.O. Rosaceæ. A sunny position in a well-drained soil is best. Plant 9 in. apart. To increase, divide in spring or autumn or sow seed in spring in a cold frame.

Varieties.—BORISII, orange-scarlet, single, 1 ft., June to September; FIRE OPAL, dazzling scarlet, single, 2 ft., June to September; LADY STRATHEDEN, yellow, double, 1½ ft., June to September; MRS. BRADSHAW, scarlet, double, 1½ ft., June to September.

Gypsophila (Chalk Plant), N.O. Caryophyllaceæ. A chalky soil grows the best plants, although they will grow on a heavy soil. They require full sun and should not be disturbed. To increase, root cuttings can be inserted in spring in a cold frame.

Varieties.—PANICULATA BRISTOL FAIRY, double, white, 2 to 3 ft., July and August; ROSY VEIL, double, pink, 2 ft., July and August.

Helianthus (Sunflower), N.O. Compositæ. They will grow in any ordinary soil in sun or semi-shade. Plant in groups 1½ ft. apart and to increase, divide in spring.

Varieties.—LODDON GOLD, double, 5 ft., August to September; MONARCH, single yellow, 6 to 8 ft., August to September.

Helleborus (Christmas Rose), N.O. Ranunculaceæ. They should be grown in a shady corner of the garden, preferably where their beautiful waxy flowers can be seen from the house. They like a leafy soil and benefit from a mulching of decayed manure in the spring and occasional applications of liquid manure during the summer. Protection by a sheet of glass in the winter is advisable to keep the rains from spoiling the flowers. To increase, divide in March.

Varieties.—NIGER (Christmas Rose), white, December to March, 1½ ft.; ORIENTALIS (Lenten Rose), white, pale pink or deep rose, February to April, 1½ ft.

Hemerocallis (Day Lily), N.O. Liliaceæ. They will grow in any soil. Plant 3 ft. apart. To increase, divide in spring.

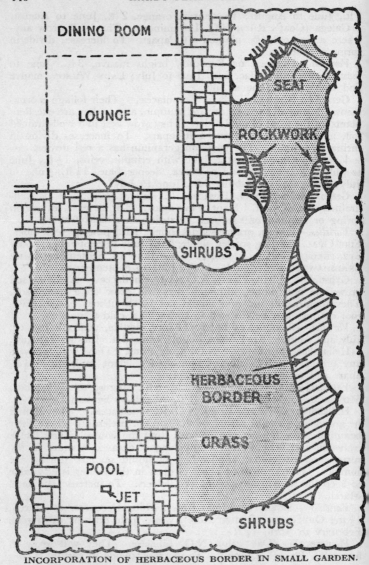

INCORPORATION OF HERBACEOUS BORDER IN SMALL GARDEN.

Varieties.—GEORGE YELD, rich orange, with inner petals flushed orange-scarlet, 3 ft., June to July; KWANSO PLENA, reddish bronze, 3 ft., June to July; MIKADO, yellow, with orange-scarlet base, 3 ft., June to July.

Heuchera (Alum Root), N.O. Saxifragaceæ. They are fine plants for the edge of the border requiring a light soil and full sun. Plant 9 in. apart. To increase, divide in spring.

Varieties.—BRIZOIDES GRACILLIMA, bright red, 2½ ft., June to July; EDGE HALL, pink, 1½ ft., June to July; SANGUINEA PLUIE DE FEU, cherry red, 2½ ft., June to July.

Iris (Rhizomatus) (Flag), N.O. Iridaceæ. Bearded irises must be grown in full sun and a calcareous soil. A heavy non-calcareous soil can be made to grow them with good results if lime is applied annually.

Beardless irises mostly require a moist position, some being semi-aquatics. All, except stylosa, dislike lime and thrive in a rich, moderately heavy soil in full sun.

Bearded irises should be moved in July. After this period new roots develop which become broken if planting is delayed until August or September. When dividing use a sharp knife and make a clean cut at the point where the new rhizome joins the old; this is easily distinguished. Plant only one fan of leaves at a time with its rhizome and roots; these fans are obtained from the edge of old worn out clumps, the central portion being discarded. It is important not to bury the rhizome beneath the soil, but it is essential to make the roots very firm. Beardless irises are planted in spring or early autumn in marshy ground, but spring planting is best. To increase, divide as given above.

Varieties.—Bearded irises are distinguished by the " beard " at the base of the falls. Plants in this group are noted for their variety of colours, free flowering and hardiness. COLUMBINE, clear and dazzling white, 3¼ ft., late; MA MIE, white, feathered blue, 2½ ft., mid-season; MILDRED PRESBY, standards ivory-white, falls dark, rich violet-edged white, mid-season; AMBER, pure yellow, 3 ft., mid-season; AMBER WAVE, standards and falls amber suffused bronze, 3 ft., mid-season; FLAMING SWORD, standards gold and yellow, falls crimson-maroon margined yellow, 2¾ ft., mid-season; APHRODITE, standards and falls violet-pink, 4 ft., mid-season; SHOT SILK, standards and falls pink blended with gold, 3 ft., mid-season; MORNING SPLENDOUR, standards and falls deep rich purplish-red, 3½ ft., mid-season; AMBASSADOR, standards smoky reddish-violet, falls dark, velvety reddish-violet, 4 ft., late.

Beardless irises usually prefer a heavyish soil. FŒTIDISSIMA, greenish-purple flowers of little show, but followed by scarlet berries, 1½ ft.; ORIENTALIS SNOW QUEEN, ivory-white, 3 ft., suitable for border or waterside; PSEUDOACORUS (Common Yellow Water

Flag), bright yellow, 3 ft., May to June, a good waterside plant; SIBIRICA BLEU CELESTE, Cambridge-blue with darker blotch, 3 ft., May to June; UNGUICULARIS (syn. stylosa), lavender blue, 1 ft., November to March. One of the most beautiful, this should be grown in well-drained poor soil, preferably against a south wall. Excellent for table decoration if cut in bud.

Kniphofia (Red-hot Poker; Torch Lily), N.O. Liliaceæ. Deep rich soil is needed as the plants are gross feeders. Top dress annually in spring, and when plants are established, give weekly applications of liquid manure in the summer. Plant 2 ft. apart. To increase, divide in spring or autumn.

Varieties.—MOUNT ETNA, intense scarlet, 5 ft., August to September; ROYAL STANDARD, rich gold below, rich scarlet above, July to September; RUSSELL'S GOLD, rich golden-orange, 4 ft., July to September; TUCKII, scarlet and yellow, 4½ ft., June to July.

Linum (Flax), N.O. Linaceæ. Light soil is best and full sun. Plant 9 in. apart. To increase, seed should be sown in spring.

Varieties.—NARBONENSE (Six Hills), sky-blue, 1½ ft., May to July; PERENNE, sky-blue, 2 ft., May to July; FLAVUM, yellow, 1½ ft., May to July.

Lupinus (Lupin), N.O. Leguminosæ. A deeply dug, well-manured soil is necessary to produce good spikes of flowers, as they are gross feeders. Although they prefer full sun they will grow in partial shade. Plant in spring about 3 ft. apart. Pea sticks are best for staking. To increase, seed may be sown outside from May to July, but to increase special varieties, divide after flowering. Lupins very quickly exhaust themselves, so it is wise to have a young stock of plants coming along every year. After a few years the old plant should be scrapped and replaced by new ones. As the seeds form they should be removed.

Varieties.—The following are a few of the most outstanding. All flower in June and grow 3–4 ft. CHOCOLATE SOLDIER, chocolate keel, bright yellow standards; CODSALL'S ORANGE, orange-coral; DOWNERS DELIGHT, dull carmine and old rose; ELIZABETH ARDEN, orange-apricot; MRS. NICOL WALKER, deep reddish-apricot with golden standards; MRS. PENRYN WILLIAMS, deep rose-red; PINK PEARLS, deep rose; RUSSELL LUPINS, mixed, a fine new strain; SUNSHINE, deep yellow.

Lychnis (Campion), N.O. Caryophyllaceæ. They like full sun and will grow in any soil. Plant 1 ft. apart. To increase, divide in spring or autumn or sow seed outside in spring.

Varieties.—CHALCEDONICA, brilliant scarlet, 3 ft., June to August; FLOS-JOVIS, bright pink, 1 ft., June; VISCARIA SPLENDENS PLENA, crimson, 1½ ft., June to July.

Meconopsis (Himalayan Poppy), N.O. Papaveraceæ. The semi-shade of trees is essential with plenty of leaf-mould in the soil.

Protect from excessive moisture in winter. To increase, sow seed in slight warmth. Plant out on a well-prepared leafy bed in April.

Varieties.—BAILEYII (betonicifolia), sky-blue pendent flowers, 4 ft., June to August; CAMBRICA (Welsh Poppy), yellow, 1 ft., June to August; WALLICHII, blue, 4 ft., June to August.

Monarda (Sweet Bergamot), N.O. Labiatæ. Any soil will suit this plant, and to increase, divide in spring or autumn.

Varieties.—DIDYMA CAMBRIDGE, scarlet, 3 ft., July to October; DIDYMA SUPERBA, purple, 3 ft., July to October.

Montbretia (Tritonia), N.O. Iridaceæ. They are useful plants for the front border, where their foliage is attractive, particularly in the autumn. They are gross feeders and should be given a rich soil. They can be lifted in October, stored in a cool, dry place and planted again in March or April. To increase, divide in spring.

Varieties.—HIS MAJESTY, yellow shading into scarlet, 2 ft., August to September; LADY WILSON, yellow, 2 ft., August to September; JAMES COEY, rich red, 2 ft., August to September.

Nepeta (Catmint), N.O. Labiatæ. A fine plant for the edge of the border. A well-drained soil is essential. To increase, cuttings can be inserted in a sandy compost in a cold frame in September, or alternatively the plants can be divided either in spring or autumn.

Varieties.—MUSSINII, 1 ft., July, lavender; MUSSINII (Six Hills Giant), lavender, 3 ft., June to July, larger than above; SOUVENIR D'ANDRE CHAUDRON, 1¾ ft., July, lavender.

Oenothera (Evening Primrose), N.O. Onagraceæ. Any soil is suitable. Plant 9 in. apart. To increase, divide in spring or autumn or sow seed in a cold frame in March.

Varieties.—FRUTICOSA FRASERI, bright yellow, 2 ft., June to August. MISSOURIENSIS, prostrate useful edging plant, yellow, 6 in.

Pæonia (Pæony), N.O. Ranunculaceæ. Pæonies are gross feeders and require a well-manured, moist soil. The young shoots are easily damaged by frost and the plants therefore should be in a position that does not get the early morning sun. Pæonies require a well and deeply manured soil. It is important to plant the pæony crowns 2 in. below the surface. They should have a top dressing of bonemeal and a mulch of well-decayed manure in the spring. Stout stakes are necessary to keep the stem upright. Allow the foliage to die down naturally. Pæonies resent disturbance, so to increase, buy new plants.

Varieties.—*Sinensis* (Chinese Pæonies), range in colour from pure white to deepest crimson, being double, semi-double or single. They are fragrant, 3 ft. high and flower throughout June. BARONESS SCHRŒDER, large, double white; ALBERT CROUSSE, double, shell-pink; PHILOMELE, semi-double, rose-pink; ADOLPHE ROUSSEAU, double, dark crimson; THE BRIDE (Grandiflora), single, snowy white.

May Flowering. Most of the species come under this heading. MLOKOSIEWICZI, single yellow, with beautiful bronze foliage, 2 ft., May; OFFICINALIS, the old-fashioned double fragrant cottage variety, flowering in May, 3 ft.; OFFICINALIS ALBA PLENA, white; TENUIFOLIA PLENA (the fennel-leaved pæony), double red with attractive feathery foliage, 1½ ft., May; WITTMANNIANA, very large single or blush pink, 2 ft., early May; AVANT GARDE, blush cream, 2½ ft.

Imperial. These flower in June or early July. The plants have pale rose outer guard petals, enclosing tightly packed narrow petaloids, often of a paler shade or entirely different in colour. They grow 3 ft. high. BEATRICE KELWAY, rose guard petals, pale rose, fawn and gold petaloids; HIS MAJESTY, maroon red incurved guard petals, saffron petaloids; MOONLIGHT, silver-white guard petals, saffron petaloids.

Papaver (Oriental Poppy), N.O. Papaveraceæ. They require full sun in a well-drained soil and should be left undisturbed. Pea sticks are best for staking. To increase, insert root cuttings.

Varieties.—CRIMSON KING, vivid crimson-scarlet, 4 ft., May to June; LORD LAMBOURNE, orange-scarlet, 2 to 3 ft., May to June; MRS. STOBART, cerise-pink, 2½ ft., May to June.

Pentstemon (Beard Tongue), N.O. Scrophulariaceæ. A light rich soil is best in full sun. To increase, insert cuttings in a cold frame in September.

Varieties.—HETEROPHYLLUS, sky-blue, semi-shrubby, 1½ ft., July to September; LARGE-FLOWERED HYBRIDS, 2½ ft., July to October; ALEXANDER MITCHELL, vivid scarlet; DOSSIE'S BLUSH, large, soft pink with white throat; GLAMIS WHITE, pure white; HON. ALAN GIBBS, cherry-red with white throat; THE BISHOP, large light purple.

Phlox. N.O. Polemoniaceæ. They require full sun and plenty of moisture during the growing season. They flower freely from July to September. Plant in spring 18 in. apart. To increase, divide in spring or insert cuttings in a cold frame.

Varieties.—DECUSSATA CAROLINE VANDERBERG, large blue-purple, 3½ ft.; DECUSSATA DAILY SKETCH, salmon-pink, carmine eye, enormous trusses, 5 ft.; DECUSSATA F. A. BUCHNER, white, 3 ft.; DECUSSATA LEO SCHLAGATER, brilliant scarlet deeper eye, 2½ ft.; DECUSSATA PROFESSOR WENT, dark crimson-purple, 3 ft.; DECUSSATA SALADIN, vivid orange-scarlet, crimson eye, 3½ ft.

Polygonum (Knotweed), N.O. Polygonaceæ. The bank of a stream is the ideal position, although they can be grown in a moist border and semi-shade. To increase, divide in spring or autumn.

Varieties.—AMPLEXICAULE, red, 3 ft., August to September; SACHALINENSIS, white, strong grower, August to September, 6 ft.;

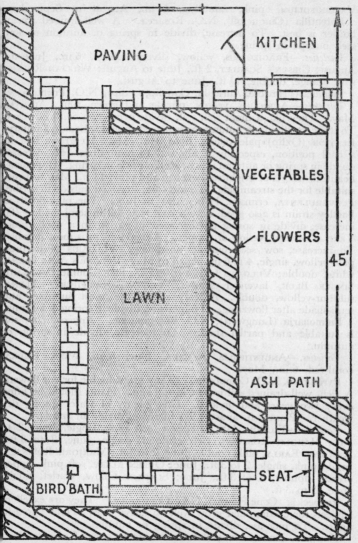

A FORMAL DESIGN FOR A RECTANGULAR GARDEN.

VACCINIFOLIUM, pink, rambling, 6 in., August to September.

Potentilla (Cinquefoil), N.O. Rosaceæ. A well-drained sunny border is best. To increase, divide in spring or autumn or sow seed outside in spring.

Varieties.—FRAGIFORMIS, yellow, silvery foliage, 6 in., June to August; GIBSON'S SCARLET, 2 ft., June to August; WILLIAM ROLLISSON, orange, double, 1½ ft., June to August.

Primula (Primrose, Auricula, Cowslip, Oxlip), N.O. Primulaceæ.

Varieties.—AURICULA, yellow, purple and green, 6 in., April to May. They like a moist rich soil, divide every two or three years. To increase, divide in autumn or sow seed in gentle heat in January. ELATIOR (Oxlip) pale yellow, 6 to 9 in., May. It grows best in a cool position, especially if allowed to naturalize. To increase, divide in spring or autumn or sow seed outside in spring. JAPONICA, beautiful whorls of bright red, orange and pink, 1½ ft., May to June, suitable for the stream side. To increase, sow seed outside in spring. PULVERULENTA, crimson, 1½ ft., May to June. The pink-flowered Bartley strain is also good, likes a cool rich soil in semi-shade. To increase, divide in spring or sow seed in spring in a cool frame. VERIS (Cowslip), yellow or copper. A heavy loam is most suitable. To increase, sow seed outside in spring. VULGARIS (Primrose), pale yellow, single, 4 to 6 in., April to May; VULGARIS ALBA PLENA, white, double; VULGARIS LILACINA PLENA, lilac, double; VULGARIS SINGLE BLUE, lavender shades; VULGARIS SULPHUREA PLENA, sulphur-yellow, double. A leafy soil is the most suitable, and semi-shade after flowering. To increase, divide in spring or autumn.

Pulmonaria (Lungwort), N.O. Boraginaceæ. Any ordinary soil is suitable and partial shade. To increase, divide in spring or autumn.

Varieties.—ANGUSTIFOLIA AZUREA, blue, 6 in., May; RUBRA, coral-red, 6 in., May.

Pyrethrum, N.O. Compositæ. They are valuable for cut flowers. A rich, well-drained soil is best in full sun. Plants should be lifted every two years and divided. Give plenty of water during dry weather. Plant 1 ft. apart. To increase, divide in spring.

Varieties.—EILEEN MAY ROBINSON, soft pink, single, June, 2 to 3 ft.; HAROLD ROBINSON, rich crimson, single, June, 2 to 3 ft.; KINGSTON EARLY, pink, double, June, 2 to 3 ft.; MARJORIE ROBINSON, bright pink, single, 2 to 3 ft., June; QUEEN MARY, soft pink, tipped cream, double, 2 to 3 ft., June; SCARLET GLOW, scarlet, single, June, 2 to 3 ft.

Rudbeckia (Cone Flower), N.O. Compositæ. They are excellent subjects for cutting, and grow well on heavy soils. Plant 1 to 2 ft apart. To increase, divide in spring or autumn.

Varieties.—HERBSTONE, yellow with a green cone, 6 ft., September; MAXIMA, yellow with a black centre, 3 ft., September; SPECIOSA (syn. Newmanii), rich yellow with a black cone, 3 ft., August to September; GOLDEN GLOW (syn. laciniata flora plena), rich yellow, double, 7 ft., September to October.

Salvia (Sage), N.O. Labiatæ.   A hot, dry soil with plenty of manure, and full sun is suitable.   To increase, divide in spring.

Varieties.—AZUREA GRANDIFLORA, soft blue, 4 ft., August to September; TURKESTANICA, gentian-blue, 3 ft., June to August; VIRGATA NEMEROSA, violet-blue, 3 ft., July.

Scabiosa (Scabious), N.O. Dipsaceæ.   A light, well-drained soil with plenty of lime is best, and full sun.   Do not move until spring. Plant in spring 1 ft. apart.   To increase, take cuttings in spring and root in a cold frame.

Varieties.—CAUCASICA CLIVE GREAVES, deep mauve, 2 to 2½ ft., July to October; MISS WILLMOTT, white, 2 ft., July to October.

Sedum (Stonecrop), N.O. Crassulaceæ.   Any soil in sun or semi-shade is suitable.   To increase, plant offsets in September.

Variety.—SPECTABILE, bright pink, 1 ft.

Sidalcea (Mallow), N.O. Malvaceæ.   A light, well-drained soil is best, in a sunny position.   Plant 1 ft. apart.   To increase, divide in spring or autumn.

Varieties.—LOWFIELD PINK, rose-pink, 4 ft., July to August; ROSE QUEEN, rose-pink, 4 ft. July to August; SUSSEX BEAUTY, pale pink, 3 ft., July to August.

Solidago (Golden Rod), N.O. Compositæ.   Any ordinary soil is suitable.   Plant 1½ ft. apart.   To increase, divide in spring or autumn.

Varieties—BALLARDI, 6 ft., yellow, September to August; BUCKLEYI, 1 ft., yellow, September to August; GOLDEN WINGS, 6 ft., yellow, September to August.

Spiræa (Meadow Sweet), N.O. Rosaceæ.   Good plants for the stream-side, where they like a rich soil and semi-shade.   An annual top dressing of well-decayed manure should be given in April. Divide every three to four years.   To increase, divide in spring or autumn.

Varieties.—ARUNCUS, cream, 6 ft., July to August; PALMATA, strawberry-red, 2 to 3 ft., July to August; VENUSTA RUBRA, red, 4 to 6 ft., July to August.

Statice (Sea Lavender), N.O. Plumbaginaceæ.   If cut when in full bloom and dried it can be used for winter decorations.   Grows in a light, well-drained soil in full sun.   To increase, sow seed outside in spring.

Varieties.—LATIFOLIA, mauve, 2 ft.; GMELINI, violet, 2½ ft.

Thalictrum (Meadow Rue), N.O. Ranunculaceæ.   A fairly rich soil is necessary.   Plant 1½ ft. apart.   To increase, divide in spring or autumn.

Varieties.—AQUILEGIFOLIUM PURPUREUM, 3 ft., July to August;

DIPTEROCARPUM HEWITT'S DOUBLE, violet, 5 ft., July to August;
GLAUCUM, yellow, 5 ft., July to August.

Tradescantia (Spiderwort), N.O. Commelinaceæ. A good plant
for the town garden, and one that will grow in any ordinary soil.
To increase, divide in spring or autumn.

Varieties.—VIRGINIANA S.C. WEGUELIN, Cambridge-blue, 1½ ft.,
July; VIRGINIANA LEONORA, violet-blue, 1¼ ft., July; VIRGINIANA
TAPLOW CRIMSON, double, crimson-lake, 1½ ft., July.

Trollius (Globe Flower), N.O. Ranunculaceæ. Ideal plants for
growing near water or in a very moist border. To increase, divide
after flowering.

Varieties.—FIRE GLOBE, deep orange, 1½ ft., May to June;
LEDEBOURII, golden queen, deep orange, 3 ft., June to July; ORANGE
GLOBE, deep orange, 2½ ft., May to June.

Verbascum (Mullein), N.O. Scrophulariaceæ. A well-drained
soil in a sunny position should be given. To increase, sow seed
outside in April.

Varieties.—BROUSSA, bright yellow, 5 to 6 ft., June to July;
COTSWOLD QUEEN, buff terra-cotta, 4 ft., June to July; DENSIFLORUM,
golden bronze, 4 to 5 ft., June to July; GAINSBOROUGH, sulphur
yellow, 4 ft., June to July.

Veronica (Speedwell) N.O. Scrophulariaceæ. A fairly well-
drained soil is necessary. Plant 1 ft. apart. To increase, divide
in spring or autumn.

Varieties.—SPICATA, 1½ ft., blue, July; TRUE BLUE, 1 ft., July.

Vinca (Periwinkle), N.O. Apocynaceæ. This is an excellent
plant for covering rough ground or growing under trees where
little else will succeed. To increase, divide in spring.

Varieties.—MAJOR, blue, 1 ft., June to August; MINOR, blue,
prostrate, 9 in., June to August.

Viola, N.O. Violaceæ. Violas are useful as an edging as well
as for groups. Plant in spring 1 ft. apart and water freely during
dry weather. Keep the seed pods removed regularly. A mulch
of manure in May or June is beneficial every ten days, and applications of liquid manure during the summer. To increase, sow seed
in a cold frame in summer and transplant in September. Cuttings
may be inserted in August or September in a cold frame. They
can be divided in September or October.

Varieties.—CORNUTA JERSEY GEM, rich violet; JACKANAPES, yellow
and brown; MAGGIE MOTT, mauve; PICKERING BLUE, china blue;
PRIMROSE DAME, yellow; SWAN, white.

The following tables are an attempt to classify, under useful
headings, a wide variety of perennials suitable for the herbaceous
border. The letter B means that the flower is raised from bulb, and
the letter S indicates that the plant is classified as a shrub.

HERBACEOUS PERENNIALS FOR

LIGHT WELL-DRAINED SOILS

Althæa	Eremurus	Inuia	Sedum
Anchusa	Gaillardia	Liatris	Sidalcea
Anemonopsis	Galega	Oenothera	Statice
Anthericum	Gypsophila	Phygelius	Thalictrum
Bocconia	Helenium	Potentilla	Thermopsis
Campanula	Heliopsis	Pyrethrum	Verbascum
Chelidonium	Hemerocallis	Salvia	Veronica
Epimedium	Heuchera	Scabious	Viola

MEDIUM LOAM

Artemisia	Galega	Polemonium	Sedum
Aster	Helenium	Polygonum	Senecio
Buphthalmum	Heliopsis	Pulmonaria	Solidago
Carlina	Hemerocallis	Ranunculus	Spiræa
Cephalaria	Inula	Rheum	Thalictrum
Chrysanthemum	Kniphofia	Rudbeckia	Veronica
Echinacea	Lupin	Saxifraga	Viola
Echinops	Phlox		

LEAFY PEAT AND MOIST

Convallaria	Erigeron	Meconopsis	Trollius
Dianthus	Funkia	Polygonatum	Veratrum
Epimedium	Galega	Rodgersia	

PLANTS FOR THE COLOUR BORDERS

BLUE

Aconitum	Campanula	Geranium	Polemonium
Adenophera	Catanche	Iris	Pulmonaria
Ajuga	Centaurea	Linum	Salvia
Allium	Ceratostigma	Lupinus	Tradescantia
Anchusa	Delphinium	Meconopsis	Veronica
Aquilegia	Echinops	Nepeta	Viola
Aster	Eryngium		

RED

Achillea	Chelone	Kniphofia	Phlox
Adonis	Chrysanthemum	Lobelia	Potentilla

Alstroemeria	Dianthus	Lychnis	Primula
Althæa	Echinacea	Monarda	Pyrethrum
Aquilegia	Gaillardia	Pæonia	Schizostylis (B)
Aster	Geum	Papaver	Spiræa
Bellis	Gladiolus (B)	Pentstemon	Tulipa (B)
Centranthus	Heuchera		

YELLOW AND BRONZE

Achillea	Doronicum	Kniphofia	Physalis
Alyssum	Epimedium	Lilium (B)	Rudbeckia
Althæa	Gaillardia	Linum	Senecio (S)
Anthemis	Geum	Lupinus	Spartium
Aquilegia	Gladiolus	Mimulus	Solidago
Aster luteus	Helenium	Montbretia (B)	Thalictrum
Buphthalmum	Helianthus	Narcissus (B)	Thermopsis
Calceolaria	Heliopsis	Oenothera	Trollius
Cephalaria	Hemerocallis	Polyanthus	Tulipa (B)
Chrysanthemum	Inula	Potentilla (S)	Verbascum
Coreopsis	Iris	Primula	Viola

CREAM AND WHITE AND GREEN

Achillea	Catananche	Gladiolus (B)	Oenothera
Althæa	Centranthus	Grasses	Papaver
Anemone	Chelone	Gypsophila	Pentstemon
Aquilegia	Chrysanthemum	Helleborus	Phlox
Arabis	Cimicifuga	Iberis	Pyrethrum
Artemesia	Dianthus	Iris	Sidalcea
Asparagus	Dictamnus	Lathyrus	Spiræa
Aster	Epimedium	Lavatera	Thalictrum
Astilbe	Eremurus	Lilium (B)	Tulipa (B)
Bellis	Eupatorium	Malva	Veronica
Bocconia	Galega	Narcissus (B)	Viola
Campanula			

PINK, MAUVE AND PURPLE

Acanthus	Crinum	Heuchera	Pentstemon
Allium	Delphinium	Incarvillea	Phlox
Alstroemeria	Dianthus	Iris	Polygonum
Althæa	Dicentra	Lathyrus	Primula
Amaryllis	Dictamnus	Lavatera	Salvia
Anemone	Digitalis	Lavender (S)	Saponaria
Armeria	Echinacea	Liatris	Saxifraga
Aster	Eremurus	Linaria	Sedum

Aubrietia
Betonica
Campanula
Chelone
Centaurea
Centranthus
Chrysanthemum
Clematis

Erigeron
Eupatorium
Funkia
Galega
Geranium
Gladiolus (B)
Gypsophila
Helleborus

Lupinus
Lythrum
Malva
Monarda
Nepeta
Pæonia
Papaver
Sidalcea

Stachys
Thalictrum
Tradescantia
Tulipa (B)
Verbascum
Veronica

HERBACEOUS PERENNIALS FOR TOWN GARDENS

Achillea
Ajuga
Alyssum
Anchusa
Anemone japonica
Antennaria
Aquilegia
Arabis
Arenaria
Armeria
Asperula
Aster
Astrantia
Bellis
Campanula
Centranthus
Cephalaria
Cerastium
Chrysanthemum maximum
Convallaria
Coreopsis
Corydalis
Dahlia
Delphinium
Dianthus
Dicentra

Dictamnus
Doronicum
Echinops
Epilobium angusti- folium
Erigeron
Eryngium
Fuchsia
Funkia
Geum
Gypsophila
Helenium
Helianthus
Helleborus niger
Hemerocallis
Hesperis
Heuchera
Iris germanica
Iris sibirica
Kniphofia
Lathyrus
Linaria Hendersoni
Linum
Lobelia cardinalis
Lupinus
Lysimachia num- mularia

Meconopsis Wal- lichii
Mentha
Mimulus
Oxalis corniculata rubra
Pæonia
Papaver
Pentstemon
Phlox
Primula
Rudbeckia
Salvia patens
Saxifraga umbrosa
Scabious caucasica
Sedum acre
Solidago
Spiræa
Statice
Thalictrum
Thyme
Tolmiea
Tradescantia vir- giniania
Veronica
Vinca minor
Viola

N.B.—Avoid woolly leaved plants in towns. Shiny or glaucous foliage will withstand a smoky atmosphere much better than plants with soft leaves.

Seaside plants easily thrive in towns, as for example the car- nation and pink family.

PLANTS FOR EDGINGS

Armeria

Artemesia stel-
  leriana

Achillea argentea

Dianthus

Heuchera

London Pride

Megasea

Nepeta

Stachys

Viola

Where there is rock work on dry wall at the edge the following plants are suitable :—

Alyssum saxatile

Arabis

Aubrietia

Helianthemum

Iberis

Saxifrage

PLANTS FOR SHADY BORDERS

Aconitum

Adonis

Anemone

Anemonopsis

Aquilegia

Artemesia

Astilbe

Astrantia

Campanula

Centranthus

Chelidonium

Cimicifuga

Convallaria

Dicentra

Digitalis

Doronicum

Epilobium

Epimedium

Funkia

Helleborus

Lunaria

Lychnis

Lysimachia

Lythrum

Meconopsis

Mimulus

Myosotis

Phlox

Polemonium

Polyanthus

Primula

Pulmonaria

Ranunculus

Rudbeckia

Spiræa

Thalictrum

Trollius

Tradescantia

Vinca

PLANTS WITH GREY AND ORNAMENTAL FOLIAGE

Acanthus mollis

Achillea argentea

Alyssum saxatile

Anthemis tinctoria

Arabis

Bocconia cordata

Buphthalmum speciosum

Centaurea

Cerastium

Cortaderia argentea

Eremurus robustus

Eryngium giganteum

Eryngium Oliverianum

Geranium ibericum

Ferula

Hemerocallis fulva

Heracleum giganteum

Lilium giganteum

Lavender

Nepeta mussinii

Onopordon acanthium

Phytolacca decandra

Pinks, Mrs. Sinkins

Santolina

Saxifraga peltata

Senecio Clivorum

Silphium

Spiræa aruncus

Stachys lanata

Thalictrum

Funkia
Gypsophila
Helianthus latiflorus

Tritoma
Verbascum
Veronica incana

PLANTS FOR BOLD EFFECTS

Achillea Eupa-
  torium
Asters
Centranthus
Chrysanthemum
  maximum
Cimicifuga
Delphinium

Echinops
Erigeron
Gypsophila panicu-
  lata
Helenium
Hollyhock
Iris
Lilium

Lupinus
Lychnis chalce-
  donica
Phlox
Rudbeckia
Sidalcea
Verbascum

PLANTS FOR FOLIAGE EFFECTS

Alyssum saxatile
Asparagus
Eryngium
Ferns
Funkia

Geranium
Heuchera
Iris
Lavender
Lupinus

Megasea
Nepeta
Pinks
Santolina
Stachys lanata

PLANTS FOR THE WOODLAND GARDEN

Aconitum
Anchusa
Anemone
Astilbe
Campanula
Centranthus

Chelidonium
Cimicifuga
Digitalis
Funkia
Geranium
Lilium

Oxalis
Primula
Polygonatum
Polygonum
Spiræa
Verbascum

CHAPTER VI

ROCK GARDENS

YOU can make a rock garden anywhere. This may sound like nonsense to a gardener of experience, but it is perfectly true. If you are prepared to accept whatever limitations the site may impose, you can have your rockery in any part of the garden site you wish. It may even be the principal feature of your garden; a rock garden of the type shown in Fig. 1, for example, fits very well into a prominent position at the end of a small fenced plot.

What do you want of your rock garden? Do you want the kind

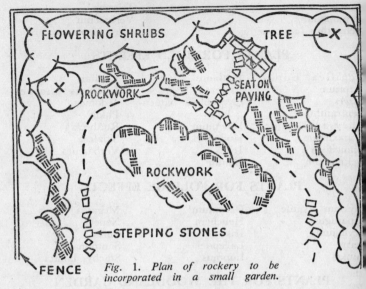

Fig. 1. *Plan of rockery to be incorporated in a small garden.*

of rock garden you see at exhibitions, where rocks are arranged in picturesque fashion and every available ledge is smothered with a carpet of colour? If so, you must make it in a very open, sunny site. Do not plan to have this brightly coloured kind of rock garden in a damp half-shady corner of the garden, where ordinary border flowers do not thrive; the brilliant splash of colour you desire just won't happen. Such masses of colour only come in response to bright sunshine.

Let us consider for a moment some possible types of rock garden for special sites. First the colourful rock garden, made on an open, sunny patch of ground.

The site may be either sloping or flat, since various levels will be arranged artificially in the course of construction. It is also possible to arrange for pockets—or ledges—of soil with a variety of aspects, and even to arrange for deep shade in parts of the rock garden, by careful disposal of the rocks. An open position is the ideal one for the rock garden to occupy, because it can be made a home for so many different kinds of plants. Fig. 2 shows how a rock garden site may be created on level ground.

An existing sloping bank or banks, perhaps with only a moderate amount of sun, means planning rather a different type of rock garden. Often it is more convenient to use such a site, in spite of the partial shade, than to begin on a flat site, where all the labour of excavation and building up must be done. A rock garden in partial shade, particularly if running water can be introduced, can be made to look very charming and natural. Some flowering plants, carefully selected for their capacity to flourish in shade, would find a home in this type of garden. Its character is intimate rather than spectacular.

Then there is the type of site which, queerly enough, is just the one that many inexperienced gardeners choose for the feature—the site in entire shade, and right under the drip of trees. There are few rock plants—few plants of any kind—that really thrive in these conditions. Ferns, and a few shrubs such as periwinkles, mahonia, and St. John's wort, and such perennials as lily of the valley, Solomon's seal (*polygonatum*), ramondia, and cyclamen are at home there; but the list of possible plants for such a rock garden is easily exhausted.

Finally there is the problem of cultivating a few rock garden plants that are special favourites, in a formal garden where an ordinary rockery is out of the question. Little rock gardens here can take the form of dry walls between various levels, bordering the sunk garden or supporting terraces; or rock work of a rather informal type can be introduced at the sides of steps, without unduly destroying the formality of the design. The spaces between paving stones provide another place where rock plants can be grown without introducing a rock garden of the accepted type. This has already been referred to in Chapter I. Rocks on a sloping bank should be arranged so that they leave pockets of soil for planting, as in Fig. 3 and *not* as in Fig. 4.

Having examined the allotted site for the rock garden, or having selected the site from among two or more alternatives, we can still

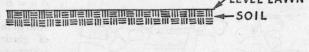

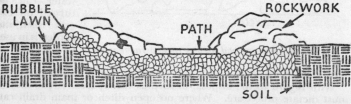

Fig. 2. Building a rockery on a level site. The lawn turf is replaced by rubble on which path and rockwork is built.

choose between several different styles. Since rocks occur in a natural state in all sorts of districts, and at all altitudes, the term rock gardening must not be limited—as it so often is—to the rocky hillside, or alpine garden.

Exquisite examples of natural rock gardening occur in such

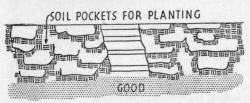

Fig. 3. Rocks on a bank, arranged with soil-pocket.

districts as the limestone valleys of Yorkshire. There the water from the hills runs among and through the limestone, forming channels, sometimes on the surface and sometimes below the ground. Where the water emerges at the surface and wears its way through the rocks, they become waterworn to curious and picturesque shapes, and the surface streams carrying seeds and soil as they tumble to the lower plains gradually clothe the watersides with plants and flowers of many kinds.

This type of rock and water garden can be imitated in quite a small garden if (*a*) a water supply exists or can be introduced, and (*b*) if some arrangement for the disposal of surplus water is made. Cost probably enters into the first requirement, but it might be remarked here that cost is not very great after the initial expense of installation, even if company's water is used. Cost can be reduced by using the same water over and over again, which means the use of a small power pump, costing from two and a half guineas upwards. It can also be reduced by using the merest trickle of water, in the form of a small cascade, the water descending from pool to pool

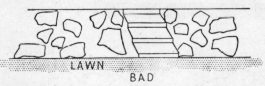

Fig. 4. Haphazard and useless rock arrangement.

down the rockery slopes. Also in this type of garden the water can be turned off except when the garden is in use, for reasons of economy. A typical plan for such a rock and water garden is shown in Fig. 5.

With regard to the disposal of surplus water, local circumstances must dictate procedure. Where no open ditch or main drain can be used, a small amount of such surplus water can be very easily disposed of by the sump method. For this a deep hole is excavated in some part of the garden to be occupied by shrubs or lawn. The hole should be at least four foot deep, and proportionately wide, and into the open hole should be thrown rough, porous clinker or other material of this character. The soil can then be returned to make the surface as before, and either turf or shrubs should be used over the sump. Turf is preferable in many ways, but chiefly because should the sump ever, in future years, become ineffective, as it might

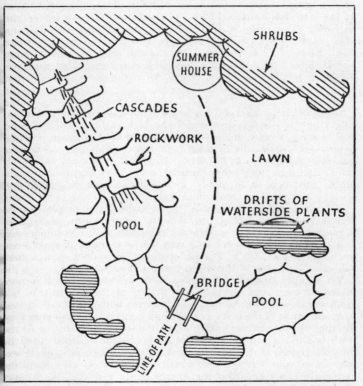

Fig. 5. A rock and water garden. This may be constructed with the help of an artificial water supply, if a stream is lacking.

if the soil silts down and consolidates, it could be opened again, and fresh clinker used.

Naturally only a small surplus can be disposed of in this way if the surrounding soil is of clay; but if the garden has a porous natural subsoil, the sump will take much more. Pipes would, of course have to be laid when the sump was built to take to it the water from the lowest end of the rock garden, unless a marshy edged pool were arranged. Such a pool, overflowing into the surrounding soil should be set below the general garden level, and a sloping trench filled with clinker, led from this to the sump.

Another type of rock garden imitates a rocky cliff such as is seen at the seaside or in mountainous districts. Here the surface crust of the earth has crumbled away, leaving a cliff more or less vertical in form. The rocky cliff surface continues to crumble, and as it does so, the finer particles are here and there caught on ledges. Birds carry seeds to these ledges, and the result is a picturesque. colourful bank in the steep cliff side, which can be imitated artificially but, if carefully done, very effectively in the garden.

"SCREE" GARDENS

Often when this kind of thing happens naturally, a fall of crumbling stones and soil will collect under the high cliff. Most of the soil will be washed away, and gradually a varied heap of stones, to which storms are continually adding, will form. This sort of heap is generally referred to as "scree." Nature is very kind, and rarely do we find such stone heaps entirely bare. They may contain what alpine gardeners value highly, such gems as androsace of various species, and the rare campanula *zoysii*.

To copy a rock garden of this "scree" type is very simple. I have seen it done on the roof of a town house, where a surprising number of plants were grown in small stone chippings, with no ordinary soil at all. Rock plants do not take very kindly to the dirty air of town districts as a rule; but in this roof garden of scree only, quite a good collection managed to thrive very well indeed.

Yet another kind of rock garden is the moraine. This is formed in nature by glacial streams. As the ice of the glacier proceeds gradually down the mountain side, it carries with it rocks of various sizes, and most of these are crushed and pounded to small stones by the time they reach the valley where the ice melts. In this way a stony bed to the melting stream of ice is gradually formed; through the greater part of the year this bed is dry at the surface, while ice-cold water runs through the underlayer of stones. Hot sunshine frequently pours down on the surface of the moraine, but always the underlayer, where the roots penetrate, is moist and cool.

Plants of certain kinds have become adapted to these particular conditions, and if they are to be brought into the garden, and to thrive there, the natural conditions must, as far as possible, be reproduced. All sorts of ingenious methods have been adopted by rock gardeners in the formation of a moraine garden, and there is still room for much originality in this direction. Moraine plants have been cultivated in shallow tanks, slightly sloping, and fed with water at the higher end. The soil has been a specially prepared compost of sandy, fibrous loam, mixed with crushed charcoal or sphagnum moss and peat, and surfaced with fine stone chips.

Another good moraine garden was made at the lower end of a rocky cascade, the water being allowed to form a bog, which was surfaced in parts with prepared peaty soil and stone chips. This question of finding a home for moraine plants is definitely one in which the ingenuity of the garden maker can find expression.

A natural spring suggests to any garden maker the formation of some water feature. Such natural springs are frequently found in districts where the subsoil is of rock, and any gardener who strikes one can call himself fortunate. It may be that such a spring occurs in a part of the plot which is open and sunny—in a quarried cliff, for instance. A rippling cascade of water tumbling over rocks and splashing on to drifts of musk, or water forget-me-nots, would suggest itself here. But should the spring be discovered in a stretch of woodland, the stream would almost naturally be planted with moisture-loving ferns and other plants suited to shade. Rather different types of rock would be preferable in the two types—small rocks suitably placed would be good in the sunny streamside, while bold cliffs of austere character would possibly be more suitable for the shady site.

A spring emerging from a wooded hillside might well be formed at the source into a natural wall fountain or dripping well, with ferns, ramondias, and such plants, set in the vertical crevices of the wet rocks.

Almost any unusual site can, in fact, be worked into a rock garden scheme, and it would be impossible to describe in detail the layout for each. As a matter of interest, the garden maker is reminded that the best rock garden firms do not offer any sort of prepared scheme beforehand for the layout of a new rock garden, but ask for their experienced craftsmen to be allowed a free hand, knowing that they will use stone, plants, environment, aspect, etc., to the best advantage if allowed to create as they work.

TYPES OF STONE TO USE

Limestone has already been mentioned as good rock for a picturesque rock garden. For a long time it was regarded by some as almost indispensable for the making of a first-class rock garden, but this somewhat unreasonable preference has largely disappeared. It is recognized that the kind of rock is actually less important than the manner in which the rock is used.

The chief kinds of rock available are limestone, sandstone, tufa, granite, and artificial cement lumps. Each has certain advantages. Limestone, if weatherworn, that is exposed to the air in its natural home so that it has become partly overgrown with moss or lichen, or waterworn, is extremely picturesque. Because of its porous nature, it forms a congenial plant home, and roots of rock plants frequently penetrate the actual rock. Landscape effects are very easily obtained with such rock, and the greyish colour tones generally with almost any kind of garden. It very quickly assumes a weathered and aged appearance, giving the rock garden an established look after only a few months.

Sandstone, of various colours, is quarried in many districts. It is very porous, and therefore a fine home for plants, particularly in districts where the soil is inclined to be dry. It weathers to an established appearance almost as quickly as limestone.

Tufa, the volcanic rock resembling the pumice stone of commerce, is also very satisfactory on account of its porousness. Its colour is dark grey, but the pleasing striations often found in limestone are mostly absent from tufa. It does not rapidly become moss and lichen covered; nevertheless, it is not unattractive, and many plants like it particularly well. It should certainly be used in the districts where it is obtainable at cheap rates.

Granite is not approved by rock gardeners who grow the rare alpines. It is hard and non-porous, and in large lumps gives an extremely rugged and picturesque air to a garden. Beautiful effects can be obtained by massing granite at the sides of a stream, which are planted with sweeping drifts of showy carpeters. It should not be despised, but it should be employed with discretion.

USE OF CEMENT IN ROCK GARDENS

Cement lumps are looked down on by some. Nevertheless, I have seen excellent rock gardens made for the most part of home-made concrete, which in the hands of an artist can be extremely attractive. From the viewpoint of the health of the plants, nothing can be said against the use of cement, except where certain calcifuges or lime-loving plants are concerned; and from the viewpoint of cheapness and availability everything is in its favour. The owner of a large garden and a small purse may be excused if he prefers to make cement rocks as and when his funds permit, instead of laying out large initial sums on imported rock.

To make useful cement blocks for a rock garden, all that need be done is this. Take one part of portland cement to four parts of coarse sand, being careful to mix them well together before any water is added. Then use enough water to make a rather sloppy mixture.

Excavate rough holes in the ground, in some available vacant corner of the garden. Drop in a layer of the mixed concrete, and then set on it any large stones, old tins—these not beaten flat, as for paths, but with the lids on, so that they remain hollow—or any other rough material. Then add more concrete, so that these tins, etc., are quite covered, leaving the surface rough and lumpy.

Gravel or rough small stones can be mixed with the concrete, and if desired, some of the coloured cements can be used. Colour should not be too lavishly employed, however, or it will add to the artificial appearance, which is what you want to avoid.

Leave the lumps untouched for a few weeks, then dig them out and make more. It takes very little time, just a few odd minutes now and then, to make enough lumps to build a small rock garden.

If just a limited amount of real stone is available, it often pays to use such cement lumps in association with the more picturesque rocks. They can usually be built up so that only the natural stone is visible after a short time, quick carpeting plants being set wherever the cement is visible, so as to hide it. In fact, as remarked previously, the manner of building is actually much more important than the kind of rockery stone used.

CHOOSING A STYLE

Before outlining the actual procedure of rock garden construction, here is a word of advice to those who hand over this feature to experts. It is best to let the craftsman on the job choose a style; but it is also wise to have some idea, beforehand, as to what you want from the rock garden. If you can tell him that you want just a picture, or that you want a home for rare alpines, or that you want to be able to walk between the rocky ledges and valleys, his task will be easier.

Further, don't expect an established, picturesque appearance immediately. Rock gardens, even when new, may look reasonably well, but such characteristic items as dwarf shrubs and drooping cascades of flower and foliage must be waited for, just as you must wait for the flowers in the herbaceous border.

If you insist on an immediate picture, you will soon have, as in so many gardens of my acquaintance, a collection of overgrown shrubs, far too large for their positions, and possibly quite unsuitable in character. An immediate effect is made by planting young, quick-growing conifers in place of the dwarf varieties, or by planting small potted shrubs of the kind that very quickly become giants. Even if you could keep them to correct proportions by regular pruning, you would find that the roots would penetrate through the rocks to such an extent that other plants would suffer.

Therefore be as explicit as possible with your instructions to the rock specialist, leave it then to him, and above all, be prepared to be patient over immediate results.

Now for the process of rockery construction. The first and essential step is to decide roughly on the general contour which will suit the garden. If water is to be used, it must be decided where it is to run from and where it is to run to, and pipes must b. laid accordingly. When company's water is to be used, instructions should be given for a supply, with tap, to be taken to the intended highest point of the rock garden.

The next step will be rough excavation and building of the contours desired; but as this proceeds, the top layer of fertile soil must be kept on one side. It is wasted if buried under infertile subsoil. Large stones and other porous rubbish might well form the foundation of the rockery hills, as they help to form drainage, and good drainage in the rock garden is very important indeed.

Paths through the rock garden will be constructed as the building proceeds. Paths in this case are really beaten soil tracks, top-dressed with stone chippings, with perhaps an occasional flat stone or stairway of stones, to make for ease in walking up and down the steeper slopes. Granite or other chips make excellent surfacing material for these paths, not only because they are picturesque, but also because many of the rock plants grown in the soil pockets will tend to creep in through the stone chips of the paths, and soften the edges. If several steps are used together, the crevices between will, of course, be set with flowering plants or ferns according to aspect.

Before beginning to set any rocks in position, a quantity of good soil should be prepared. The ideal mixture for most parts of the rock garden is made by rubbing old leaf-mould and old stable manure through a coarse sieve, and mixing it with coarse sand or gritty soil. Certain lime-loving plants do best if some crushed mortar rubble is added, and certain peat-loving plants like peat in the compost if it is obtainable, though generally the peat-lovers will do well in any mixture free of lime.

Do not be afraid that light sandy soil will wash away from the necks and roots of the plants. Perhaps it will, but the plants in their native haunts grow in just such soil, and rains do wash it away frequently. Rains also bring down from upper slopes enough new soil to take the place of that which is washed away. The rock gardener performs

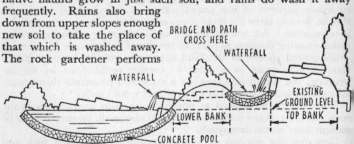

Fig. 6. Cross-section of a rock and water garden, showing building of two banks and concreted pools.

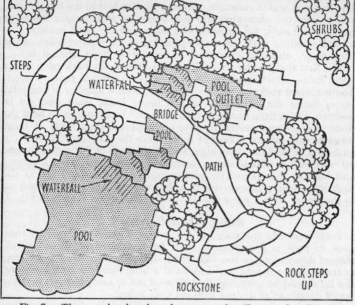

Fig. 7. The completed rock and water garden illustrated in Fig. 6.

the same service when he top-dresses—as he must do every now and then—with fresh soil.

In the initial stage of rockery construction it is not necessary to use artificial fertilizers in the compost, though it must never be presumed that all rock plants will thrive in poor infertile soil. Where flowering plants are to be grown, bonemeal can, if desired, be used in the compost, as it is slow-acting, and encourages flower production.

In addition to a supply of mixed compost, you need to have by you a quantity of small stones or breeze or other porous material. You will find this useful to fill in at the bottom of very deep pockets, so as to keep the drainage free in all parts of the rock garden.

When an artificial stream is planned, or a small cascade of water runs from pool to pool down a steep slope, this part of the rock garden should be constructed first. It is almost impossible to give detailed instructions, since so much depends on the kind of stone, the kind of site, and various other points that differ widely in different gardens. I have in mind at the moment a small rock garden made by an amateur on a flat site. Fig. 6 shows how it was constructed. The first step was to excavate a wide, irregular hole in the foreground, and to pile the excavated soil into a sort of semicircular bank, or rather two banks, for between one ridge and the back horizon was a small winding path. A water pipe led to the highest point of the back ridge, and was concealed by arranging rocks around it.

The first rocks to be set in place were round the back edge of the open hole—which was to become a pool with a marshy edge. Tooth-shaped rocks set vertically behind, with a number of irregular stones lining the back wall of this lower bank, were next set in position, and a little concrete used here and there, partly to hold the stone in place and partly to make a non-porous waterway. A large concrete slab formed a kind of bridge over the " stream " to link the pathways behind the first ridge, and at the back of this was arranged a " waterfall." These stones again were partly cemented together, and built so that the water was brought over the stony bed of the stream, to drop a foot or two in a thin sheet of water, and splash on to the stones with a noisy chatter. The final effect is seen in Fig. 7.

ROCK GARDEN POOLS

Pools made in the rock garden, where a series of cascades from pool to pool is constructed, need be nothing more than saucer-shaped depressions in the soil, lined with concrete. The front edge of the concrete should stand forward a little from the rock face, and the lip should be very slightly hollowed out in one place, so that the water overflows as desired into the pool below.

If a real stream is to be constructed artificially, the course must be excavated, and concreted or bricked all along, before any water is introduced. A series of small cascades can be achieved by the method shown in Fig. 8.

When it comes to the placing of the main rocks, the garden artist must try to visualize the result of his labours before they happen, and try to create the effect of a natural scene. He should always arrange the rocks so that they appear to be a part of a natural rocky subsoil that has been washed by rain. Natural stone will have this appearance if the weathered parts are exposed.

Another point is that where natural strata are visible in the rocks, the lines of each should be generally parallel, as they would naturally be. True, occasionally through a " fault " rocks tilt and overturn, or are pushed out of position by pressure from surrounding rocks; but the general " lie of the land " should be traceable in the rocks. Very round rocks or very thin flat rocks are awkward to place well and should generally be avoided. The flat ones will do for path-making, and a round rock of large size might make an impromptu seat; but in building rock pockets, it will need to be disguised. Only a part of each rock should generally be visible—roughly

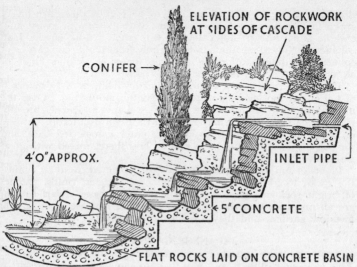

ELEVATION OF ROCKWORK
AT SIDES OF CASCADE

CONIFER →

4'0" APPROX.

INLET PIPE

5" CONCRETE

FLAT ROCKS LAID ON CONCRETE BASIN

Fig. 8. A series of cascades in the rock garden, artificially constructed with water supply from an inlet pipe.

about a third—the rest should be buried under the soil (Fig. 9). Each rock should rest firmly on another rock, or be so well buried in the soil as to be perfectly secure, even when trodden on. It is quite probable that most of the exposed rocks will, at some time, be used as stepping stones by the gardener, and stones insecurely placed are then a nuisance, if not a danger.

I think a little might be said here concerning one or two less common styles in rock gardening. All are built on much the same principles as the simpler styles, but there are some rather important differences.

One is the style now known as the alpine meadow. In the mountain valleys, where sun and rain are both plentiful, and where

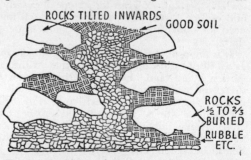

ROCKS TILTED INWARDS   GOOD SOIL

ROCKS ½ TO ⅔ BURIED

RUBBLE ETC.

Fig. 9. Rocks, at least half buried in soil, are tilted in and down to catch moisture.

streams and rich fertile valleys are to be found, there are lovely green meadows, starred in springtime with flowers of every hue, and in late summer still coloured with such plants as the lilac colchicum. These meadows differ entirely from the alpine garden of convention, though affording a home for some similar kinds of alpines; and they are very easy to construct.

The first requisite is a stretch of meadowland, or a sown patch of soil of not too level character, but gently undulating. Over the meadowland are disposed rocks of varying shapes and sizes, carefully set into the turf, so that they appear as a natural outcrop. At one or both sides of the larger rocks a soil patch can be left bare, and the soil displaced by the rocks can be laid there, mixed with good compost.

Plants of suitable character will then be planted, nestling against the rocks, in irregular drifts. Ornamental grasses, bulbs, patches of bright rock-carpeting plants, and in some cases dwarf shrubs, are all materials that the landscape gardener can use in an alpine meadow garden, and they are all equally effective.

JAPANESE GARDENS

Another distinctive style in rock gardening is the Japanese garden. This is a wide subject, and one that, to the Japanese gardener, is worthy of a lifetime of concentrated study. The chief difference between a Japanese garden and a European garden is this. In our gardens, we plant either for a landscape picture, to a formal pattern, in order to complete our collection of horticultural specimens, or to produce perfectly grown plants for exhibition. The Japanese design their gardens symbolically, and every stone set in position in a Japanese rock garden must have its meaning, and must be chosen for the suitability of its size and shape, and set in just the right position for that kind of stone. A Japanese gardener searches perhaps for years for a stone of exactly the right proportions and outline. We, however, merely search for stones that satisfy a need for something more or less picturesque, and then leave it at that.

It is impossible to go fully into this subject in a limited space; but as an illustration, let me explain that in the conventional Japanese garden you would always find three stones (or three plants, for there might be the same idea worked out in other materials), representing God (or the Guardian), Man (or Worship), and Earth (or material things). There would also be stones or other material of secondary importance, but still full of meaning, each with its name and place in the scheme. There might be many more such items, but each and every item must be known, named, and valued in the layout of the garden.

It is an interesting subject to study, for any gardener with time to devote to it. Since the size of a Japanese garden can be anything from 6 in. to many acres, this is an ideal phase of gardening for the owner of a tiny plot. There are a number of good books on the subject in most libraries, and any who care to tackle the task of making a Japanese garden are advised to read these.

A new rock garden is best left for a few weeks after construction, before planting is begun, so that the soil and rocks can settle well. Although the utmost care is taken to ram soil well into all crevices as the building proceeds, so that no large air spaces are left in which plant roots can become starved and dry, a certain amount of settlement or movement is inevitable, and it is best that this should take place before there are any plants to be disturbed in the process.

Rock plants are usually bought in pots, or just tipped from pots, and they should be set out in the prepared soil pockets with as little disturbance as possible. In the case of home-raised seedlings, set out from boxes, the planting process is similar to that of ordinary bedding out. Care must be taken not to damage the tender necks of small plants, but all plants must be set firmly, and have the soil well pressed down over the roots.

Rock plants like a cool, moist root-run; they rapidly die off if the soil surrounding them cakes and dries. Until the plants themselves are large enough to cover the soil surface of the whole pocket, small granite or limestone chippings, or pea gravel, can with advantage be used as a cover to the surrounding soil. These prevent much surface evaporation, and do not interfere with the normal development of roots and foliage.

WHAT ARE SOIL " POCKETS "?

It may be worth while to explain to the novice in rock gardening that a soil " pocket " so frequently referred to is a flat bed of soil, supported by rocks. The rocks are tilted slightly into the bank of the rockery, so that rains falling on them are carried into the soil, to feed the plant roots. Soil is then filled in wherever it will remain, and forms a series of flat-surfaced pockets, or ledges, down the banks of the rock garden.

Many a beginner has tried the method of making first a bank of soft soil, and then pushing in rocks here and there—with disastrous results. The first heavy rains wash the soil down, and probably unsettle the rocks. In any case the rock garden so made looks " like a decorated trifle, with almonds over it," as one writer has aptly said, instead of looking like a piece of natural scenery.

Arrangement of the plants in a rock garden is a matter of artistic expression. A good plan when water is included in the picture is to begin with the water feature, arranging drifts of colour or foliage along the waterside. It will seem more natural if these drifts are irregular in form and size, and certainly no attempt must be made

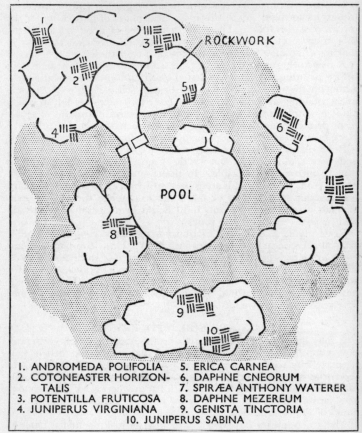

Fig. 10. A suggested use of shrubs in the rock and water garden.

to alternate colours along a streamside. Rather should groups be collected—several patches of musk in one part of the stream, and several patches of forget-me-nots in another, and so on.

Bold colour masses in the dry parts of the rock garden can be arranged as desired, but with some effort to dispose these so that the various seasons are represented in all parts of the picture.

Dwarf shrubs, particularly those of characteristic form, such as pyramid conifers or columnar conifers, or broad spreading shrubs

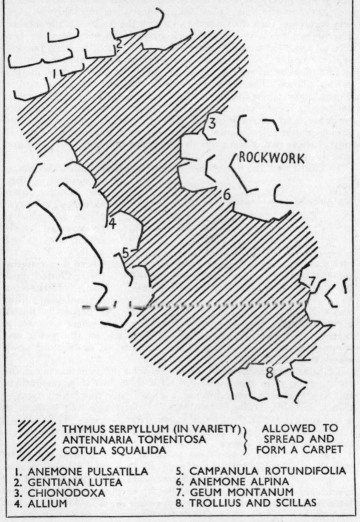

ROCKWORK

THYMUS SERPYLLUM (IN VARIETY)	ALLOWED TO
ANTENNARIA TOMENTOSA	SPREAD AND
COTULA SQUALIDA	FORM A CARPET

1. ANEMONE PULSATILLA   5. CAMPANULA ROTUNDIFOLIA
2. GENTIANA LUTEA   6. ANEMONE ALPINA
3. CHIONODOXA   7. GEUM MONTANUM
4. ALLIUM   8. TROLLIUS AND SCILLAS

Fig. 11. A suggested arrangement of flowering upright and carpeting plants to give variety to the rock garden.

that drape gracefully over rocks, will be used by the artist where they are most effective. This is often somewhere near the eye-level; very rarely are such shrubs satisfactory on the horizon of the picture. The highest point of a small rock garden can very often be best used as a site for a garden seat, this serving much the same purpose as the " mount " which is made to overlook Tudor gardens.

The mention of shrubs brings to mind the wide variety in rock garden plants. There are, in fact, all the kinds of plants used in the ordinary landscape or garden—shrubs, bulbs, grasses, carpets, herbaceous perennials, annuals, biennials—available for the rock gardener, and the majority of plant families are also represented among the smaller plants suitable for rock gardening. Figs. 10 and 11 show two of the ways in which the different kinds of plants may be used by the rock gardener.

In most cases, the use of the various plants on the rockery slopes is similar to their use in the main garden. The carpet plants are allowed to spread their colours over the soil as they will, except where they outgrow their allotted position. Herbaceous perennials are lifted and divided occasionally, as in the herbaceous border. Annuals are sown under glass and pricked out, or sown where they are to bloom. Biennials are treated as are biennials for the spring and summer flower beds, though these too can, if desired, be sown where they are to flower.

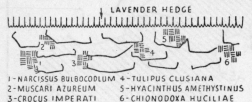

I—NARCISSUS BULBOCODLUM 4—TULIPUS CLUSIANA
2—MUSCARI AZUREUM   5—HYACINTHUS AMETHYSTINUS
3—CROCUS IMPERATI   6—CHIONODOXA HUCILIAE

Fig. 12. *Bulb planting in the rock garden.*

Bulbs and shrubs are both used in rather a different manner in the rock garden from that employed with them in the larger garden. Bulbs are chosen from among the available miniature types— dwarf daffodils, scillas, snowdrops, chionodoxas, tulip species of a daintier type than the florists' tulips, dwarf iris, etc. They are not replanted every year, but form a part of the permanent planting scheme of the rock garden (Fig. 12).

One of the best ways to use bulbs in the rock garden is to set them in the same pockets as some of the carpet-forming plants, so that the bulb foliage and flower spike come up through the green carpet and flower early, while the carpeter carries its flowers later in the same pocket. Snowdrops with arenaria *balearica*, scillas with globularia *nana*, and the dwarf types of narcissus with mossy saxifrages all result in two seasons of flower from the same pocket.

Shrubs are differently used in the rock garden for the chief reason that masses of shrubbery are never desirable in this planting scheme. Shrubs used should be either outstanding specimens, or low-growing drapery shrubs designed to soften the hard outline of the rocks (Fig. 13).

That is the reason why rock shrubs must be very carefully placed, for the least suggestion of " shrubbery " will quickly become obtrusive in the picture. This does not mean that shrubs must be always isolated specimens. In a large rock garden a bank of shrubs, growing from almost vertical crevices in huge quarried rocks, is a

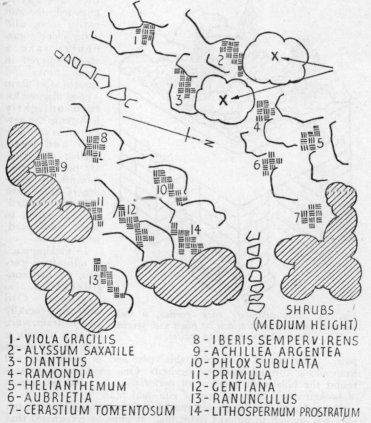

SHRUBS
(MEDIUM HEIGHT)

1- VIOLA GRACILIS
2- ALYSSUM SAXATILE
3- DIANTHUS
4- RAMONDIA
5- HELIANTHEMUM
6- AUBRIETIA
7- CERASTIUM TOMENTOSUM

8- IBERIS SEMPERVIRENS
9- ACHILLEA ARGENTEA
10- PHLOX SUBULATA
11- PRIMULA
12- GENTIANA
13- RANUNCULUS
14- LITHOSPERMUM PROSTRATUM

Fig. 13. A suggested mixed arrangement for the rock garden.

delightful background; but shrubs in a rock garden should never be allowed to obscure a view.

Miniature rock gardens (Fig. 14) can be made in stone sinks or troughs. This is a very popular type of rock gardening, and by no means limited to those gardeners who have insufficient space to accommodate the ordinary rock garden. In fact, stone sinks and troughs form an accompaniment to many rock gardens, and are also useful in various other parts of the garden.

They have a big advantage in that plants can be raised so that

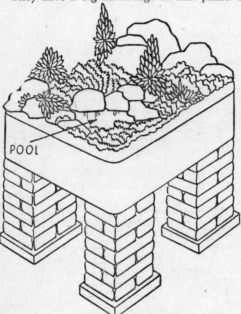

POOL

they are easily attended to and easily seen, and many elderly gardeners take a special interest in them. Sinks and troughs also form a good disguise for such unsightly features in the new garden as manhole lids and open drains; and they are naturally welcomed by gardeners who must confine their horticultural efforts to some small yard, or to a roof.

In making such a miniature garden, the first consideration is drainage. Old sinks are generally easy to drain, since there is already a hole in the lowest

Fig. 14. This miniature rock garden, a sink standing on brick pillars, can be filled with special dwarf plants, including conifers.

part. Some means of keeping this open and of preventing soil from silting through must be devised. One good way is to surround the hole with a collar of perforated zinc, and pile pieces of broken crock over the top of zinc and hole.

The soil used for the garden must be of open porous nature, but also rich enough to support plant life. It must be recognized that sink gardens generally need artificial watering at some seasons, as it is impossible to use sufficient humus in the under soil to hold moisture during drought.

The sink can be filled loosely with soil, and the rocks then set in place, as effectively as possible, and in such a manner that soil can be filled into the pockets. Fine soil of good consistency is then sifted over the garden, and allowed to fill the pockets and silt down among the rocks. This is best left a day or two to settle, and then the garden is planted with all kinds of dwarf plants.

If possible, one or more dwarf conifers should be used, but these should certainly not be set at the pinnacle of the highest " hill." Rampant growers, even those of dwarf type, should generally be avoided. If they are inclined to spread through the soil they will very quickly choke the other plants in the rock garden.

Rock garden specialists generally offer special collections of plants suitable for the sink garden. If these are purchased, care should be taken to give to each the kind of site in which it will thrive. The use of top-dressings of fine stone chippings is almost' essential for success, while sand should also be kept handy for the same purpose. Many of the finest alpine plants find a happy home in a sink garden; and sinks of not too large a size can if desired be wintered in the alpine or cold greenhouse, and moved to the open air of the garden for the summer months.

WHEN TO MAKE A ROCK GARDEN

The time to make a new rock garden is any time when the work can conveniently be tackled. Rock plants, as already mentioned, are mostly raised in pots, and can be set out at any time if handled carefully. A good time to choose in many ways is late summer, when most rock plants are resting, i.e., not in full flower, and are not likely to suffer from a move so much as when the flowers are all open. Also, late summer is a period when, if ever, the home gardener can take a little rest from his ordinary labours. Plants have all reached their flowering quarters, with the exception of those to be flowered in winter under glass, and except for propagation, there is not much " extra " work to be done in the main flower garden.

However, a new rock garden can be made at any time, and in the same way it would be possible, though not advisable, to remodel a rock garden at any season. Gardeners generally choose, however, to remodel the rock garden, when necessary, just before the winter, when alpine plants are preparing to sleep beneath a canopy of snow.

After a rock garden is made and planted, it will take a few months for the plants to become established. By that time it will be necessary to keep a sharp lookout for weeds, and also to watch the vigorous growers among the plants and see that they do not encroach on the slow growers. Rock plants do not like to be smothered by decaying humus. From time to time, therefore, the pockets must be carefully gone over, and all old decaying leaves trimmed away. Leaves that blow on to the pockets from nearby trees in autumn are particularly dangerous to the health of alpines.

Occasional top dressings of gritty soil, or stone chippings, or, in the case of lime-loving plants, of crushed mortar, should be given to roots which are bared by rains or frost; and any plants that have been loosened in the soil by weather action should always be made firm again.

Whenever a plant has finished flowering, it should be attended to according to the type. Carpet plants of vigorous habit such as arabis, the white rock cress, should be cut hard back after flowering, or they will quickly become a nuisance. If an increase in stock is desired, the pieces cut away can be inserted in sandy soil in a shady part of the garden, or in a frame or propagating pit, where they will root well in time for autumn planting.

Dead flowers should generally be snipped off with scissors; but if rock plants are to be raised from seed, some of the seeds can be left to ripen on the plant. Most rock plants grow readily from such freshly gathered ripe seed, if it is sown at once, though in some cases it is better to wait until the following spring before sowing. Methods of raising the fine seed of certain rare alpines are described below under the heading " The Alpine House." A few rock plants have decorative seed heads, and in such cases they should, of course, be left to ripen on the plants.

PROTECTING THE ROCK GARDEN AGAINST WINTER

At the end of each summer, before the worst frosts come along, the rock garden should receive its winter coverings. Some plants winter best if liberally top-dressed with stone chippings but otherwise unprotected. Other rock plants, particularly those with rough, hairy, or woolly leaves, winter very badly in this climate, though they are perfectly hardy in alpine regions. They cannot stand the constant moisture of our fogs and rains. It is not always convenient to winter these in an alpine house, and if they must remain in the open, they should be protected by glass. The erections called " alpine protectors " are specially valuable, because they are simple pieces of glass held over the plant so that most of the rains are diverted, and do not enter the heart of the plant and cause decay.

Ordinary bell glasses can be used, but must never remain closed for so long that they shed condensed water into the centre of the plant, or they will prove worse than useless. They should be lifted off daily in fine weather and replaced at night.

A well-made rock garden should not need frequent renovation, though in all rock gardens, certain pockets need to be cleared out now and again and refreshed with some new compost. If faulty drainage or extension of the rock garden necessitates rebuilding, remove the large rocks one by one, and carefully lift out the plants. Pack them into boxes, and stand these in a sheltered shady corner while remodelling takes place. Lift all the soil possible with the roots, so that they do not suffer. Then rebuild as desired, and put back the plants at the earliest opportunity. If they are moved carefully, the plants will not suffer even if they are disturbed while in active growth; but the replanting must be firm, and afterwards the soil must be kept moist for a time.

Increase of rock plants is effected by the ordinary methods of increase as described in Chapter III. A number of the more vigorous subjects can be roughly pulled apart and replanted, or pieces can be pulled away and inserted without further preparation in boxes of sandy soil or in a shaded nursery plot. Arabis and cerastium are well-known plants that can be roughly handled in this manner without any apparent harm.

VALUE OF AN ALPINE HOUSE

With many rock plants, however, a greater amount of care is needed in handling than is required by the inhabitants of the herbaceous border. An alpine house as an adjunct to the rock garden makes it possible to give them this extra care, and so to propagate all kinds of rock plants.

A further use for an alpine house is in the winter culture of rare rock plants that will not stand our damp, foggy winters. It should be recognized by the rock gardener from the outset that the alpine house is not a warm house. It is not intended as a protection against frost, which rarely kills alpine plants, but as a protection against the damp air and rains which cannot be avoided in the open in this country.

Heating apparatus certainly exists in many alpine houses, but its purpose is to dry the atmosphere, and usually the cooler the house can be kept the healthier will be the plants.

BLOOMS THAT NEED GLASS SHELTER

Still another reason for cultivating certain alpines under glass is the delicacy of their blooms. Some plants flower when our weather is, generally, rather showery, and if we are to make certain of having flowers in perfection, glass shelter is necessary. In some cases, too, as with some of the rare saxifrages, the plants are grown in pans all the year round under glass, partly because of their real beauty and interest at all seasons.

The best alpine house is a span-roof type with rather low roof, so that the shelves, while showing off the plants well, are not too far removed from the glass (*see* Chapter IX). For the same reason the shelves are usually on each side, allowing for a central path. A cool staging is desirable, and this usually takes the form of a 2-in. layer of pea-sized gravel.

Although good ventilation is absolutely essential, care must be taken not to allow a draught through the alpine house, as plants that are used to the still air of the house suffer keenly in unaccustomed draughts. Strange as it may seem, when we think of the blazing sunshine on the high alps, certain of the rare alpines do need a little shading in the hottest part of the year, and for these specimens whitewash over the glass is the simplest and most common method for protecting delicate growths against the direct rays of the sun.

CLEANING THE ALPINE HOUSE

Cleanliness is another important point in the general care of the alpine house. Fumigation is the only really safe method to adopt for ridding the house of various glasshouse pests, such as scale insects and wood lice. The preparation of composts for use in the alpine house is also very important, and all soil used should be sterilized.

Fibrous loam, with some leaf-mould and a good proportion of gritty sand (i.e., sand that is fairly coarse, not fine sand which cakes almost as badly as clay in some circumstances) makes a good general compost, and a supply of stone chippings of various degrees of coarseness should also be to hand.

USE OF ALPINE PANS

Alpine pans are sold by all sundriesmen. These are like broad flower pots, several inches deep, and raised a little from the saucer. Wide drainage holes are provided, and in planting alpines for the alpine house these holes are first covered with about 2 in. of coarse drainage material. Broken crocks (i.e., ½-in. pieces of broken flower pot) with a few larger stones make a good drainage layer. The idea of this layer is that when the plants are to be watered, the pans can stand in water 2 or 3 in. deep, and the moisture will gradually percolate to the upper layer of soil.

In a great many cases the pans stand permanently in water, so that the roots can always be kept supplied with enough moisture. The fact that the top soil is of a very open nature, that is, at least one-third sand, allows for the circulation of air to the roots, so that the growth remains healthy.

In potting the rare alpines for under-glass culture, the idiosyncrasies of each should be catered for, crushed mortar being given to the lime-loving saxifrages, and sandy peat provided for such plants as the dwarf campanulas, and the rock daphne (D. *rupestris*). Special care should be taken over this.

A full list of rock plants suitable for the alpine house, with culture for each, would occupy a volume on its own; but here is a short list of a few subjects that the beginner might use to stock his shelves, adding to them from time to time as he becomes better acquainted with these interesting plants.

THE COMMONER ROCK PLANTS

Androsace sarmentosa. The rock jasmine, with rose and white flowers, appearing in early summer. Plant in peaty loam with plenty of grit, and top-dress the pan with small limestone chips. Give plenty of sunshine and water in summer, but do not over-water in the cold weather. Increase by cuttings in September, or by seeds or division in spring.

Campanula pulla. A small violet bellflower blooming in the summer months. Plant in lime-free or peaty loam, and winter in the cold frame. Increase by seeds or division.

Daphne rupestris. Pink flowers, on a tiny plant 3 or 4 in. high in February. Plant in peaty loam, with a little lime, and stand outside during the summer months. Increase by cuttings or layers.

Dianthus alpinus and **Dianthus neglectus.** Both rose-coloured pinks that flower in June. Plant in gritty, lime-free loam, and winter in the cold frame. Increase by seeds, layers or cuttings.

Gentiana verna. Blue, spring flowering gentian. Plant in two parts loam, one part sand, and one part coarse grit or small stone chips. Stand in the open during summer. Increase by seed, or by division in March.

Oxalis adenophylla. Lilac-flowered wood sorrel, blooming in March. Plant in gritty loam. The method of increase is by seeds or division.

Primula farinosa. The " bird's eye " primrose. Plant in ordinary good potting soil, and re-pot annually after the flowers fade, in May or June. Winter in a cold frame. Increase by seeds or division when re-potting.

Ramondia pyrenaica. Violet flowers with orange centres, in April. Plant in loam, with limestone chips, and give plenty of moisture. Shady position preferred.

Saxifrages. A great number of species, names of which will be found in catalogues. Plant in gritty loam and leaf-mould with top-dressings of stone chips. Beyond care over watering in winter, these usually present no difficulty. Increase by division. Some saxifrages do not need the shelter of the alpine house at all.

Silene acaulis. The moss campion. Pink flowers in June, on plants only 2 in. high. Plant in moist gritty loam and increase by seeds or summer cuttings.

Wahlenbergia serpyllifolia. The thyme-leaved harebell. Violet flowers in June. Plant in sandy peat and keep fairly dry in winter. Increase by seed, cuttings or division.

BULBS FOR THE ROCK GARDEN

JANUARY TO MARCH
Anemone Apennina
,,   blanda
Chionodoxa
Crocus Susianus
,,   Tommasinianus
,,   imperati
,,   Sieberi
,,   versicolor
Cyclamen Coum
,,   ibericum
Eranthus hyemalis
Galanthus Elwesii
,,   Byzantinus
Iris Histrio
,,   histrioides
,,   reticulata
Scilla bifolia

Narcissus bulbocodium
,,   cyclamineus
,,   minimus
,,   triandrus
Trillium
Tulipa Clusiana
,,   Kaufmanniana
,,   praecox
,,   pulchella

JUNE
Allium trigustrum
Brodiaea
Lilium tenuifolium
Sisyrinchium
Zephyranthes carinata
Calochortus

APRIL TO MAY
Anemone fulgens
,,   hepatica
,,   nemorosa
Chionodoxa Luciliae
,,   gigantea
Crocus
Cyclamen repandum
Dodecatheon alpinum
Erythronium
Fritillaria meleagris
Leucojum vernum
Muscari botryœides

JULY AND AUGUST
Allium
Babiana disticha

SEPTEMBER TO OCTOBER
Colchicum
Crocus Clusii
,,   sativus
,,   speciosus
,,   zonatus
Cyclamen africanum
,,   europaeum
Leucojum autumnale
Zephyranthes candida

ROCK PLANTS FOR SHADE

Acaena
Anemone
Arenaria balearica
Bellis Dresden China
Campanula
Cyclamen
Dodecatheon
Dryas octopetala
Epimedium
Gentiana

Geranium
Omphaloides
Oxalis enneaphylla
Ramondia
Ranunculus
Saxifraga
Tiarella cordifolia
Trillium grandiflorum
Viola
Vinca

ROCK PLANTS FOR DRY SUNNY POSITIONS

Achillea
Alyssum
Androsace
Arabis
Aster alpinus
Aubrietia
Cistus
Dianthus
Erigeron mucronatus
Erinus

Erysimum
Gypsophylla repens
Helianthemum
Iberis
Papaver alpinum
Saponaria ocymoides
Saxifraga
Sedum
Thymus
Veronica

DWARF SHRUBS FOR THE ROCK GARDEN

Berberis buxifolia nana (Barberry)
Cistus (Rock Rose)
Cotoneaster adpressa
    ,,   horizontalis
Cytisus Beanii (Broom)
    ,,   kewensis
Daphne Cneorum
Empetrum nigrum (Crowberry)
Epigaea repens
Erica carnea (Heath)

Gaultheria procumbens (Winter Green)
Helianthemum (Sun Rose)
Hypericum aegypticum (St. John's wort)
Phyllodoce coerulea
Potentilla fruticosa pyrenaica
Rhododendron kamtschaticum
Vaccinium angustifolium
Veronica Hectorii

CONIFERS FOR THE ROCK GARDEN

Cupressus obtusa nana gracilis
    ,,   pisifera filifera aurea
    ,,   Fletcheri

Juniperus hibernica compressa
Picea Albertiana Conica
Thuya rosedalis

CHAPTER VII

FLOWERING TREES AND SHRUBS

IT is only necessary to take a look at any newly built housing estate, to appreciate the feature value of trees and shrubs; and it is only necessary to walk a mile or two through the streets of such an estate on a hot, dry day in summer, to appreciate the comfort and blessing of their shade. The new garden, made from a plot of old pasture or moorland, and bare of any kind of tree or shrub, is unsatisfying, even though its owner fills it with colour the first summer. It has but two dimensions, and the lack of height is a disadvantage that every gardener wants to eliminate as quickly as possible.

To some extent height can be given to the picture by constructing a pergola and trellis screens, and by covering them with annual or very quick growing climbers; but these features do not provide much in the way of shade. Even the pergola fails in this matter, because it is, after all, only a walk, and one does not want to sit for hours on a sunny day in the middle of a walk.

Shade in the garden is desirable, too, because of the picturesque quality of the shade itself—are not the shadows of tall trees falling across a lawn among the most attractive features of the garden?

Trees are very varied, not only in their form and size, but in their colour, which changes with the seasons, and in their floral beauty. We are apt to classify trees according to whether they flower or not, forgetting that all trees flower, though there is much difference between the trees that carry catkins, such as the poplars and willows, and the so-called flowering trees, such as the various fruit trees and their near relatives.

I suppose there is no tree which would not be welcome in some garden, but of course there are some trees that seem to give a great deal more beauty to the small garden than others. In particular the trees which carry ornamental flowers and ornamental fruits, and that also turn to rich colours in the autumn are valuable; so are the conifers and other evergreens, and so are the tall Lombardy poplars, that add to other virtues a habit of quick growth. But whatever we choose, some trees are needed in almost every garden. A garden layout like the one in Fig. 1, for instance, would not be one half as attractive without its carefully placed trees.

MISTAKES DIFFICULT TO RECTIFY

One of the most common mistakes on the part of the novice in gardening is to think that any plant can be made to grow anywhere. When initial mistakes in planting are made in the herbaceous borders, the plant either dies or becomes sickly, and it is then removed either to the bonfire or to a more congenial border, and its place taken by something more suitable. Replacements of this kind are simple among the smaller plants, but when it comes to trees, mistakes cannot so easily be rectified. It is, therefore, very important that full understanding of the problem should be attained in the early days of garden planting. As with most garden problems, we can turn to nature for a solution.

Trees growing in the wild garden of nature sort themselves out by processes of natural selection. Certain trees thrive best in certain soils or in certain districts, in sheltered or exposed positions, etc. etc., and these trees, naturally adapted to the conditions, will oust their rivals. So we find that alders and willows group themselves by riversides, and that bay trees flourish on the warm chalk downs of the southern counties and the Isle of Wight. We find that Scotch pine grows in sandy soil in all districts of the British Isles. We find rhododendrons growing freely in woods in lime-free or peaty soils, and birches growing almost anywhere.

Such observations help us to choose trees for the particular kind of soil and situation at our disposal. At the same time, there may be special reasons why trees not exactly suited to the soil are desirable. As a rule it is best to keep to the species we know will thrive in the garden, but if for any reason we want others, there are ways of improving the existing conditions. For instance, if the natural soil of the garden is stiff clay, and we specially want to plant in it a strawberry tree (arbutus *unedo*), we can do so, provided the tree is given a good start in soil congenial to it. The strawberry tree prefers a somewhat peaty soil, well worked. To establish it in a clay soil garden therefore, a deep wide hole should first be excavated, say 3 ft. deep and 4 or 5 ft. square. The roughest material available

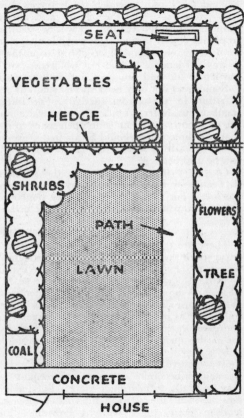

Fig. 1. *A typical small garden, illustrating the use of trees in such a layout.*

will be thrown in at the bottom, and over this should be put either some fresh, imported soil of light leafy or peaty nature, or the excavated clay soil, sifted and mixed with leaf-mould and sand. Planted like this, the tree will establish itself without difficulty.

It would, on the other hand, be useless to plant rhododendrons in the same way on a garden of chalky soil, for it must be remembered that rhododendrons hate lime or chalk, and will not live in it. Since the roots of large trees travel a long way through the soil—far beyond the extent to which the branches spread—they would in a few years penetrate the chalk, and the rhododendron would immediately sicken and die. It will be seen that there are limitations to planting, and that it is not possible altogether to overrule nature's limitations by human effort. So that on the whole the best advice to any gardener is to find out what trees are likely to thrive in the particular soil and situation, and to keep mainly to them.

Some trees not only need special soil, but definitely need a special situation in the garden design. For instance, the well-known monkey puzzle tree (araucaria *imbricata*) should not be grown in a mixed group; it demands an open space to itself. In the same way many of the conifers should be planted as specimen trees, on an open lawn, if possible, so that the full beauty of their mature symmetry can be appreciated.

One very important point in the selection of trees for garden decoration is to look ahead and choose them for their use when mature. Too often one sees a grey poplar set in a small garden, where it must either become a nuisance or be constantly mutilated.

SLOW AND QUICK GROWERS

There are trees that grow comparatively slowly, and never make large specimens, and there are trees that grow so rapidly that after ten years they are almost giants. Some cypress trees, for instance, will attain 30 ft. in about ten or twelve years. On the other hand there are cypress and pine trees, intentionally dwarfed by the cultivators, as much as a hundred years old, and still not too large to be used as indoor decorations. Between these two extremes is an enormous variation in rate of growth, and it should be possible for the garden maker to find the type that will suit his particular purpose.

It is easy enough in some cases to plant both slow growers and those which run up rapidly. When the quick growers have reached the stage of becoming a nuisance on account of size, the slow growers may be ready to take their place. But though this arrangement is possible in a large garden, the small garden cannot usually accommodate many trees without crowding, and crowding almost invariably means a loss of natural symmetry.

On the other hand, crowding may at times be deliberate, in order to attain a definite habit of growth. This is often done when large estates of park land are being developed, and a group of trees is planted where perhaps only one mature specimen will be wanted. The reason is that the slight crowding induces the trees to run up tall, with a length of bare or branchless stem near the ground. As the years pass, the unwanted specimens are removed, leaving the most suitable tree to attain maturity.

These remarks perhaps indicate to the novice what a big subject tree selection can be, and how much there is to consider, even in planting a single specimen. You will probably do best to make your choice first, and then, before actually ordering the trees, discuss your plans with a tree and shrub specialist. Any reliable nurseryman will give sound advice.

If you order trees from a distance, tell the grower what kind of soil you have, whether there is any special difficulty, and whether the trees are to be in any particular aspect, facing the sea, for instance, or on a dry stony bank, or by the waterside. You will always find that it pays to take the grower into your confidence, for he will be able to guide you round many unforeseen obstacles.

CHOOSING COLOUR AND OUTLINE

Now just a word about trees from the purely æsthetic point of view. I know a suburban district where every house is of red brick, and when I visited the place last it seemed to me that every front garden had (a) one almond tree, (b) one purple-leaved plum, and (c) one laburnum. If there was any difference in the planting scheme, it was usually that a red thorn had been substituted for the plum or almond.

I suggest that almond trees, though as pretty as any that grow in this country, do not look their best against red brick, but show up far better if set against grey stucco or dark green hollies or cypress. I suggest, too, that red brick is the very last background to choose for a purple-leaved plum; and further, that the very monotony of this planting scheme is enough to make it unsatisfactory.

Most (though not all) of the flowering trees carry their blossom in the early part of the year, and it is quite easy to have a gay background to the garden picture then. Some of the flowering trees also carry berries in the autumn. The well-known rowan tree is one. Some trees become gaily coloured when autumn tints the foliage with gold or red, but some have the advantage of such brilliant colouring all the year through, or at least, all the spring, summer and autumn. The crab family includes several species that flower, leaf, and fruit gaily : pyrus *eleyi* is one, and the John Downie crab another. A collection of conifers in gold and blue varieties, mixed with the ordinary dark greens gives a colour variation that is permanent, even in winter.

Then most tree families have one or more representatives with a drooping or " weeping " habit, and these, not too freely used, are extremely valuable in adding character to a garden planting scheme. I have said not too freely, because to use more than one such tree in a group is a fatal mistake. In the little garden where colour is important, a weeping cherry could be chosen, but by a grass and water garden, where form is more important than brilliance of colour, a weeping birch or weeping willow might be a better choice.

Tree and shrub specialists mostly issue descriptive catalogues, and since the choice of specimens of this kind must always be an individual affair, I do not propose to make recommendations, but refer the gardener to these catalogues. But better still, in my opinion, is the practice now becoming very common of visiting the specialist nursery in the height of the growing season, and selecting trees on the spot. Only by seeing them in full growth can their true beauty be judged.

Just one other point in this connection. A young tree, particularly a young conifer, often varies very much in habit from the mature specimen. A young cedar of Lebanon, for example, presents a soft feathery appearance, very unlike the characteristic silhouette of the older tree. It is almost always best to plant with the mature tree in mind, even though it may take years for the tree to reach anything like its characteristic form.

And finally, regarding selection on the spot, always remember that a young specimen transplants more easily and certainly than an old one, and that it usually makes a more shapely tree than one which is rather old when it is acquired.

WHEN TO PLANT YOUR TREES

Planting time for trees of deciduous character, such as the flowering cherries, plums, apples, laburnums and so on is any time when the leaves are absent, i.e., from about October to March, but with most of them the best month of all is October. A few rather tender trees, such as the magnolias, are better planted late in winter, so that they have the warm spring weather to help them recover from the shock of transplanting. Evergreen trees, such as conifers, are best planted during the showery weather of April or May or of September. They are inclined to die back in the cold weather if they are not well established in the soil.

Evergreens, because they carry their leaves at all times, need special care in moving, as there is a constant evaporation from leaf surfaces. When roots have been damaged, as they are always to some extent during a move, they cease for a time to do their normal work of absorbing moisture from the soil. Thus there is a greater loss of moisture from the leaf surfaces than is being made good by damaged roots, and the plant is likely to die from this cause. The loss from evaporation can, however, be checked by frequent watering or spraying overhead; if the weather is showery, the evaporation will be checked naturally. That is why spring and autumn, when showers are likely to occur, are the best times to move evergreens. Moreover, the soil is a little warmer

hen than in the depth of winter, and the roots more quickly
become settled into warm soil.

There should never be any delay in setting once the plants have
arrived from the nursery, unless they should chance to come along
during a period of hard frost or excessive rains. If this happens,
the roots must be kept moist and frost-free until better weather
arrives.

A hole, dug in preparation for a tree, should be at least 2 ft.
deep, and sufficiently wide to take the roots spread out horizontally
in all directions. If possible it should be even deeper and wider.
Tree roots, when the tree is fully grown, will extend many yards,
and a tree cannot be moved for the soil to be refreshed as can a
plant in the herbaceous border, so that it is important that the
soil should be right before any planting is done.

THE IMPORTANCE OF DRAINAGE

Rough, porous compost at the bottom of the hole will allow
for good drainage, which is generally of the utmost importance.
In badly drained soil there is no air, and where there is no air
in the soil plant roots become unhealthy.

Over the drainage material should be thrown some good, well
broken, top soil—not cold, sticky clay subsoil, nor stony gravel.
Rest the tree in position, with its roots on this finely broken top
soil, and immediately drive in a stake to support the tree. If
you plant single-handed, the tree can be tied to the stake at this
stage.

Fill in more fine, good soil, to cover the fibrous roots, and tread
each layer of soil well down. Loose planting allows air pockets
round the roots, and these dry out in consequence. Moist, porous
soil should be in immediate contact with the root hairs. Try to
plant so that the old soil mark on the main trunk is just at the
new soil level. Never pile the soil up against the tree trunk in a
kind of mound. This will divert the rains so that the young tree
may possibly lack moisture at the roots. Setting the tree in a
slight hollow in the ground is a good practice if you are planting
on dry soil. The stages of planting are shown in Figs. 2 and 3.

SHOULD TREES BE MANURED?

Rake the soil surface after it has been finally trodden firm round
the tree, so that you leave a crumbly surface layer. This lessens
soil evaporation, prevents soil cracking, and generally assists the
tree in the way that hoeing assists herbaceous plants.

As a general rule, do not use any manure at planting time. If,
however, you are planting a tree in very poor soil, and you know
that it is a tree that needs plenty of moisture, it is a good plan to
bury a layer of manure well down out of reach of the roots. Manure

in direct contact with the roots is not advisable, even if it is old manure.

Some time after planting, say in the spring if you planted in the autumn, a surface mulch of manure can be given. This means a layer of manure 3 or 4 in. thick spread over the soil surface round the tree, to be washed in by rains. The surface mulch helps the soil to retain moisture during the first summer, and may save the life of the tree if the summer should be unusually hot and dry.

When staking newly planted trees, be very careful how the tree

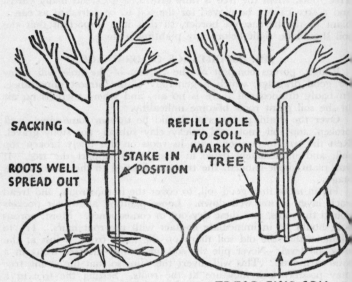

Fig. 2. *How to plant a tree. The hole should be at least 2 ft. deep, wide enough to take the roots, and well drained.*

is tied to the support. In the case of a standard tree it may be best to use three stakes, set round the trunk, so that there is no possibility of its swaying in the winds. It is wind that causes most damage to the roots of newly planted trees, by swaying the trunk and so tearing at the roots, and the only way to avoid this is to stake so that the trunk is rigid. It is important, however, not to restrict the growth of the tree by ties that are too tight. Generally the cord used for tying should be twisted between the trunk and

If turfy loam is used, to improve the synthetic in the root, it is best to do so at least a few weeks after planting, as the friable stock is dangerous food for the tree. Trees moved from the nursery in late autumn have usually been grown with a tidy root supply.

The method of planting evergreens is the same as with deciduous trees, except that they are usually lifted with a good ball of soil round roots which are packed in sacks. This ball of soil must be maintained during planting, so it should be quickly placed in contact with good fresh soil, with as little delay as possible.

Fig. 3 gives a view of how this may be done. The soil ball is not removed from the roots, but the sacking or other covering material is carefully undone to allow the roots to move freely.

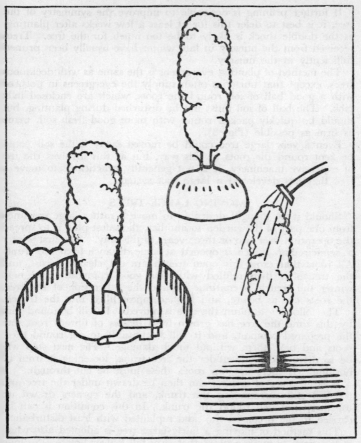

Fig. 3. Planting an evergreen. (Top) Ball of soil round roots tied in sack. *(Left)* Set tree in place and tread each layer of soil down firmly. *(Right)* Water the tree overhead as well as at roots.

the stake. It should be examined frequently after planting and loosened if the cord has become too tight.

Occasionally roots and branches get torn or broken during the move. These broken and torn parts should be cut cleanly away with a sharp knife before the planting takes place. Torn rough wounds are dangerous, as they encourage tree disease spores.

If further pruning is desirable to improve the symmetry of the tree, it is best to defer this for at least a few weeks after planting, as the double shock is likely to be too much for the tree. Trees received from the nursery in late winter have usually been pruned sufficiently in the nursery.

The method of planting evergreens is the same as with deciduous trees, except that nurseries often supply the evergreens in pots, or with a good ball of soil round the roots, which are enclosed in a sack. The ball of soil must not be disturbed during planting, but should be quickly packed round with more good fresh soil, made as firm as possible (Fig. 3).

Even a very large tree could be moved safely if the soil could be kept round the roots in this way, but as this involves the use of expensive machinery, it is not generally practicable to move a tree that has developed a large root system.

MOVING LARGE TREES

Should it be thought desirable to move a rather large specimen from one part of the garden to another, the safest plan is to spread the operation over two or three years in this way. The first winter a semicircular trench is opened at some distance from the trunk. All roots that cross this open trench are cut cleanly across, and the trench is then refilled with fine good compost. The next winter the trench is continued round the other side of the tree, the roots cut as before, and fresh compost filled into the trench.

The following autumn the tree is moved. It will be found that by this time the tree has grown fresh masses of fibrous root into the prepared compost, and it will be possible to dig round these roots and bare them without much damage. The next step will be to drive the spade under the tree trunk, loosening it from its position. If there are tap roots, these must be cut through.

A large piece of sacking can then be drawn under the tree and the soil still surrounding the trunk, and the corners drawn up together, and tied round the trunk. In this condition it can be carried to the prepared site, and replanted with least disturbance.

This method of moving a fairly large tree is adopted also when it is desired to move a plant that is in full leaf or flower. So long as the soil is not shaken from the roots, a move can often be made successfully in the height of the growing season, and by dragging the sacking under the ball of soil, and temporarily tying up the roots, many a plant can be safely moved that would die if transplanted by any other means.

The pruning of garden trees, if we leave out the problem of fruit trees, is not a subject that need cause much trouble to the amateur gardener. An ornamental tree is usually best left to grow naturally, and apart from the removal of broken branches, and occasional cutting back if a tree loses its symmetry through wind damage or other cause, there is little pruning to be done.

The best type of pruning, if any has to be carried out, is the ' finger and thumb " kind. That is to say, when a tree is quite young, any small growths that threaten to develop into unwanted branches are removed immediately they are seen. Similarly, if a tree makes only one or two main stems, and a bushy habit of growth is wanted from it, then " finger and thumb " pinching of the growing tips while they are still young and tender is the best way to induce the required new side growths.

Almost any season of the year can be chosen for pruning old trees that must be restricted, except the spring, when the leaves are just bursting. If large branches have to be removed, the wounds should be made cleanly, right back to a joint, and the cut portion should at once be painted over or tarred so that moisture is excluded. Neglect of this simple rule of painting wounds is one of the chief causes of disease in trees.

Large forest trees, of the kind not recommended for small gardens, often have to be lopped severely so that they do not unduly over-shadow the garden. Where such lopping has to be done, it is wise to call in an expert. If it is tackled by the owner himself, he should endeavour to leave a tree that is not an eyesore, but will quickly attain a good symmetrical outline. Spreading branches, if cut half-way back, should all be cut proportionately and the cuts made at a joint. When the tree is in leaf again it will look quite natural and show few signs of the recent pruning.

TREES FOR THE SMALL GARDEN

The following list gives some of the most valuable trees for the small garden, together with their chief characteristics.

Acer japonicum aureum and **Acer palmatum atropurpureum.** Two varieties of maple, the first golden leaved and the other with purple foliage, of dwarf, bushy growth. These require a sheltered position in the sun, and good soil for the best results. Deciduous. Many other good maples are listed in catalogues.

Aesculus carnea. Crimson flowered chestnut. Grows anywhere, and makes a fine specimen on a lawn. Deciduous.

Ailanthus glandulosa. The Tree of Heaven. Grown naturally it makes a very large tree, but it can be kept to any size by regular hard pruning in February. The long leaves are very ornamental, and turn yellow in autumn. Deciduous.

Catalpa bignonioides. The Indian bean tree. Flowers of white, yellow and purple in late July and August. Makes a broad spread-ing tree. Grows in ordinary soil. Deciduous.

Cercis siliquastrum. The Judas tree. Rose-purple pea flowers on the bare stems in May. Suited to southern gardens. Deciduous.

Cratægus coccinea. Scarlet-fruited thorn. A standard tree makes a fine specimen. May flowering. Deciduous. Several other thorns make good trees for small gardens, and all grow well in ordinary soil.

Mespilus germanica. The medlar. A useful lawn tree that keeps its yellow foliage late in the autumn. The fruits are both decorative and edible. It will grow in any ordinary garden soil.

Prunus amygdalus. The almond, in dwarf and tall varieties and with double or single flowers. Standards or half-standards make fine specimen trees for lawns. Deciduous. Ordinary soil.

Prunus Blireiana. A plum with coppery foliage and early flowers (before the leaves) of double pink. As attractive in the garden as the better known purple-leaved plum (P. *Pissardii*). Grows in ordinary soil.

Prunus cerasus serrulata sekiyama. The hizakurea cherry, with coppery young foliage and masses of double pink blossoms. Deciduous. Ordinary soil.

Pyrus malus. The fruiting crab family and the flowering crab family both come under this heading. There are many varieties, all of which are suitable for the small family garden, and trade lists should be consulted. All are deciduous and grow in any ordinary soil.

Pyrus aucuparia. The common mountain ash is as decorative a tree as one can find. There is also a weeping variety obtainable which makes a fine lawn tree. Deciduous, flowering and berrying. Prefers a rather moist loam, but is not generally difficult to cultivate.

WHAT IS A SHRUB?

There is very little difference between a tree and a shrub. One might almost say that there is no difference, since the distinction is purely one of size. When dealing with ornamental trees and shrubs, however, the distinction most generally accepted is that a tree is limited at the base to a single stem, from which branches radiate to make a " head," either a standard head of the usual type grown in the little garden, or a more bushy head, in which the branches come from perhaps only 1 ft. or 18 in. above the soil level. A shrub, on the other hand, frequently has many stems growing from the ground level, and is encouraged to make bushy growth from the ground upwards. Two kinds of shrub outline each of them useful and decorative in the garden scheme, are shown in Fig. 4.

All the remarks made concerning the selection and planting of trees apply to shrubs, but there is this difference, that whereas the ornamental tree in a garden should be allowed freedom to develop and display its natural characteristic form, the shrub in garden design is generally made to conform to the gardener's wishes. I

FASTIGIATE DWARF SPREADING

←STANDARD

Fig. 4. *Two shrub outlines useful in garden design. Standard shrubs, which may also be classed as trees, are on the whole more formal than dwarf spreading shrubs, and are useful for single planting.*

may be pruned to some formal outline, as is often done with specimens of box and bay. It may be pruned less formally, perhaps with the idea of producing more flowers and berries, or just to restrict the growth to the situation. In any case, pruning is one of the important features of shrub culture, and it is one of the points that most often seem a stumbling block to the inexperienced gardener.

The old idea of shrub culture was often limited to a " shrubbery," in which all the shrubs were collected. Modern gardeners allow themselves greater freedom, and use shrubs in the borders with herbaceous flowers and even with annuals, in the rock garden, as lawn specimens, as a screen for the kitchen garden, as material for a mixed hedge, and so on. (Some of these uses are illustrated in Figs. 5, 6 and 7.)

In fact, shrubs are valued for their permanence and brilliance even more than are the herbaceous perennials. It is quite a common thing today to find a fairly small garden in which the borders are more than half filled with shrubs, the reason being that these plants are labour-saving. Beyond an occasional clean-up of the soil in autumn, and the use of the secateurs at the appropriate season, they demand little attention, and remain attractive all the

year round. Fig. 8 shows a small front garden of shrubs an
roses, Figs. 9 and 10 show layouts for shrub borders and Fig. 1
the type of border that can be overhung by trees.

The principle of a shrub border can be very simply outlined. I
should be arranged so that there is a " skeleton 𝄞 of evergree
shrubs that will furnish the border in winter.

There should als
be a sufficiency o
flowering shrub;
with different sea
sons of blooming, t
give some specia
interest to eac
month in the yea
As an example o
this one migh
plant a borde
with the followin
twelve shrubs
chimonanthu
fragrans (January
berberis *beal*
(February)
hamamelis *moll*
(March), forsyth
(April), lila
(May), philade
phus (June)
olearia (July
hibiscus (August
tamarix (Septen
ber), caryopter
(October), coto
easter (berries
November)
laurustinu
(December).

OPEN COUNTRY   GRASS

1 - BUDDLEIA & POTENTILLA
2 - MAGNOLIA LENNEI & VERONICA
3 - COTONEASTER SIMONSII & BROOM
4 - SILVER BIRCHES

*Fig. 5. The use of shrubs and small trees in an
informal corner of the lawn.*

Such a list cou
be repeated wi
variations over and over again, for the arrangement of a shru
border never loses its interest to the keen gardener.

Shrubs in the mixed border should generally be of the rathe
compact growing type, that need little pruning, but this depend
entirely on the size of the border. In a small border of 5 ft. wi
daphne *Mezereum*, cistus in variety, and veronicas of several kin
would be suitable, with lavender, senecio *Greyii* and santoline
add a variation of foliage. The planter will easily be able to wo

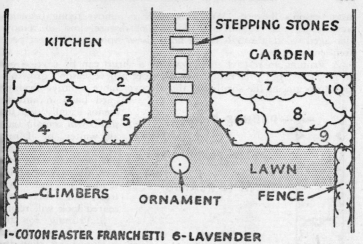

Fig. 6. *A shrub border is ideal for screening a kitchen garden from the main garden, thereby adding beauty to both.*

out schemes for himself from the lists that are given elsewhere, and will find plenty of satisfaction in this task.

So much depends on a variety of factors—amount of pruning, for instance, and the question of when such pruning can be done, as well as the questions of soil, foliage colour, habit of growth, flowering and berrying colours—that it is useless to plan a border without some knowledge of the site. A few suggestions will be seen in the planting plans given with this chapter, and still more will be gathered from the description of a few favourite shrubs given below.

On the question of shrub pruning in general a few hints may be given in summarized form.

1. The reasons for pruning shrubs are varied. We prune to restrict the growth to the amount of space available in the border, or to let more light and air to the remaining branches so that the season's new growth ripens and becomes " woody " instead of soft and sappy. Ripening the wood makes it less likely to be killed back by winter frosts, and more likely to develop flower buds for

next season's flowers. We prune also to remove dying branches and stems, and so obviate the risk of disease, and to remove damaged wood, through which both disease spores and insect pests frequently enter.

2. Pruning to restrict the growth of a shrub can be carried out at any time, but preferably shortly before a new season's growth is due to begin, as the shrub will then recover more rapidly. Pruning hard back in autumn means usually that the shrub will remain bare all winter, or if new growth should break out just before the cold weather, it will be too tender to stand the frost, and a blackened seared look will result.

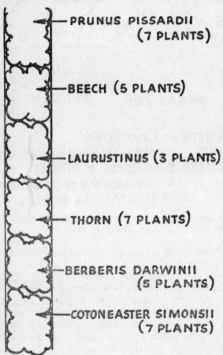

PRUNUS PISSARDII (7 PLANTS)

BEECH (5 PLANTS)

LAURUSTINUS (3 PLANTS)

THORN (7 PLANTS)

BERBERIS DARWINII (5 PLANTS)

COTONEASTER SIMONSII (7 PLANTS)

Fig. 7. A suggestion for a well-balanced mixed hedge, giving the proportionate number of plants needed to set it out.

3. Pruning for the sake of better flower is timed so that the new growth coming from the remaining parts of the shrub will have as long a season of growth as possible prior to flowering time. Thus the shrubs that flower on stems which grow newly each season are pruned in early spring, leaving just sufficient dormant leaf buds to develop into the desired strong stems and finally to carry the season's flowers in late summer. Shrubs that flower on wood of the previous season's growth are pruned hard back immediately each flowering season passes, as the new long stems have then time to grow and become well developed and ripened before the winter.

A few shrubs that flower like fruit trees on short old spurs, close to the main stems, are regularly pinched back, like the trained fruits, to induce the formation of these fruiting spurs. Very often

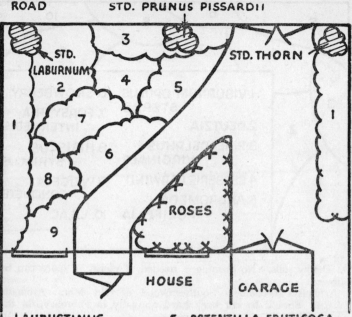

Fig. 8. A small front garden stocked with shrubs, flowering trees, and roses. The addition of a formal bed of roses to the plan adds variety to the shrubbery.

however, shrubs of this character are best left to their own devices, and should not be as strictly pruned as the others.

POPULAR GARDEN SHRUBS

These are the general principles, and as far as possible, details of the most popular of garden shrubs will be given in the following list.

Amelanchier canadensis. The snowy mespilus. The foliage is slightly hairy and greyish, the flowers white in April, and the berries and tints of the leaves decorative in autumn. It thrives

1. VIBURNUM OPULUS STERILE
2. DEUTZIA
3. PHILADELPHUS VIRGINALE
4. BERBERIS DARWINII
5. ANDROMEDA POLIFOLIA
6. SNOWBERRY
7. FORSYTHIA INTERMEDIA
8. HIBISCUS SYRIACUS
9. WEIGELA CONQUETE
10. LILAC

Fig. 9. A shrub border for a town garden.

on chalky soils. No pruning is needed, if plenty of space can be allowed.

Artemisia abrotanum. Southernwood or Old Man. Aromatic foliage. Should be cut back hard annually in February, for the best results.

Aucuba japonica. Variegated laurel. Male and female are on separate bushes, and both should be grown together so that the female one may carry bright red berries. No pruning is necessary, unless the bushes are straggly, when they can be cut hard back in April.

Azalea. A deciduous section of the rhododendron family, suitable only for cultivation on lime-free soil. No regular pruning except to cut off the dead flower heads.

Berberis. A large family of shrubs, of varied character. B. *aggregata* has masses of coral berries and brilliant autumn foliage. Deciduous. B. *Darwinii* has tiny holly-like leaves, and rich orange flowers followed by purple berries. Evergreen, excellent for hedges. No pruning. B. *stenophylla* is narrow leaved, evergreen, with masses of paler yellow flowers, scented, on long arching stems in April and May. Prune just after flowering, cutting back the long arching stems nearly to the old wood. If grown as a formal hedge plant, trim back once more, in August. Evergreen. B. *Wilsoni* has coral red translucent berries in profusion. Rather spreading growth. Deciduous. No pruning. B. *aquifolium* is the holly leaved mahonia.

March flowering, in clusters of yellow flowers, followed by purple berries. Evergreen. A good subject for under-tree planting. No pruning. Many other useful members of the berberis family are listed in catalogues.

Buddleia are another group of flowering shrubs, which may be either evergreen or deciduous. B. *alternifolia* is a dainty June flowering buddleia, about 5 ft. high, useful as a lawn specimen. The flowers are pale lilac, and pruning consists of shortening the branches a little after the flowers fade. B. *variabilis* is purple, flowers in late summer. Cut back the previous year's shoots to within a few inches of the old wood in February. B. *globosa*, the orange ball tree, flowers in June. No regular pruning is needed to keep the shrub attractive.

Calluna vulgaris or **Scotch heather.** Several species of this family make good shrubs for the wild garden or for the rock garden, the double-flowered ling calluna *vulgaris flore pleno* being particularly pleasant. No pruning.

Chimonanthus fragrans. The Winter Sweet. One of the best of winter flowering shrubs on account of its fine scent. The parchment-coloured flowers open in December and January, whenever the sun shines, and scent the air even on a frosty day. Needs a warm situation, preferably against a south wall, and warm light soil. To train as a wall climber, cut back the side shoots after flowering to leave two to three eyes. Flowers are borne on the wood made the previous summer. As a bush no regular pruning is required. Deciduous.

1. PHILADELPHUS   4. CHIMONANTHUS
2. SYRINGA (LILAC)   5. SKIMMIA
3. OSMANTHUS   6. VIBURNUM
7. DAPHNE MEZEREUM   CARLESII

Fig. 10. A border of shrubs which will grow well in a shady position.

Ceanothus. The spring flowering species are evergreen, with flowers of various shades of blue. These need no pruning, unless trained to a wall, when they should be cut back after flowering. The later flowered species include blue and pink varieties. These are deciduous, and bloom on wood of the current season. They are pruned hard back in February or March. There are recent hybrids between the two types, and the pruning of these will be adapted according to the nature of the hybrid.

Choisya ternata. Mexican orange blossom. Evergreen, but slightly tender shrub suitable for sheltered positions only. No regular pruning is required, but trim for shapeliness if necessary in April.

Cistus. Rock rose. (Near relative of the small rock roses grown on rock gardens.) Very showy, June and July flowering shrubs, evergreen, but not specially ornamental in winter. Young shrubs should be "stopped" to induce the formation of bushy specimens, but later the shrubs need no pruning.

Cotoneaster. Shrubs grown chiefly for the charm of their freely produced berries. They vary greatly in habit. *C. horizontalis* with stems resembling the skeleton of a skate, is useful as a wall shrub, as well as on the rock garden. Evergreen. No pruning, except where needed in tying it to supports on a wall. *C. microphylla* is a good seaside shrub, and will grow under the drip of trees. Evergreen. No pruning. This makes a good hedge plant. *C. frigida* makes an erect bush or small tree. White or pinkish flowers are followed by crimson berries (or yellow berries in the variety *fructulutea*). Deciduous. No pruning. Many other useful varieties are listed in catalogues, and can be grown quite easily.

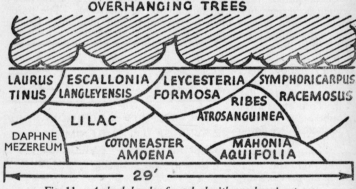

Fig. 11. *A shrub border for a bed with overhanging trees.*

Daphne Mezereum. A rose-purple or white-flowered deciduous shrub, bearing its scented blossoms on bare stems in February. Dwarf habit, useful for small borders. Needs a moist, cool soil. No pruning.

Deutzia candidissima. Deciduous June flowering shrub, of easy culture, growing to 6 or 8 ft. high. Thin out the growths every three years or so, to prevent crowding.

Diervilla or **Weigela.** Pink trumpet flowers in May. Deciduous shrubs of arching, spreading growth. No pruning is necessary, but they can be pruned if it is desired by cutting back secondary branches annually to the next strong shoots below the flowers.

Erica. The heath family. All good plants for the wild garden, but generally best on lime-free or peaty soils. E. *carnea* and its varieties will succeed on soil with some lime present. No regular pruning needed.

Escallonia. Donard seedling. A pink-bloomed, June flowering shrub, possessing very fine arching sprays, and growing to 10 ft. if desired. Grows in any ordinary soil, and unless growing against a wall it needs no regular pruning. Makes a good hedge, and should then be cut back after the flowers fade. Evergreen.

Forsythia. March flowering, golden bell trees. Will grow anywhere, and can be hard pruned or left unpruned as desired. If pruned, cut back after flowering. This results in stronger and more floriferous stems next season. Deciduous.

Hibiscus. Late summer flowering shrubs, very decorative. Flowers of white, rose, peach or purple. Deciduous. No pruning needed.

Hydrangea hortensis. The florist's hydrangea, a good shrub for sheltered districts. Growth round and bushy. Moist soil preferred. The older shoots can be thinned out after the flowers fade, but the young growths should be left full length, as the flowers come at the tips. Deciduous. H. *paniculata* is a late-flowering shrub of hardy character. Flowers white, turning pink. Prune in February, severely or lightly according to situation. The shrubs will grow to 8 ft. if required.

Hypericum. Several species are useful in the garden, particularly the evergreen H. *calycinum* and H. *Moserianum*, both of which do well under other shrubs or trees.

Kerria japonica. Single or double orange flowers in spring. Deciduous, suitable for any soil. No pruning required. Height up to 8 ft.

Lavandula. The common lavender, and various near relatives, are all suitable for ordinary, well-drained soil. Evergreen. Cut back after flowering, but not into the very old wood.

Lilac. Deciduous, spring flowering shrubs, of which there are numerous new good hybrids. Remove suckers regularly, but do not prune further unless the plants are large and flower poorly. In this case some of the stems can be shortened about half-way, to the junction of two stems, soon after the flowering season. This allows more light and air to the remainder, and so encourages the formation of flowering buds for another season. Occasional doses of liquid manure are appreciated.

Lupinus arboreus. One of the best shrubs to associate with herbaceous plants in the mixed border. Makes a spreading rather large bush, covered with yellow or white scented flowers. Evergreen. Should have old wood removed, and the last year's shoots shortened in February. Many hybrids. Height 4 to 7 feet.

Olearia. Daisy bushes. O. *Haastii*, late summer flowering and evergreen, is useful as a hedge plant or specimen. It has small greyish leaves, and masses of white daisy flowers, over a roundish bush.

Philadelphus. Mock orange, or sometimes erroneously called syringa. Scented, white flowers towards the end of June. Deciduous, and rather large. Thrives in any soil. Most species can be left unpruned, but some of the hybrids such as P. *Lemoinei* are better if cut back a little after the flowers fade. Cut to a strong shoot half-way down the stems that have flowered.

Rhododendron. A large genus of (mostly) evergreens, with conspicuous flowers. Suitable mainly for large gardens on lime-free soils. The finest for the little garden is pink pearl. Prune only occasionally, beyond the removal of flower heads, which is desirable immediately after the flowering season.

Rhus cotinus. The smoke plant. The variety *folius purpureus* is one of the best for purple foliage during the summer. Flowers June and July, and thrives in poor soil. Deciduous. Rhus *typhina*, the stag's horn sumach, turns a fine orange and red in autumn. Can be left unpruned, except if it grows unshapely, or can be cut hard back every February, in order to obtain extra large leaves. Deciduous.

Ribes of various kinds all thrive in ordinary soil, and flower in spring. The flowering currant. Deciduous. No pruning needed.

Santolina incana. Cotton lavender. Will grow in any garden but is best in full sun. Trim regularly if required as an edging to a shrubbery. Yellow daisy flowers are borne in July. Valuable for its silvery foliage.

Spiræa arguta. A deciduous shrub smothered with white flowers in April. No pruning needed. Deciduous. S. *japonica Anthony Waterer* has corymbs of deep carmine flowers in late summer. Should have old weak wood cut out in February, and the remaining shoots shortened. Deciduous. Other species are pruned according to their habit of growth. All succeed in ordinary soil, but prefer ample moisture.

Syringa, or mock orange. A member of the lilac family, treated in the same way as lilac (q.v.).

Veronica. Evergreen flowering shrubs, particularly useful in small gardens and in towns. V. *Simon Deleaux*, crimson, autumn flowering; V. *Traversii* white, July flowering; and V. *Alicia Amherst*, deep blue, autumn flowering are some of the best. All prefer sheltered positions and thrive in ordinary soil. V. *Traversii* is the hardiest and best for difficult gardens. No regular pruning is required.

Viburnum. Evergreen and deciduous shrubs, including the guelder rose, the scented viburnums, and laurustinus (winter flowering). All thrive in ordinary soil and need no regular pruning. Height 5 to 10 ft.

The books that have been written on the subject of rose cultivation would make a whole library of literature. Specialist growers will naturally turn to such books of reference, and not to a general work of this kind for information concerning the various aspects of rose culture. I propose therefore to deal with roses only in the simplest way, in order that the novice in garden matters may be induced to take up rose growing with confidence.

A great many inexperienced gardeners are dubious about the question of pruning, and listen to the expert who distinguishes so glibly between tea roses and pernetianas, between ramblers and wichuraianas, with many misgivings. They need not get alarmed, for rose growing, sufficiently intelligently practised to get ordinarily good results, can be reduced to comparatively simple principles.

ROSE VARIETIES AND THEIR HABITS

First let me state at once that the majority of roses grown in gardens are hybrids, that is to say they are the result of inter-marriages arranged by the growers, between various rose species. In many cases the growers themselves are uncertain of the exact parentage of some of the roses, so it would seem quite unnecessary for the amateur gardener to worry unduly about this matter.

What the gardener does want to know is the general habits of growth of the roses in his care. This he could find out by observation, but he can also find it out by the name and classification of the plants he buys. I am going to explain the main classification in a somewhat unorthodox way.

First there is a division into two groups. In one, the rose plant grows like many other shrubs, by adding more new stems to the old wood each season. In the other the new season's growth comes mainly from below the soil level, or from just above it, and this gradually supersedes the old wood. In this second class there are plenty of roses that send out some new growth from the upper parts of the old stems, but their chief annual growth comes from the soil level.

Look at the garden roses, and you will easily be able to distinguish the two groups. All the roses growing as dwarf bushes in the rose beds, the standard tea roses, and some of the climbing roses have the habit of sending out new growths from the old wood. The rambler roses, such as Dorothy Perkins, send up fresh long stems from the soil level each year. These rambler roses are therefore a class apart when it comes to pruning. They are the " wichuraiana " roses.

Now look at the others; some of them make bushy rounded growth, but occasionally we find varieties that tend to climb. There is a bush, Mrs. Herbert Stevens, for instance, but there is also a climbing variety. Apart from the fact that the long climbing framework of old wood is retained when the rose is trained on a wall or pillar, there is not much difference between the methods of pruning the two. Both are cut back enough to develop fresh growths.

The beginner need not worry much concerning the differences

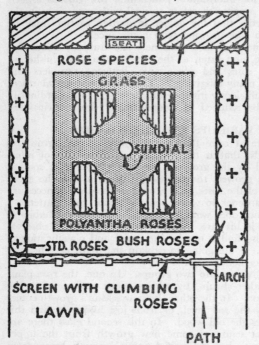

between the bush roses. Some have the habit of one rose species, and some the habit of another, but in view of the mixed blood in most of them, the differences are not always very marked. It is sufficient for ordinary purposes to recognize the difference between a bush rose and a standard rose, and this is simple enough. The standard has a single main stem, with a "bush" at the top, i.e., the bush is elevated to a point nearer the eye level.

Occasionally the rambler type of rose is grafted on to a standard, and is sold as an

Fig. 12. A small enclosed rose garden, illustrating the use of bush, standard and polyantha roses.

"umbrella standard." This merely signifies that the rambler will grow its new stems from the head, instead of from the soil level.

Now for the use of roses in the small garden. Ramblers are useful to cover all sorts of screens, or sometimes to hang over banks. Climbing roses, which, because they keep growing from the old wood, sometimes run up to 20 or 30 ft. on a house wall, are obviously better plants for walls and other permanent sites. The climbing Mrs. Herbert Stevens type does well on pergolas, too, or in any position where the rose can extend to an almost unlimited extent.

Standard roses are useful in all sorts of odd places; in enclosed small gardens of the kind suggested in Fig. 12, alongside front garden walks, as " dot " plants in odd places in the garden design, here and there in the ordinary flower-beds or borders, or in groups in parts of the large rose garden.

Bush roses make a brave display in small rose beds— small for preference because if there are too many roses in a bed, pruning and attending to them becomes difficult. If space permits, the grouping of roses of a single colour in each bed is recommended, and formal rose

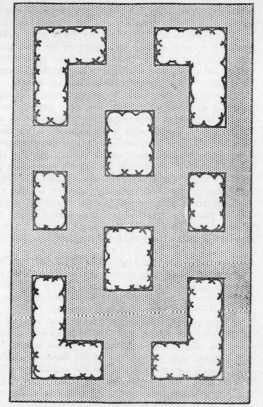

Fig. 13.   A rectangular arrangement of rose beds suitable for a formal garden.

gardens like the one in Fig. 13 are delightful if the colours are graded and the cultivation is of a high standard.

Planting roses is exactly similar to the planting of any tree or shrub. Deep soil cultivation is necessary, and sufficient humus should be present in the soil to hold moisture in dry weather. There is a popular belief that roses like clay. They do prefer a heavy loam, usually, but certainly will not thrive in unworked clay. Bone-meal used in preparing the beds is a great help, and nitrate of potash and superphosphate of lime are both useful fertilizers (apply separately, the superphosphate in spring, and nitrate of potash during growth). Lime in the soil is also an essential of success in rose culture.

November is regarded as the ideal rose planting month. The season's growth should be complete by that time, and if the roses are moved then, the roots have time to establish themselves well before pruning time, which is in late March or early April, according to district. If roses are planted in late winter—and any time until April will do—they must be pruned much harder than if they were planted in November, and the new growth will be less vigorous.

One important item regarding planting—roses should invariably be clearly labelled with a waterproof label that will not become illegible. This is a matter which does not appear of great importance to the novice, but later, when visitors ask the name of the rose, or when he wants to consult an expert regarding pruning, he will be glad to know the correct names. Roses planted late in the season are often pruned before being supplied by the nursery. If they are not, all roses planted in March could advantageously be pruned before planting. If the pruning seems likely to cause budding a little early it does not matter, since the shock the rose receives by the move will delay its growth for another week or two.

TIME AND METHOD OF PRUNING

Pruning, as already stated, is done mainly at the end of March in the south, and beginning of April in the cold districts. This applies to the bushes and standards and climbers, but not to the rambler roses, which are pruned in late summer.

Spring pruning is designed to rid the rose of its thicket of young stems, each of which has leaf-buds at every joint. If these stems were all allowed to remain, the result would be such a crowd of weak stems that the quality of the flowers would be poor—in fact, they would generally revert to the wild type after a few years.

The time for spring pruning is selected for this reason : as soon as the pruning has been done, the bud left at the end of the shortened woody stem begins to swell and grows into a new shoot. This will carry the first crop of roses. Should this growth of new season's flower buds be allowed too early in the year, there is a great probability that May frosts would ruin the buds. Delay beyond the chosen pruning times is less dangerous, but it probably means delay in the arrival of the first flowers, and so there may be fewer flowers through the season than might have been produced. Beginners should note that it is not the weather in February or March that dictates the rose pruning dates, but the probable weather in May; the advent of fine days in February causing the roses to " break " into growth should not be taken as a sign that pruning can be done earlier than usual.

Now for the question of how to use the secateurs. (Secateurs of the Rolcut type, or a sharp knife, used with an upward cut, are recommended by the National Rose Society.)

Newly planted (first season) bushes are pruned in this way. First any broken stems are cut away cleanly; then any old or weak wood is removed, leaving if possible a skeleton of stems radiating in all directions, so that they leave an open heart to the bush.

Each stem is examined carefully, and a bud (or the scar that is often the only sign of the bud) selected that is on the outer side of the stem, about two-thirds of the way down. The stem is cut immediately above this bud, so that when the bud develops, as it will, a new stem will push out away from the heart of the rose. Thus a sort of goblet-shaped skeleton will be built up.

After the first crop of roses fade, they should be cut away with long stems, as this automatically prunes the bush again, and fresh stems come for the second crop from a point low down on the plant.

At the end of summer, the last roses are snipped off without stems, but no pruning is done. The flower

WRONG   RIGHT   WRONG

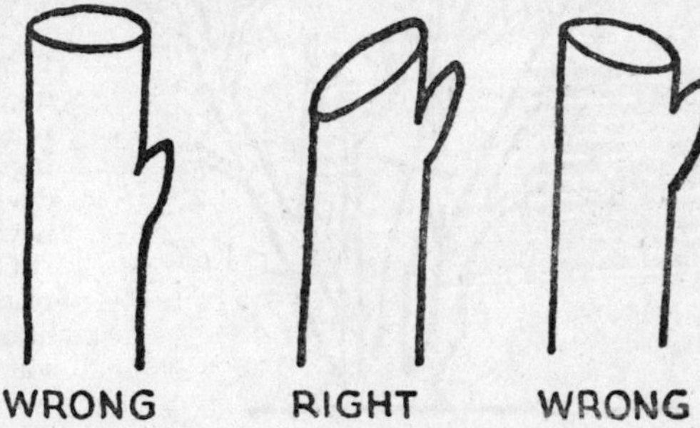

Fig. 14.   When pruning a bush the cut should be made immediately above a " bud " with the cut made at the angle shown in the centre above.

stems remain long during the winter, and are a kind of protection to the lower portion of the plant. Should some of the wood be killed back by frosts, the lowest parts, with fully dormant buds, will generally come through unscathed.

Rose beds where bush roses are growing should be dressed with lime every winter, and when the pruning is done in spring, they should be forked over, with either animal manure or bonemeal as a dressing just before forking.

Polyantha roses, that is the roses that grow in clusters, of the dwarf or bush type, are not so hard pruned as the ordinary bush roses; but they can be cut back a little, and also thinned out in March to prevent overcrowding.

Standard roses of similar varieties to the bush roses are pruned in exactly the same way, regarding the head of the standard as the bush, and carefully removing any suckers, or any side shoots that come from the main stem below the head.

Suckers, if they appear in a rose bed, should always be removed.

Roses are grafted on to common stocks, and the suckers come from these briar roots. If they are allowed to grow, the strength of the rose will go to the sucker, and the results will possibly be fatal to the rose you want to keep.

Now for the pruning of the rambler roses. These flower on the long growths sent from the base of the plant the previous year. They

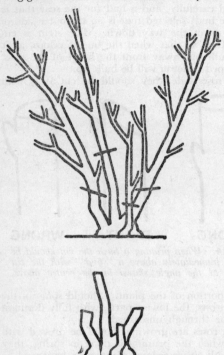

should be pruned as soon as the flowers fade, all stems that have borne flowers being cut away right to the base and the new ones tied in to replace them. Pruning is illustrated in Figs. 14 and 15.

Manuring or a good dose of liquid fertilizer is advisable after pruning, to encourage the development of strong new growth.

Certain of the pillar roses seem to have a habit of growth that is something between the two types described. The only thing to do in such cases is to use your discretion. If there are no fresh basal stems, but some very strong new growths coming from somewhere near the top of the old stems (as in the rose Alberic Barbier) it would obviously be absurd to cut the whole growth away, though if the rose is

Fig. 15.   *The right way to prune a bush rose with the result after pruning.*

overgrown, it would do no permanent harm. Alberic Barbier grows very well indeed with a minimum of pruning, the new growth being tied in with the old, and allowed to make a real smother. On a stout pillar, set in a small bed of its own, it makes a fine lawn specimen treated in this way. So also do a number of other roses, Albertine, Mermaid, etc.

It will be seen that the principles of rose pruning, once understood, are capable of wide adaptation by the grower of experience, and the novice is advised to grasp these fundamental principles and then to experiment freely, rather than to fly to a reference book for a detailed description of the right way to prune his particular varieties of rose.

Another difficulty that presents itself is that of pests and diseases. Clean healthy cultivation, regular and sufficiently hard pruning, hoeing the soil to keep it open and weed free, will do more than anything to solve these problems. There will always be times, however, when greenflies or other pests will appear, or when such diseases as " black spot " will prove a menace to the rose beds. Nicotine sprays used freely among the roses, or Derris dust dusted over them, to keep down most of the pests (handpicking of maggots may be required also), and the use of Bordeaux mixture (the best-known fungicide) when disease seems troublesome, are the recommendations I make to the novice. For the rest I should be inclined to let the problem arise before considering it, and I doubt if the gardener who is supplied with a syringe, nicotine wash, and Bordeaux mixture will ever have much trouble in his rose garden.

Lists of roses suitable for various purposes follow this chapter.

DWARF SHRUBS FOR ROCK GARDENS

In a previous chapter we have mentioned the value of dwarf shrubs in the rock garden. They are particularly useful there because the rock garden is a feature that should be a picture at all seasons, and, as all rock gardeners know, the springtime is the time when rockery plants are in bloom in the greatest profusion. Some of the flowering shrubs, however, flower much later than the spring carpet plants, and help to colour the pockets all through the summer months. Rock roses, sun roses, heather, and the shade-loving hyperica are very useful in this respect. Dwarf conifers of characteristic habit of growth are also specially useful as outstanding features of the rock garden, and certain of the trailing or prostrate shrubs are indispensable. A short list of some of the best rockery shrubs is given below.

Berberis buxifolia nana. A 2-ft. barberry that can be used like box edging. On the rock garden it can be kept as small as required by regular pruning after the flowers fade in May. The flowers are large, yellow, and solitary. Evergreen.

Daphne. This group includes D. *Cneorum*, with clusters of rosy pink, scented flowers in May. Grows to a spreading bush about a foot high. Prefers moisture and some lime. Evergreen. Cut back after blooming.

Genista saggittalis. An unusual genista, with green, winged, leaf-like branches and bright yellow flowers, which appear in June, growing to less than 1 ft. in height. Deciduous. Prostrate.

Helianthemum. Sun roses. Dwarf shrubs with flowers in a great variety of colours and shades flowering from May to July. Evergreen, and can be kept quite dwarf by pruning back after the flowers fade, or in very early spring.

Hypericum reptans. A 2-in. high trailer, with yellow flowers in summer. Deciduous.

Potentilla fruticosa nana argentea. Deciduous shrub about 1 ft. high, giving a constant succession of golden flowers all summer. Prefers scree. Several other members of the family are useful in the rock garden.

Senecio Monroi. Yellow flowered deciduous shrub, flowering from June to August. Ordinary soil, with plenty of sun. Height up to 2 ft.

Veronica pimeleoides. Evergreen shrub, 6 in. high, violet flowered in June and July. Foliage glaucous. Ordinary soil, full sun.

Below will be found a selective list of conifers suitable for rock gardens.

Abies nobilis glauca prostrata. A glaucous fir, of prostrate habit, growing up to 2 ft. Moist, lime-free soil.

Cedrus libani nana. Cedar. A compact pyramid form. Ordinary rockery soil.

Cupressus obtusa nana. Deep green cypress, with arching growth. Another variety of cypress is C. Lawsoniana Fletcher. Glaucous and pyramidal, and compact. Very good for the small rock garden. Ordinary soil.

Juniperus communis prostrata. Very low-growing, grey-green juniper, almost creeping. Ordinary rather moist but well-drained soil.

Picea albertiana conica. Cone shaped and dense foliaged, bright green. One of the best of the spruces for the rock garden. Ordinary moist soil.

Thuya occidentalis compacta. Bright green, grows to a ball shape, eventually making a globe 5 ft. across.

SHRUBS AS CREEPERS

Nearly all the plants we commonly use to clothe walls, fences and screens, to smother porches, and to furnish foliage and flower over the pergola, are shrubs. There are a few annual plants, and perhaps one or two herbaceous plants such as the perennial hop that are used when occasion demands, but for the most part the gardener prefers climbers to be of the kind that furnish the garden all the year round, or at least from early spring to late summer.

Evergreen climbers such as ivy and certain of the honeysuckles are delightful when well grown, and when not allowed to become too unruly. The most decorative flowering climbers are, however, in the class of deciduous shrubs, and it is to that class that we usually turn for plants to grow against house walls and over porches, in schemes such as the one suggested in Fig. 16. The fact that a house climber loses its leaves in winter may often be regarded as a virtue. It allows for the necessary repairs to the wall, prevents the accumulation of too much rubbish, which is a harbourage for insects, and also avoids much of the dampness associated with some wall climbers. All the same, ivy, the climber that has perhaps the worst reputation of all, is by no means so bad as it is believed to be, and if it is well cared for, it is possibly the finest of all wall shrubs for this climate.

Planting a wall shrub is done in exactly the same way as for any other shrub, with special care over the moisture-holding condition of the subsoil. Walls divert much of the normal rainfall, and climbers set against a house wall, particularly if there are overhanging eaves, often suffer badly from lack of moisture. When they are well established, no doubt, the roots penetrate some distance in search of moisture, but while the

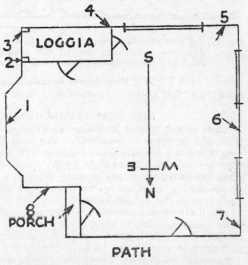

1-CEANOTHUS   5-HONEYSUCKLE
2-CLEMATIS   6-GARRYA ELLIPTICA
3-AKEBIA QUINATA 7-ACTINIDIA
4-VITIS   CHINENSIS
  COIGNETIAE   8-WINTER JASMINE

Fig. 16. *An arrangement of climbing shrubs to decorate the walls of a house.*

climbers are young it is wise to make a practice of throwing a few bucketfuls of water over the roots once or twice a week. This alone will prevent many losses, and double the growth of the climber, so that it becomes really established in a year or two.

Climbing shrubs are useful, too, for a background for a herbaceous

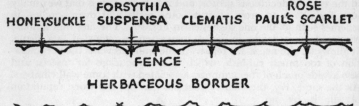

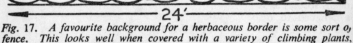

Fig. 17. *A favourite background for a herbaceous border is some sort o, fence. This looks well when covered with a variety of climbing plants, which will harmonize with the border, as in this diagram.*

border, as in Fig. 17; they should be chosen both for their screening qualities and, of course, as part of the colour scheme of the bed.

THE BEST CLIMBING SHRUBS

Some of the best of climbing plants are listed here, and many more will be found in catalogues. But from this short list it will be seen that many more varieties might well be used in the small garden than are now grown, with the happy result of making gardens less monotonous than they are in some districts, where Virginia creeper or golden ivy seem to be the only house climbers known to the gardeners of the neighbourhood.

Abutilon megapotamicum. Scarlet and yellow flowers, continuously produced from May to September. Semi-arching habit. Needs winter protection except in warm districts. South wall. A well-drained soil is very important.

Actinidia chinensis. Deep green foliage, grey below, good to cover a pergola.

Aristolochia sipho. The Dutchman's pipe. Yellow and brown pitcher-shaped flowers and large green leaves. Useful over a pergola in a warm garden.

Celastrus articulatus. Should be grown for its winter beauty, when the scarlet and gold fruits are very striking. Ordinary soil, and plenty of room. Will grow on a north wall.

Hedera canariensis variegata. The best of the variegated ivies. Self-clinging will grow on any aspect, and in any soil, but does best in sheltered gardens.

Humulus lupulus aurea. A golden-leafed form of the common hop. Ordinary soil, and a position where it can ramble freely.

Hydrangea petiolaris. A variety with large flat corymbs of white flowers in June. Does well over an old tree stump. Ordinary soil.

Jasminum nudiflorum. Winter flowering golden jasmine. A shrub that will grow anywhere, and can be pruned as desired when the flowers fade. It should be in every garden, for its fine show of colour in winter.

Jasminum officinale. The white-flowered summer jasmine. South or west walls, or over pillars and fences.

Clematis. A varied race of climbers, all extremely decorative. The early flowering kinds are best unpruned, or pruned immediately the flowers fade. Late flowering kinds are pruned hard back in February. The various hybrids respond to slightly different pruning, and fuller particulars are usually given by the growers in their catalogues. All grow best in rich light loam, moist but well drained, and with some mortar rubble or lime. Ideal climbers for the modern pergola of concrete or brick.

Lonicera or Honeysuckle. *Japonica aureo-reticulata* has golden veins to the leaves. No pruning. L. *japonica periclymenum Belgica* is the early Dutch scented honeysuckle. No pruning. L. *japonica periclymenum Serotina* is the late Dutch honeysuckle, rather more vigorous than the early type. All these are useful where they can twine and ramble. No pruning.

Passiflora coerulea. The blue passion flower. An excellent climber for south walls and sheltered gardens. Ordinary good soil. Prune in February, cutting back secondary growths to within a few eyes of the old wood.

Solanum crispum autumnalis. Lavender-blue, potato-like flowers make this a distinctive climber. Useful for sheltered walls south or west aspect.

Vitis. Vines, of many different kinds, including the self-clinging, small-leaved Virginia creeper (Ampelopsis *Veitchii*), the five-fingered creeper (V. *quinquefolia*), the hardy grape vines, and many others. All grow easily in ordinary good soil. The grape vines can be pruned back in January, to leave two or three eyes at the base of the previous year's wood, or if desired they can be less severely pruned. The creepers need no pruning. Propagation is by seeds and layers.

Wistaria chinensis. The well-known wistaria with trusses of mauve flowers. Grows best on pergolas or on south walls. Prune in summer and winter. In July and August shorten the young shoots a little, and in winter cut them well back to leave only two or three buds. This results in short spurs, as on fruit trees.

ROSE PRUNING

H.T.=Hybrid Tea. H.P.=Hybrid Perpetual.

Bush H.T., H.P. and Pernetiana. After planting cut back to 2 in. of the base. In succeeding years, prune at the end of March.

Remove all dead and worn-out wood, cut back weak growers to three or four eyes, and strong growers to four to six eyes, according to strength, to a good dormant, but pointing towards the outside of the bush.

For exhibition purposes harder pruning is necessary.

Climbing T., H.T., H.P. and Noisette. Prune in mid-March. Remove all dead and worn-out wood. Shorten weak shoots to two to three eyes, but strong shoots should only have the unripened tips removed.

Bush T. and Noisette. Prune in April. Remove old and dead wood. Remove weak growers to three or four eyes and strong ones to six or eight eyes.

Polyanthas. Prune mid-March. Thin where branches are weak or overcrowded and remove old flower stems.

Ramblers and Weeping Standards. Prune immediately after flowering. Cut out at ground level all shoots that have flowered, and tie in new growths. Where there are secondary shoots on these new growths they should be cut back to about half an inch.

BUSH ROSES

Red
Etoile de Hollande
Charles P. Kilham
Christopher Stone
Pink
Betty Uprichard
Dame Edith Helen
Picture
Mrs. George Geary
Mrs. A. R. Barraclough
Mrs. Henry Bowles
Ophelia
Orange and Apricot Shades
Talisman

Mrs. G. A. van Rossem
Lady Forteviot
Emma Wright
Barbara Richards
Duchess of Atholl
Mrs. Sam McGredy
Shot Silk
Yellow
Julien Potin
Mabel Morse
Christine
White and Cream Shades
Frau Karl Druschki
Clarice Goodacre

POLYANTHA ROSES

Red
Karen Poulsen
Kirsten Poulsen
Pink
Else Poulsen
Coral Cluster

Ellen Poulsen
Orange
Gloria Mundi
Paul Crampel
Yellow
Poulsen's Yellow

ROSES FOR SPECIMENS

Wich.=Wichuraiana.   H.T.=Hybrid Tea.   Pern.=Pernetiana.

Weeping Standards.   Prune in autumn.   Thin out old wood and make shapely.

	Class	Colour
Alberic Barbier	Wich.	Cream
American Pillar	Wich.	Bright red with white eye
Chaplin's Pink	Wich.	Pink
Dorothy Perkins	Wich.	Pink
Excelsa	Wich.	Crimson
François Juranville.. ..	Wich.	Orange pink
Lady Godiva	Wich.	Pink
Paul's Scarlet	Wich.	Scarlet
Shower of Gold	Wich.	Yellow
White Dorothy	Wich.	White

Standards, or Half Standards.   Prune in March, keeping in mind the shape of the head, as for bush roses.

	Class	Colour
Betty Uprichard ..	H.T.	Rose
Caroline Testout ..	H.T.	Pink
Etoile de Hollande ..	H.T.	Red
Lady Forteviot	H.T.	Golden
Madame Edouard Herriot (Daily Mail Rose) ..	Pern.	Coral
Mrs. Henry Bowles ..	H.T.	Glowing rose
Mrs. G. A. van Rossem ..	H.T.	Orange
Mrs. Henry Morse ..	H.T.	Silvery rose pink
Swansdown	H.T.	Creamy white

ROSES FOR WALLS AND FENCES

Cl.=Climbing.   T.=Tea.   N.=Noisette.

North-facing Walls.

	Class	Colour
Alberic Barbier	H.Wich.	Cream
Allen Chandler	H.T.	Scarlet
Dr. van Fleet	Wich.	Blush
Gloire de Dijon	Cl.T.	Cream

South-facing Walls.

	Class	Colour
Chaplin's Pink Climber	Wich.	Pink
Climbing Lady Hillingdon ..	T.	Apricot
Climbing Ophelia	H.T.	Flesh
Fortune's Yellow	Cl.N.	Yellow
Mermaid	H.Bracteata	Yellow

East-facing Walls.

	Class	Colour
Climbing Caroline Testout ..	H.T.	Pink
Dr. van Fleet	Wich.	Blush
Gruss an Teplitz	Cl.H.T.	Crimson
Paul's Scarlet Climber	H.T.	Scarlet

West-facing Walls.

	Class	Colour
Banksia Lutea	Banksia	Yellow
Chaplin's Pink Climber	Wich.	Pink
Climbing MadameAbel Chatenay	H.T.	Rose
Mermaid	H.Bracteata	Yellow
Zephyrine Drouhin	H.Bracteata	Carmine

ROSES FOR PERGOLAS AND PILLARS

Wich.=Wichuraiana (Rambler). Cl.H.T.=Climbing Hybrid Tea. Cl.H.P.=Climbing Hybrid Pernetiana. N.=Noisette.

	Class	Colour
Alberic Barbier ..	Wich.	Yellow buds, creamy white
Albertine	Wich.	Coppery chamois passing to salmon
Allen Chandler ..	Cl.H.T.	Vivid scarlet
American Pillar ..	Wich.	Clear rose pink centre
Chaplin's Pink Climber	Wich.	Bright warm pink
Conrad F. Meyer ..	Rugosa	Rose
Climbing Hugh Dickson	Cl.H.P.	Crimson

	Class	*Colour*
Climbing Lady Waterlow	C.H.T.	Salmon
Climbing Mme. Abel Chatenay	Cl.H.T.	Salmon pink
Dorothy Perkins ..	Wich.	Rose pink
Emily Gray	Wich.	Golden yellow
Excelsa	Wich.	Bright rosy crimson
Gruss an Teplitz ..	Cl.H.T.	Crimson
Mermaid	H.Bracteata	Sulphur yellow
Paul's Lemon Pillar ..	N.	Sulphur yellow
Paul's Scarlet	Wich.	Scarlet
Zephyrine Drouhin ..	H.Bourbon	Carmine

SHRUBS

Evergreen, with showy flowers or fruit

Andromeda
Berberis aquifolium
Berberis Darwinii
Berberis Gagnepainii
Berberis stenophylla
Cistus—all varieties
Choisya ternata
Ceanothus dentatus
Ceanothus rigidus
Cotoneaster congesta
Cotoneaster lactea
Cotoneaster microphylla
Daphne retusa
Escallonia langleyensis
Escallonia C. F. Ball
Escallonia edinensis

Ilex
Lavandula
Olearia Haastii
Olearia stellulata
Osmanthus
Pernettya
Phlomis fruticosa
Pieris floribunda
Polygala
Rhododendron
Senecio Greyii
Skimmia
Ulex europæus
Veronica
Viburnum Tinus
Yucca

Berried and Fruiting

Acanthopanax
Actinidia arguta
Ailanthus glandulosa
Berberis aggregata
Berberis concinna
Berberis Gagnepainii
Berberis polyantha
Berberis Thunbergii
Berberis verriculosi
Berberis Wilsoni
Celastrus articulatus

Daphne Mezereum
Gaultheria
Ligustrum sinensis
Lycium chinense
Pyracantha
Pyrus baccata
Pyrus malus
Rosa
Ruscus aculeatus
Sambucus
Skimmia japonica

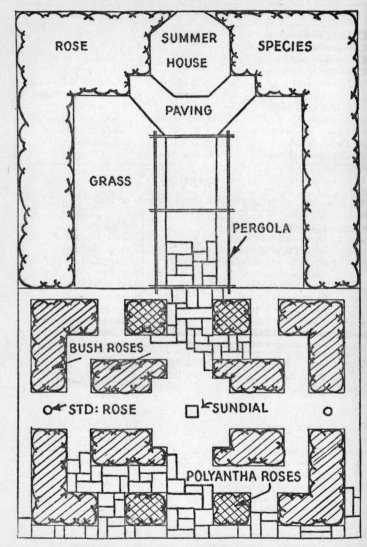

HOW TO ARRANGE A GARDEN OF ROSES

SHRUBS (*continued*)

Colutea arborescens
Cotoneaster (in variety)
Cydonia japonica
Cydonia Maulei

Symphoricarpus
Viburnum opulus
Viburnum lantana

Catkin-bearing

Alnus glutinosa
Alnus sitchensis
Betula Maximowiczii
Betula nigra
Betula pubescens
Betula verrucosa
Carpinus Betulus
Carpinus caroliniana
Castanea sativa

Corylus Avellana
Corylus maxima
Garrya elliptica
Populus tremula
Populus tremula pendula
Salix Bockii
Salix caprea
Salix gracilistyla

No Regular Pruning (thin when crowded)

Acer
Andromeda
Aucuba
Azalea
Buddleia globosa
Camellia

Chimonanthus
fragrans
(bush form)
Choisya
Cistus
Cornus
Coronilla

Cotoneaster
Daphne
Erica
Exochorda
Fothergilla
Gaultheria

Magnolia
Pernettya
Rhododendron
Skimmia
Ulex
Vaccinium

For Seaside Planting

Aucuba japonica
Berberis
Buddleia globosa
Buddleia variabilis
    magnifica
Calluna
Cistus
Cornus sanguinea
Cotoneaster

Euonymus
Fuchsia
Garrya elliptica
Griselinia littoralis
Hydrangea
    hortensis
Laurus nobilis
Lavandula
Leycesteria formosa

Ribes
Rosa
Rosemarinus
Spiræa
Symphoricarpus
Syringa
Tamarix
Ulex europæus
Veronica speciosa

SHRUBS (*continued*)

Cratægus   Escallonia   Prunus laurocerasus
Cytisus   Olearia Haastii   Veronica Traversii
Deutzia   Phillyrea   Viburnum Tinus
Elæagnus

For Windy Places

Aucuba japonica   Prunus spinosa
Berberis vulgaris   Rosmarinus
Colutea arborescens   Ruscus aculeatus
Cratægus   Sambucus
Escallonia   Spartium junceum
Euonymus   Tamarix
Griselinia   Ulex europæus
Hypericum calycinum

Shady Places

Aucuba japonica   Olearia Haastii
Berberis Darwinii   Philadelphus
Berberis stenophylla   Prunus laurocerasus
Buxus sempervirens   Prunus lusitanica
Cornus alba   Rhododendron ponticum
Cotoneaster microphylla   Ribes
Gaultheria Shallon   Ruscus aculeatus
Hedera   Sambucus
Hypericum calycinum   Skimmia japonica
Leycesteria formosa   Symphoricarpus
Ligustrum   Viburnum Tinus
Mahonia aquifolium   Vinca

Beneath Trees

Aucuba japonica   Rhododendron ponticum
Buxus sempervirens   Ruscus aculeatus
Cotoneaster Simonsii   Sambucus nigra
Hedera helix   Skimmia japonica
Hypericum calycinum   Viburnum Tinus
Ligustrum   Vinca
Mahonia aquifolium

SHRUBS FOR DIFFERENT SOILS

For Chalk Soils

Aucuba japonica
Berberis
Buddleia variabilis
Buxus
Cistus
Cornus
Cotoneaster
Cratægus

Cydonia japonica
Diervilla
Forsythia
Helianthemum
Hypericum
Jasminum
Ligustrum
Philadelphus

Prunus
Ribes
Rubus
Spartium junceum
Spiræa
Syringa
Veronica
Yucca

For Non-calcareous (Lime-free) Soils

Andromeda
Azalea
Calluna vulgaris
Cornus canadensis
Daboëcia
Daphne
Empetrum

Erica
Gaultheria
Kalmia
Laurus nobilis
Leucothoe
Magnolia
Oxydendrum

Pernettya
Pieris
Rhododendrons
Skimmia
Vaccinium
Zenobia speciosa

Poor, Stony, and Sandy Soils

Berberis
Calluna vulgaris
Cistus
Colutea arborescens
Cotoneaster micro-
    phylla
Cratægus

Cytisus
Genista
Helianthemum
Lavandula
Prunus amygdalus
Prunus cerasus
Prunus padus

Rosa spinosissima
Rosmarinus
Rubus
Santolina
Spartium junceum
Ulex europæus

For Clay and Marl

Aucuba
Berberis
Buddleia variabilis
Cornus
Cotoneaster
Cratægus
Cytisus
Deutzia
Diervilla
Escallonia

Forsythia
Genista
Hypericum
Ligustrum
Lonicera
Philadelphus
Prunus
Pyracantha
Pyrus
Ribes

Rosa
Rosmarinus
Senecio
Spartium junceum
Spiræa
Symphoricarpus
Syringa
Ulex europæus
Viburnum

Moisture Loving

Andromeda polifolia	Myrica Gale
Arundinaria (Bamboo)	Oxycoccus macrocarpus
Bambusa (Bamboo)	,, palustris
Cratægus	Salix

CLIMBING SHRUBS

1. Climbers that need no regular pruning but should have crowded shoots thinned and the straggling ones shortened in winter

	Colour	Season	Aspect	Remarks
Ampelopsis Veitchii	—	Autumn	S.W.	Bright autumn foliage
Cotoneaster horizontalis	White	Autumn	N.E.	Brilliant foliage and berries
Hydrangea scandens (petiolaris)	White	June	Any aspect	Self-clinging
Vitis quinquefolia	—	Autumn	Any aspect	Vivid autumn foliage Self-clinging

2. Climbers that flower in spring and early summer on shoots formed the previous year must be pruned immediately after flowering. Cut the flowering shoots fairly hard back to the old wood to encourage the production of strong young growths for flowering the following year.

	Colour	Seasons	Aspect	Remarks
Abelia grandiflora	White	July	S.W.	Evergreen
Ceanothus dentatus	Dark blue	June–Aug.	S.W.	Evergreen
Ceanothus rigidus	Blue	April–May	S.W.	Evergreen
Chimonanthus fragrans	Cream	Nov.–Mar.	S.W.	Fragrant
Clematis montana	White	May	S.W.	Deciduous
Clematis patens ..	Various	May–June	W.	Deciduous
Cydonia japonica	Scarlet	April–May	N.E.W.	Deciduous Scarlet berries
Forsythia suspensa	Yellow	April	Any aspect	Deciduous
Garrya elliptica ..	Green	Nov.–Feb.	N.E.	Catkins. Evergreen
Jasminum nudiflorum	Yellow	Nov.–Feb.	Any aspect	Deciduous Blooms before leaves appear

3. Climbers that flower from early summer onwards on shoots formed the same year are pruned in early spring to encourage the production of strong growths, giving as long a growing period as possible. Cut the shoots that bloomed the previous year hard back, leaving a few of the best to replace old worn-out wood.

	Colour	Season	Aspect	Remarks
Clematis Jackmanii	Purple	July–Oct.	W.	—
Clematis viticella	Bluish-purple	July–Oct.	S.W. or pergola	—
Passiflora cœrulea	Blue	June–Sept.	S.W.	"Passion Flower"
Solanum crispum	Mauve	June–July	S.W.	—
Tecoma radicans	Orange and scarlet	Aug.–Sept.	S.	—

4. Climbers that should have the old wood removed and the new tied in place in autumn after flowering.

	Colour	Season	Aspect	Remarks
Escallonia Langleyensis	Crimson	June–July	N.	Evergreen
Jasminum officinale	White	June–Oct.	Any aspect or pergola	Fragrant Deciduous
Lonicera japonica	Yellowish White	June–July	N.E. or pergola	Fragrant Deciduous
Lonicera japonica aureo-reticulata	Yellowish White	June–July	N.E. or pergola	Mottled yellow and green foliage
Polygonum baldschuanicum	Creamy white	Summer and autumn	Any position	Evergreen Rampant

5. Climbers that are pruned by cutting back to within a few buds of the old wood in early spring.

	Colour	Season	Aspect	Remarks
Wistaria sinensis	Mauve	May–June	S. or Pergola	Fragrant

On the following pages will be found comprehensive lists of flowering and fruiting trees which will be found suitable for the small garden and also reasonably easy to cultivate. The main characteristics of each are also given.

FLOWERING TREES FOR THE SMALL GARDEN

	Colour	Season	Remarks
Amelanchier (snowy mespilus) ..	White	April	—
Arbutus Unedo (strawberry tree)	White	Winter	Best near sea. Scarlet fruit in autumn
Catalpa bignonioides (Indian bean)	White, yellow and purple markings	July–August	—
Cercis siliquastrum (Judas tree)	Pink	May	Full
Crataegus oxyacantha (hawthorn)	White, pink or crimson		—
Halesia carolina (snowdrop tree)	White	May	—
Laburnum Vossii	Yellow	May	Requires a chalk-free soil
Liriodendron tulipifera (tulip tree)	White	May–June	—
Magnolia	White	—	Any soil
Prunus amygdalus (almond)	Pink	March–June	Slow growing
Prunus avium (bird cherry) ..	White	March	
Prunus cerasus vars. (cherry) ..	White and pink	May	
Prunus padus vars. (cherry) ..	White	May	
Prunus persica vars. (peach) ..	Pink	April	
Prunus serrulata vars. (cherry) ..	White and pink	April	Grow against a dark background if possible
Prunus subhirtella vars. (cherry)	Pink	May	
Pyrus malus (crab apple) ..	White	May	Abundant fruits in autumn
Robinia pseudacacia (acacia) ..	White	June	Slightly fragrant
Syringa standards (lilac) ..	Various	May–June	—
Sophora japonica (pagoda tree)	White	Aug.–Sept.	No flowers until mature

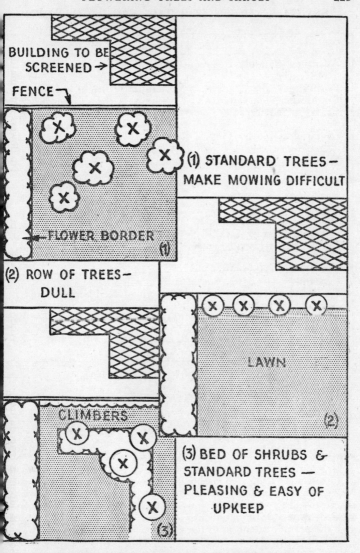

THREE WAYS TO USE TREES FOR SCREENING

FRUITING TREES FOR THE SMALL GARDEN

	Season	Remarks
Ailanthus glandulosa (Tree of Heaven)	Autumn	Brown "keys"
Cornus mas	September	Bright red berries
Cotoneaster Henryana ..	Autumn	Crimson brown berries
Cratægus Carrieri ..	Autumn	Pendant clusters of scarlet berries
Cratægus coccinea (hawthorn)	Autumn	Scarlet berries
Hippophae rhamnoides (sea buckthorn)	Sept.–Dec.	Orange berries Plants of both sexes required
Ilex aquifolium (holly) ..	All winter	Red berries
Pyracantha coccinea ..	All winter	Red berries
Pyrus aucuparia vars. (mountain ash)		
Pyrus malus vars. (crab apple)	Autumn	Red and orange fruits
Pyrus sorbus vars. (white-beam)		
Sambucus racemosus .. (golden elder)	June–July	Red berries. Golden foliage
Arbutus Unedo (strawberry tree)	Autumn	Like strawberries
Taxus baccata (yew) ..	August onwards	Red fruits

CHAPTER VIII

VEGETABLES AND FRUITS

THE British are reputed to be a nation of gardeners, yet one seldom finds home-grown vegetables on the table of the average British household. Possibly, there is a reason. Vegetables of the common kinds—cabbages and peas, beans and marrows—are so cheap to buy in their season that most small garden owners do not think it worth while to cultivate them and give their whole attention to the æsthetic side of gardening.

This argument is sound, as far as it goes, but it results in a deplorable monotony in vegetable diet, for the rarer vegetables, because they are not grown in gardens, become rarer still, and the prices almost prohibitive. I should like to see globe artichokes in suburban gardens as they may be seen in the cottage gardens of France, and a bed of asparagus to each family garden on the new housing estates.

Even those who prefer to limit their efforts in kitchen gardening to the more common vegetables could do much better than they usually do, if a little more discrimination and a little more care in management were exercised. Hints for the kitchen garden layout are given in Figs. 1 and 2. The main points to concern the gardener are these:—

1. A vegetable plot should be mainly open to full sunshine, and though it is an advantage for some shelter to be present, the plot should not be so confined that it is airless.

2. The plot or plots should be arranged so that lines of vegetables can run north and south, or nearly so, and so that these lines shall not be too long. A length of 20 ft. is plenty for each row, and longer rows do not make for ease in management.

3. Paths through the vegetable garden should be made to take a heavily loaded wheelbarrow, and

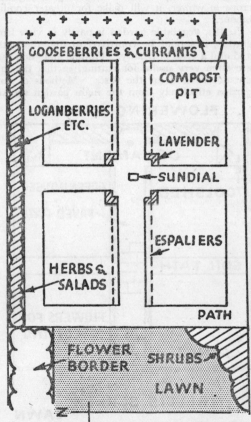

Fig. 1. *A mixed fruit and vegetable garden; the four rectangular beds contain vegetables.*

should not be of grass, which harbours slugs. Gravel paths, paving, or breeze on well-rolled foundations are suitable.

4. A frame or frames are an almost essential adjunct to the vegetable plot if the plot is to keep a family supplied all the year round with vegetables. There should also be, within reasonable distance, a place to store manure—preferably under cover, though manure can be stored in the open under a covering of soil—and a tool and potting shed where tools, insecticides and artificial fertilizers can be stored dry. If this shed is large enough for the storage of root crops in winter, it will make for greater comfort and save much labour.

5. If a vegetable garden is partly in view from the main flower garden, it should be contrived so that the paths are flower-lined, and add a vista of beauty. Flowers alongside the plots of vegetables are often very useful for cutting, so that the main garden borders are not robbed for the vases. Methods of screening the kitchen garden effectively from the main garden are suggested in Fig. 3.

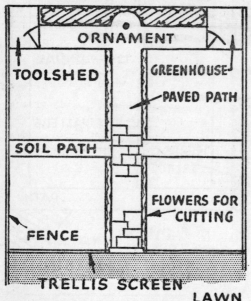

FLOWERING SHRUBS

ORNAMENT

TOOLSHED

GREENHOUSE

PAVED PATH

SOIL PATH

FLOWERS FOR CUTTING

FENCE

TRELLIS SCREEN

LAWN

Fig. 2. A layout for a self-contained kitchen garden, which need not be unattractive.

Vegetable gardens should be planned; they should not seem accidental or afterthoughts. In an ideal garden there would be three or four plots devoted to annual crops, one plot for use as a nursery bed, and sufficient room for the cultivation of perennial vegetables such as asparagus and artichokes. It is sometimes convenient to wall in the vegetable garden, and when this is done the annual crops are well placed in the middle, open portion, while the nursery bed, a salad bed, herbs and perennial or permanent crops occupy the long side borders. The walls are used for trained fruit trees such as apricots, nectarines, peaches and dessert pears.

The reason for the allotment of three or four separate plots for the main vegetables raised annually is that by so doing a proper rotation can be arranged and thus effect an economy in manuring. The principle of rotation of crops is that each crop takes from the soil only a proportion of the various plant foods present, and that the proportion of each varies according to the crop. If the same crop is not grown on the same ground a second season, it is not necessary to use so much extra plant food. For instance, plants of the pea and bean family have the habit of forming nodules on their roots. In these nodules are bacteria

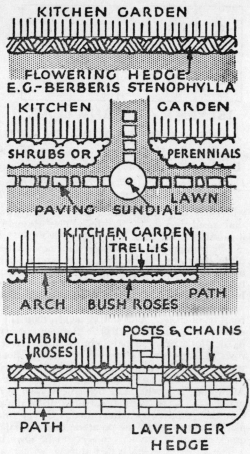

Fig. 3.   Four ways of screening a kitchen garden, combining trellises, shrubs and climbing plants.

which have the power to fix nitrogen in the soil and make it into assimilable plant food. If the peas and beans are cut off just above the soil level after the crop is gathered, and the roots dug into the ground, the soil will be richer in soluble nitrates for the succeeding crop. It will therefore need less nitrogenous fertilizer, and

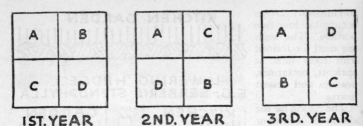

Fig. 4.   *A suggested rotation of crops in the kitchen garden.   This method*
does much to prevent soil exhaustion.

will be in a good condition for the cultivation of all green crops
that need plenty of nitrates. The system of crop rotation is
illustrated in Fig. 4.

The average home gardener does not want to go too deeply into
plant chemistry—if he does, there are specialized books available
on the subject. But he does want to appreciate the reasons underlying garden practices, otherwise he may be tempted to shirk small
but important tasks, such as this one of planning a rotation.

Intensive culture is a gardening term often associated with
rotation of crops. This simply means that no part of the plot should
ever be idle, except when it is " under the spade," and by no part
of the plot I mean *no* part, not even the unoccupied space between
rows of newly sown seeds. For instance, potatoes (which, by the
way, are the finest possible crop for virgin soil, because they help
to break and clean it properly) can be followed immediately by
April-sown broccoli. The broccoli is sown in the nursery plot, and
planted out after the final earthing up of the potatoes, or after the
first earlies have been harvested. Celery or leeks could also be
planted out to follow the potatoes, or small salads, spinach, or other
quick maturing summer crops could be sown between potato rows.

The broccoli is harvested during winter and spring, and the
ground is then sown with beet, carrots and parsnips, most of which
will be harvested the next autumn, though the parsnips will remain
for winter digging.

Early peas, broad beans and onions (autumn sown) might occupy
the ground the third year, and after the ground has been well dug in
winter, potatoes, celery and leeks would occupy it during the
fourth summer. The other plots would take a similar succession
beginning with a different group, so that a complete supply of

vegetables would be available each year without any part of the soil being either overworked or left fallow.

The keen cultivator will be ever on the alert for an opportunity to sow a catch crop of some quick maturing salad, such as radishes or lettuce, or a row of spinach, and will find that this method not only allows for a maximum yield of produce, but also tends to save labour. This it does because the frequent preparation of the soil for the sowing of catch crops prevents the appearance of weeds, and to a limited extent takes the place of hoeing.

The nursery plot in the kitchen garden is of great importance. It pays the gardener to get this going at the earliest opportunity. The ground should be dug deeply and carefully, all weeds being removed as the digging proceeds. This is much more important here than on the larger plots, where the hoe can be used.

It is not wise as a general rule to sift soil so that no stones are present. Stones do much to assist good drainage, the plant roots do not mind them, but find them cool and moist in the dry weather. And even surface stones, so long as they are not large enough to interfere with the use of the hoe, are best ignored, as they prevent excessive evaporation. Instances are known where cultivators have stripped fields of stones, employing a band of boys for the purpose, only to find that they had to take the stones back and dig them in again before plants would grow well !

PREPARING THE NURSERY PLOT

In the nursery plot, however, we are dealing mostly with tiny seedlings, and here it is rather important that there should be no stones of any considerable size. On stiff clay soils it pays to dig the plot well as for ordinary cultivation of crops, and then to top dress all over it with a 3 in. layer of prepared compost similar to that used for seed boxes, i.e., half ordinary soil, one quarter old crumbling leaves, and one quarter sharp sand, all rubbed through a $\frac{1}{2}$ in. sieve. Seeds sown on a bed so prepared generally germinate very quickly and transplant much more easily and safely than if sown on coarse, lumpy soil.

Cleanliness is very important on the nursery plot; that is, cleanliness from weeds and from pests. It pays to fumigate the plot thoroughly with soil fumigant if it is made from virgin soil that is likely to be troubled with wireworms, leatherjackets, woodlice and millipedes. Slugs can be controlled best by the double method of soil fumigation and laying a trail round the nursery plot of bran and crushed Meta.

An annual dressing of lime should be a part of the routine of the nursery as of the main vegetable garden. Lime is most effective used in small doses annually, rather than in large doses at infrequent intervals. Two ounces per square yard will be an average dressing.

The use of the nursery plot is twofold. In the early spring or late winter, crops such as cauliflowers and brussels sprouts are sown in the frames. Very soon the seedlings become large, and crowd each other, so that they cannot remain in the seed boxes. If a sheltered spot has been chosen for the nursery, the seedlings can be pricked out into it, about a foot apart, and left to grow on for a time. Then they are ready for transference without much root disturbance to their permanent quarters, and the move can be made whenever the ground is ready to receive them and the weather right.

The second use of the nursery is for actual seed sowing. It may also be a home for salads at the same time. Lettuce seeds sown thinly, broadcast, with radish sown thinly over the same patch is an instance of double cropping. The radish seeds mature rapidly, and as they are pulled the lettuces have more room left for development. Or the lettuces can be transplanted to another home as the radishes are gathered. Onions and radishes are frequently grown together in the same way.

As soon as the worst of the frosts are over, the nursery plot is sown with a variety of vegetables that will be transplanted to the main vegetable garden as the earliest crops are gathered. Thus, the nursery plot can, in a sheltered garden on warm light soil, become a substitute for a cold frame, though, as suggested previously, the best way is to have both frame and nursery, the frame being used to see the seedlings through the baby stage and the nursery used for their further development up to the time when there is room for them on the main plot.

DIFFERENT KINDS OF VEGETABLE CROPS

For the convenience of the beginner, I propose to deal with vegetables in groups according to their manner of cultivation. First let us consider the ordinary roots grown on every allotment—carrots, parsnips, beetroots, turnips.

All these are crops that are sown where they are to remain. They do not succeed when transplanted, the reason being that transplanting is a shock to the system, and a shock to a plant usually makes it grow old before its time. That is, it makes it cease to grow stems and leaves, and set about the work of reproduction.

In the case of these root crops we do not want them to reach this second stage of plant life. We want them, if possible, to build up an exceptionally rich store of food, packed away in the swollen tap root, so that we can make use of the food on our tables. Any kind of shock during the growing season, such as lack of water for a few days, or disturbance of the soil while hoeing, or an attempt to transplant, or the shock to the root system of meeting with very large stones or with lumps of hot, fresh manure, is likely to make these

plants send up flower stems, and when this happens the roots grow
coarse and fibrous and unfit for the table.

The first necessity, therefore, is to have a bed dug for these crops,
with the soil well broken to a considerable depth, and more or less
free from large stones. If the natural soil is particularly stony, it
pays to make large deep holes with a crowbar, worked round and
round in the soil, and then to fill into these holes some prepared
sifted soil, in which the roots will grow happily (Fig. 5).

The seeds are usually sown in lines, thinly, and when the seedlings
appear they are thinned out. To be sure of making the lines
parallel and straight, stretch a line of string across the plot from side
to side, attaching it at each end to a sharpened stick, which can be
pushed into the soil to hold the line taut. (Remember that the
lines should run north and south if possible.) Then, with the edge
of the hoe or rake, draw a narrow drill about an inch deep along
the line, and scatter the seeds thinly from end to end. If you prefer,
or the seed is expensive or scarce, sow just a pinch here and there at
intervals of 9 in. or more, according to the distance apart that you
intend to leave the mature plants. If you prepare special stations,
as suggested above, these too will be spaced according to the amount
of space needed by the mature plants.

It is sometimes advisable to thin out in easy stages. For instance,
when carrots are sown along a drill, they need not be thinned at first
to 8 or 9 in. apart, but may be left about 2 in. apart when the first

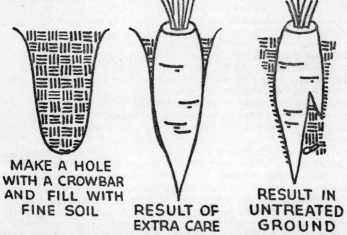

MAKE A HOLE
WITH A CROWBAR
AND FILL WITH
FINE SOIL   RESULT OF
                   EXTRA CARE   RESULT IN
                                       UNTREATED
                                       GROUND

*Fig. 5. Poor soil needs preparation before vegetable planting. Above is
seen the difference between a carrot in prepared and unprepared soil.*

thinning is done, i.e., when the seedlings are first large enough to handle. Then as the roots grow, alternate ones can be pulled while still small, to flavour soups or to use in the salad bowl, while the others are left to grow on for a bit. At the second thinning alternate roots are once more removed, so that finally as much room as the plants seem to need is left.

Cabbages, cauliflowers, broccoli, brussels sprouts, savoys, come next in the list of common garden crops raised from seed. It is possible to grow many of these in much the same way as one grows carrots, i.e., by sowing where they are to grow, and thinning out unwanted seedlings. This is not generally done, however, partly because it pays to sow many of these crops early in the year, when outdoor sowings would be inadvisable, and partly because it is a waste of space to grow seedlings that develop slowly, as do most of these, in the main vegetable plot. It is better to use the nursery plot for their culture until they have, say, six or eight leaves, and then to transplant them to the main garden.

HOW TO GROW CABBAGES

Cabbages and their relatives mostly need somewhere about 2 ft. space each way for a single plant—certainly more than 15 in. To try to sow them at this distance, or to thin them out to it, is obviously a waste of garden space because, by raising such plants as brussels sprouts on a nursery plot, the gardener is able to use for their later culture the same ground that was previously occupied fully by some early crop such as peas or potatoes.

Cabbages are sown at various seasons, and as the plants are hardy enough to stand frosts, this method of sowing results in a supply practically all the year round. Cauliflowers are tender and are sown under glass in the early part of the year, and grown on through the summer only. At the end of the season, if any heads are not quite ready, a leaf or two is bent over them to protect the white flower head from the first early frosts.

Broccoli, the winter form of cauliflower which is grown through the cold weather for spring use, is, of course, hardier. There is the large white-headed broccoli and the so-called " sprouting broccoli " which develops numerous small flower heads. Good soil and plenty of nitrogenous fertilizer are the requisites for first-class crops of any of these vegetables. They respond readily and satis-factorily to small, frequent doses of nitrate of soda, or to the use of sulphate of ammonia. Such stimulants should be given after the seedlings have become established in their permanent quarters.

The chief difficulty in the cultivation of the brassicas, as the cabbage family are called, is in fighting pests and " club root." Club root is a trouble on lands deficient in lime, and where it has taken hold it is difficult to keep down entirely. The best cure for club root on a vegetable plot has been found to be treatment with mercuric chloride. One ounce of this dissolved in twelve gallons of water, is used over the seed bed before sowing at the rate of one pint to a 5 ft. run of plants. Twice the quantity of the same solution is used when the plants are 2 in. high. Half a pint of the same solution is used in each hole when planting out. In addition, lime is used freely during soil preparation, and these precautions are sufficient to guarantee the crop against the dreaded disease.

Several of the cabbage family can be made to serve a second term of usefulness. For instance, the large cabbage heads cut in winter will be followed by a good crop of spring greens if the remaining stem is cut across and across with a sharp knife. Brussels sprouts have a longer season if the bottom yellowing leaves are regularly cut away, and the bottom sprouts plucked first. The tops should never be removed until all the buttons have been gathered.

Potatoes may be regarded as in a class by themselves. It should be remarked here that it does not pay most gardeners to cultivate main crop potatoes. They are so cheaply raised in fields, where machinery is used, that it is wiser for the home gardener to grow a little extra of the more valuable groups of vegetables, and to buy main crop potatoes for home consumption. Nevertheless, many gardeners prefer to raise all their own vegetables for the year, or prefer certain varieties of potato which are not easily obtained from farmers or from greengrocers.

POTATO CROPS GROW EASILY

Potatoes are a useful crop. They do not need rich soil, though some of the best crops have been raised in soil well manured with farmyard manure. I have seen potatoes set directly into fresh manure, dropped into an open trench, and the resulting crop has been all that could be desired. I have also seen good crops of potatoes grown on rather poor pasture land, where the grass has been turned in and the potatoes planted at the same time, and no additional manure or fertilizer given. Potatoes are frequently employed in this way to break and clean new land, and if they are hoed up once or twice during the season the soil is generally well cleaned by the time the potatoes are harvested.

In a great many home gardens it is not possible to use farmyard manure and an alternative must be found in fertilizers. Where prize crops are wanted, both manure and fertilizers may be used, and a good method to adopt is this. After double digging (see page 65) the spade is used to open a narrow trench, and manure is thrown all along the bottom of this, about 2 in. thick. The potatoes, which have been previously stood on end in boxes to sprout, should have one or two good strong shoots to each. If they have more some of them should be rubbed away, as it is not advisable to plant potatoes with too many growing stems.

A good idea is to obtain potato seed early and set the tubers to sprout at once. Tubers set in the sprouting boxes immediately after the previous season, and left in them all winter, make only a few stout growths in place of many weak ones. They must, of course, be kept entirely free from frost, but it is not necessary to exclude light. All that should be done is to set them rose end upwards in shallow trays. The rose end is the end where the "eyes" are clustered.

In planting, press the tuber into the soil, still with the rose end uppermost, and immediately draw over it about 4 in. of soil. Thus, it will be necessary to make the trench about 6 in. deep in the first place. Immediately afterwards, dust along the rows about three ounces to the yard of the following fertilizer : three parts kainit, two parts sulphate of ammonia and five parts superphosphate. This will ensure a good crop even from poor soil.

WHEN TO HOE AND SPRAY POTATOES

As soon as the tops of the early potatoes show through the soil, the first hoeing up should be done, i.e., a little of the soil from the sides should be drawn up over the tips that are showing. This prevents trouble from frosts, which can completely ruin the first early potatoes in a cold spring. All potatoes must be hoed up during growth, that is, the soil should be drawn up against the stems, leaving the potatoes apparently growing from the top of a ridge. This is done to cover the new potatoes, which tend to grow just at the surface of the soil. If they are not covered, they become green and are unfit for the table. Late potatoes, which make a smother of top growth that shades the ground surface, can sometimes remain without hoeing up, but generally speaking they too are better hoed.

Early potatoes do not require to be sprayed as they are seldom attacked by the potato blight, and are not intended for storing. Late varieties, which are to be stored during winter, must always be sprayed. Potato blight is a very common disease, which turns the tops yellow prematurely. It prevents the proper development of the tubers, so that the crop is smaller than it should be. But it is even more harmful in another way. The disease travels down from the leaves to the tubers, and so affects them that they turn brown, and gradually decay into an offensive slimy mass of putrefying matter. Some of the tubers will show signs of the disease when they are lifted, but others may appear healthy at the time of storing. Later they may decay and the trouble will spread to healthy tubers stored with them.

Spraying with Bordeaux mixture or with Burgundy mixture while the potatoes are growing is the cure for this disease. Spraying should be done from the middle of June onwards at intervals of three weeks—two or three sprayings being desirable. The cultivator should never wait for the disease to appear, but should regard the spray as a preventive measure. Bordeaux and Burgundy mixtures are well known to horticultural sundriesmen, and can be purchased with instructions for use.

When sufficient potatoes are grown in the home garden to warrant storing, they can be packed into sacks, after being allowed to dry and being rubbed fairly clean of soil, and if the sacks stand in a frost proof shed, and light is not allowed to reach the tubers, they will keep well all winter, to be used as required. If sufficient room for such storage is not available, a clamp can be made in the open, as for other root crops such as carrots and parsnips. Choose the highest part of the plot for your clamp, or one end that can be spared for a few months. Lay the roots on to the soil over a layer of clean, dry straw or sand.

Then cover the potatoes with straw, making a sloping ridge or roof to the clamp. Take a large digging fork and open a trench all round the clamp, packing the excavated soil solidly over the straw. Here and there along the top ridge a wisp of straw should be arranged to protrude, chimney fashion, so that the clamp is ventilated. Fig. 6 shows a cross section of the finished clamp. Built in this way, a store of roots will keep through the worst winter, but the layers of straw and soil must each be several inches thick, so that frosts are really excluded.

Onions, from the point of view of the home gardener, are a very important crop. From the horticultural point of view, they are a test of the gardener's skill, since a well-made onion bed, resulting in a good crop of onions, is something that never just happens, but is the result of really good cultivation.

Onions rarely do very well on newly broken land, but succeed best on ground that has been under cultivation for some time, thoroughly cleared of weeds and pests, and brought into

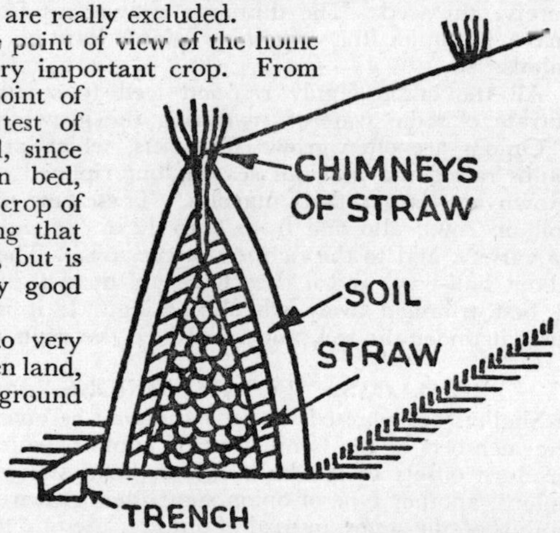

Fig. 6.   Cross-section showing how root crops are stored in a ventilated "clamp" of soil-covered straw.

" good heart " to a considerable depth. They like well-dug soil, well manured, but with the manure already partly decayed before it is dug in, and thoroughly mixed with the soil. The bed should be prepared some time before the onions are sown, and allowed to settle, so that the underneath soil is pretty well consolidated. Onions do not like loose, shifting soil. The largest stones should be removed when preparing an onion bed, and throughout the soil lumps should be well broken.

RAISING ONIONS UNDER GLASS

If desired, onions can be raised under glass in autumn and kept in a frame until spring, when they are planted out in rows on the onion plot. Or they can be sown direct on the plot, either in autumn or in spring, thinned out gradually as they appear to crowd, and so left at the required distance apart according to the variety of onion. The largest exhibition onions are usually autumn sown, and autumn sowings are advisable for most purposes, as the onions so raised have developed tough " necks " by May, when the onion fly is about. The onion fly is a pest that lays eggs in the tender neck of young onions, and these hatch out into grubs which destroy the crop.

Onions to be transplanted can be sown broadcast in boxes or on the nursery plot. Those which are to mature where sown should be arranged in lines, making a drill about 1 in. deep to receive the seed. The thinnings drawn out from time to time to make room for the remaining plants can be used in soups and salads.

All the onion family respond well to small frequent doses of nitrate of soda, watered in during the growing season.

Onions are often grown from sets, which are really tiny onion bulbs raised the previous season, but ripened off before they have grown any larger than marbles. These sets are pushed into the soil, in rows, allowing from 6 to 12 in. between them (according to variety, and to the richness of the soil). They should be buried about half-way, and if they have old dead foliage still present, this is best trimmed away when planting. If it is left, worms often drag it under the soil, and so disturb the roots of the onion.

SHALLOTS, " POTATO ONIONS " AND LEEKS

Shallots are planted in the same way as onions, and so also are the members of the family called " potato onions." Both of these produce offsets to the bulb, which form the season's crop. Tree onions, another type of onion sometimes grown as a curiosity, form bulbils on the stems, instead of flowers; these, if left, gradually weigh down the stem to soil level and root there to form new plants.

Leeks, also members of the onion family, are grown in a little different manner. They are usually sown under glass in March, set out in the nursery in April, and planted in prepared trenches, or in heavily manured soil, in June or July. For success rich soil is essential, and it is common on poor soil to open wide, deep trenches, and to fill in a 4 or 5 in. layer of animal manure at the bottom. Then, as growth develops, the earth from the sides of the trenches is gradually drawn up against the plants, with the result that the lower portion of the leaves becomes blanched. It is this lower portion that is cooked for the table, and it is essential that there should be a good length of blanched growth, of good substance. Quite satisfactory leeks for ordinary purposes can be grown if a wide hole is made for each by working a dibber round and round in the soil, refilling the hole with rich, sifted soil, so that the surface is just a little lower than the surrounding ground. Seeds can be sown direct on this prepared site, and thinned to leave one strong seedling, the soil being hoed up round the plant as it develops. It should be noted that whereas celery plants are allowed to grow to full size before they are blanched by earthing, leeks are earthed in stages as they grow.

Celery is another vegetable worth special treatment. For this seeds must be sown under glass in late winter or early spring, and grown on to produce good plants by June or July. It is best to sow in ordinary seed boxes, and to prick out the seedlings either into a frame of good soil, or into rather deeper boxes of soil, as the plants have a long season of growth under glass and should not be starved during that time.

PREPARING CELERY TRENCHES

Before the seedlings are ready for the open, the trenches should be prepared. Celery is a native of marshlands, and needs plenty of water during the summer. That is why it is grown in trenches, and the deeper and richer the trench prepared, the larger and better will be the crop, though as many a home gardener has discovered, small plants of very fine flavour can be grown in shallow trenches, where the larger trenches cannot well be made.

A 15 in. deep trench, with 4 in. of rotten manure or other humus, and 4 or 5 in. of soil over it is best. The remaining soil should be stacked at the trench sides, so that the trenches will actually appear to be somewhere about 1 ft. deep at planting time.

Plant firmly, in a double row if the trench is wide enough to allow for this, but allowing 1 ft. between the plants. Keep up the water supply, and when the plants are fully developed, which may be at any time after the middle of August according to the date of planting out, make a paper collar to each and tie it loosely in position. Then earth up in easy stages, say at weekly intervals, drawing a little more soil up against the collar each time. The purpose of the paper collar is to keep the stems as clean as possible, and to ensure that they are quite blanched, as green parts are not edible.

Celery is very liable to attacks of soil pests such as slugs, and soot dusted frequently along the rows is a useful insecticide and fertilizer. Liquid manure, preferably made from animal droppings, is very beneficial to the plants throughout the growing season.

Peas and beans are very popular vegetables, which for convenience can be grouped together in one of the plots in the kitchen garden. Peas are hardy, and the first sowings can be made as early as February in the open, successive sowings being made at intervals of two or three weeks from then until June. An easy way to cultivate peas in a small garden is to sow a wide row of the dwarf variety, which need no pea sticks. The soil must be good, and manure in the underlayer to hold moisture in dry weather is an advantage. Take out with a spade a shallow trench 6 in. deep and the width of the spade (Fig. 7) and scatter the pea seeds over the bottom, about 2 or 3 in. apart. Then draw about 2 in. of soil over them, leaving them in the shallow trench to grow to maturity. This diverts the maximum amount of rainfall to the plants. If any support is necessary, give it by running a line of string or wire along each side of the peas, about 6 in. from the ground level. The trench should have a flat bottom.

Peas grown for exhibition must be sown more carefully. For these drills are drawn, and the peas sown 3 or 4 in. apart in a single or double line. Pea sticks must be provided immediately, so that the tender seedlings, as they push through the soil, are protected a little from winds.

Occasional watering may be necessary, as the finest peas cannot be grown where moisture is lacking. Liquid manure given every fortnight or so after watering, beginning when the peas are showing their first flower buds, will prove of great benefit. Any general fertilizer can be used for this. Gather the pods immediately the peas are well formed in them, not before the pod is full, but well before the skins toughen. They should then be at their best both in quantity and flavour. As soon as the last peas are gathered, cut down the tops and throw them in the compost pit, leaving the roots to be dug into the ground. There are numerous varieties of peas, dwarfs, medium and tall growers, and the

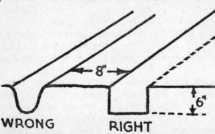

WRONG   RIGHT

Fig. 7. *Trenches for peas should be flat-bottomed, 6 in. deep and 8 in. apart.*

stringless peas known as sugar peas. These last are gathered younger than usual, and are eaten without shelling, as the pods have none of the stringy lining common in the other peas. Culture is otherwise the same.

Beans are of two distinct types. Broad beans are hardy beans that will stand the winter in the open. They are best sown in November, as the beans so sown generally reach maturity before the appearance of black fly, which is one of the great curses of this crop. It attacks the tender growing tips of the plants. As soon as the flowers are well open on the plants the growing tip should be pinched out, and in this way the fly will be discouraged. Spring sown beans are often badly attacked before they have had time to reach the fruiting stage, but frequent sprayings with insecticide will ward off the pest.

Broad beans are sown in a shallow trench 3 in. deep, with the seeds in a double row, about 5 in. apart. Leave 3 or 4 ft. between the rows if more than one row is sown.

RUNNER AND FRENCH BEANS

Runner and French dwarf beans are similar in character. They are only half hardy, and must be sown either under glass, or in the open in April or early May, so that they do not appear above the soil before the frosts are past. Runners are sown in rows with about 4 in. between each seed, and 10 ft. stakes or bean poles are needed for their support. Plenty of water is needed in dry weather, or the buds may drop badly. Gather the beans as they form, and never leave any to become old, or the supply of fresh beans will cease.

Dwarf French beans, and the climbing French variety, are also sown in rows in the open. They should be thinned to leave plenty of room between the plants, as the resulting crop is better and heavier.

Some dwarf French beans are useful for winter use. If they are grown for this purpose, they should be allowed full room for development, and the beans should all be allowed to ripen on the plants. About the middle of September they should be gathered, dried and stored. The easiest way is generally to lift the plants, strip off the beans when they are ripe (at once, or after storing in a dry shed for a time) and immediately shell them. Pack quite dry into jars for winter use.

So far the culture of the most common garden vegetables has been described. There are, however, many little gardens where the owner does not really want to grow his own vegetable supplies for all the year round, but where he is glad to grow a few of the best varieties, or a few crops of the kinds which are not generally available in shops, or which suffer considerably by market handling, such as the fresh salads, spinach, etc. The essentials for the cultivation of such crops are given below. For other information regarding times and seasons, the table of sowing given on pages 268–271 should be consulted.

Artichokes. The Jerusalem and Chinese artichokes are roots, grown from tubers, which are planted 6 and 3 in. deep respectively, in early spring. They are lifted and stored in October. These artichokes can be grown as a wind screen along one end of the plot.

Globe Artichokes are the unopened flowerheads of a perennial plant of not unattractive appearance. Plants should be bought in early April, and set in rich soil. The first season's flowerheads should not be allowed to form, but after that the plants send up many stems annually, and crop for six or seven years. Grow these in the part of the kitchen garden reserved for permanent crops.

Asparagus is another permanent crop. A well-made asparagus bed will last for a quarter of a century without disturbance, though annual dressings of animal manure are required. The soil should be very deeply dug—2 or 3 ft.—and well manured. Beds 4 ft. wide, with a beaten soil track between them are best. Set the plants in rows 18 in. apart, and cover the crowns with 4 in. of soil. Do not cut any shoots until the plants are well established. If one-year plants are set out, wait for two years before cutting. (There are certain strains now sold which the growers claim to be fit to cut the first season after planting.) When the tops turn colour in autumn, cut them down and top dress the bed with old manure. In March use artificial fertilizer, made by mixing two parts sulphate of potash, two parts nitrate of soda, three parts superphosphate and six parts agricultural salt, at the rate of three ounces to the square yard.

Aubergine, or Egg plant. This is grown usually in pots in a frame or cool greenhouse, but in warm gardens and in favourable summers, crops can be grown like tomatoes in the open ground after the plants have been raised under glass. Sow the seeds in February, and prick out each seedling into a 6 in. pot of good soil, if the crop is to be grown on the greenhouse shelves. Pinch out the tips when about 6 in. high to make a bushy plant. The fruits are purple or white according to variety, and are eaten when as large as eggs, or larger. If the plants are to grow in the open, the seedlings can be set into 4 or 5 in. pots until June, when it is safe to move them outdoors.

Mushrooms. These should be grown in a cellar or shed, away from frosts and rains. Light is unnecessary. The method is this. Fresh manure is placed in a heap, and about every fourth day it is turned over. During this time the manure should remain moist, and a little tepid water should be used if needed. At the end of three weeks, or longer if the manure contains shavings or sawdust, the heap will be ready to make up into a bed. It should have lost its disagreeable odour by this time, and the temperature should have dropped to about 120 degrees centigrade.

The bed can be flat, 10 in. deep, or built to a ridge shape. When the temperature has dropped to about 70 degrees centigrade, pieces of mushroom spawn about 2 in. square are pushed in so that they are covered by about an inch of manure. The surface should be beaten firmly after the spawning, and a layer of soil an inch or two deep should then be added all over the heap. Tepid water may be needed to prevent the beds drying out, but this is not usually required.

When the first small buttons are seen, gather them and immediately dress the whole bed with a little more sifted soil. More mushrooms will appear, for perhaps several months, the supply being dependent on the weather and other conditions. It is possible, in a frostproof shelter, to grow mushrooms continuously all the year round, and fresh beds can be made up in succession so that the supply is maintained. When a bed has ceased to bear, the manure is no longer valuable in the mushroom house, but is very useful for making up beds for vegetable marrows or for other garden manure.

Rhubarb. Although rhubarb is not regarded by the housewife as a vegetable, it is definitely a crop for the vegetable garden or allotment, and should be given one of the permanent positions. Plants are set 5 ft. apart, in March, in good rich soil. The crown of each should be 1 in. below the soil surface. No sticks should be gathered the first season, but in subsequent years, particularly if the rhubarb is given a good mulch of rotted manure (the manure from an old mushroom bed is ideal) in the summer, sticks will be available from early spring to midsummer.

Early supplies are obtained either by lifting roots in late autumn, and packing them into boxes of moist soil to stand under the greenhouse staging, or by inverting boxes over the plants in the open garden, old manure being piled over and round the boxes to keep the plants warmer and to exclude light. Such forcing weakens the plants, and should not be too freely practised. Plants can be lifted and divided every three or four years, at any time except when they are in active growth, or when the soil is frosted.

Seakale. Roots can be bought in March and planted 15 in. apart. At the approach of winter they are lifted, the foliage is trimmed away, and the roots replanted close together in deep boxes of moist soil, which stand under the greenhouse staging. They need a temperature of 60 degrees centigrade, and will, in this heat, develop new growths which are cut when they are about 6 in. long. If preferred, the roots can be forced in the open ground by inverting seakale pots over them, and covering them with leaves.

To propagate, take some of the roots at the end of the year and cut them into pieces 6 in. long. Store them in sand until March, when they can be planted in open ground to replace old plants.

Vegetable Marrows, Pumpkins and Gourds are all grown in much the same way. All are edible, though the marrow is the commonest.

Seeds can be sown in thumb pots, singly, in April, and planted out at the end of May on to a well-manured bed or an old hotbed, or a pile of old rotted manure, over which a 3 in. layer of soil has been laid. Alternatively, the seeds can be sown direct in the open, but if so they should be watched carefully for fear of frosts. If a late frost should threaten, invert a large flower pot over each seedling every night, and remove it in the morning. Plenty of water and occasional doses of liquid manure or fertilizer are well repaid by an abundance of good marrows. As marrows, particularly the trailing kind, take up a good deal of space, it is usually found convenient to grow them in some unsightly corner of the plot, where they can ramble at will and perhaps hide from view a rubbish heap or an old shed.

GROWING GREEN SALADS

Quick growth in good rich soil, with never a check to the water supply is the culture secret of small green salads.

Chicory is gaining favour as a salad or vegetable in this country. It is sown in lines in late spring, allowing 1 ft. between the rows, and thinning the seedlings to 9 in. apart. In autumn the plants are lifted, the tops trimmed back, and the roots replanted in boxes of moist soil with 5 or 6 in. of sand over the plants. The boxes stand in the dark, but in some warm corner of the greenhouse, and as the new growths appear through the sand cover, they are ready to cut. These blanched parts are the parts used in the salad bowl, and they are called " chicons."

Lettuces, which are perhaps the salad crop most in demand, are grown most of the year in the open garden, the method being extremely simple. On well dug and rich soil, drills are drawn about 9 in. or 1 ft. apart and 1 in. deep. Along these lettuce seeds are scattered thinly, and a little soil is used to cover them.

As soon as the plants are large enough to handle, some can be transplanted to other positions, the remaining seedlings being left about 9 in. apart. Crowding should be avoided, as it causes the plants to bolt into flower, which is what the cultivator wants to avoid. The hoe is used to keep down weeds, and occasional doses of nitrate of soda or liquid manure are useful to encourage rapid development of the leaves.

There are two types of lettuce, the tall cos lettuces and the broad round cabbage lettuces. Formerly, the tops of the cos varieties had to be tied together when the plants were partly grown, so that the blanched heart would develop, but there are now varieties that form the desired shape naturally without tying the tops together.

Lettuces can, if preferred, be raised by broadcasting seed in a nursery bed or in boxes under glass, and pricking out the seedlings into the frame or on to the plot when they can be handled.

Mustard and Cress are familiar to everyone. Both these are sown thickly in patches, either outdoors or under glass. The seed need not be covered with soil, but can be pressed well down on to moist soil, as thickly as possible over the surface, and then shaded with brown paper until it has germinated. The shading is then removed and watering is the only further treatment needed. The crop is cut when the seedlings are uniformly green all over, and an inch high or more, but before a second pair of leaves forms. Successive sowings are required to keep up a supply.

Cress takes a few days longer to germinate than mustard, and for use together should be sown at least three days before the mustard.

Radishes are sown in lines in any available corner of the nursery garden or salad patch. They grow quickly and as soon as the roots form they should be pulled, as old roots are stringy and worthless.

Watercress can be grown in any garden if a good water supply is maintained. A bed a little below the general level of the garden should be prepared by deep digging, and pieces of watercress (tops) should be dibbled in about 6 in. apart. If planted like this in March, a supply of watercress will be available during the late summer.

It is almost impossible to state in general terms what produce can be grown on a given area devoted to vegetables. Naturally, it depends on the fertility of the soil, on the general management of crops, and on the choice of crops—since some vegetables are far more valuable than others.

The average allotment of ten rods is regarded as capable of producing the bulk of the vegetables for an all-the-year-round supply for a family of four or five persons. It may be taken that if the same area is devoted to the small vegetables and salads, and well cropped, it will produce sufficient for a family twice the size, assuming that the family would purchase the main crop potatoes and perhaps some of the other roots from market supplies. If smaller space, in proportion, is available for vegetable culture, certain of the cheaper and easily bought vegetables should be left out, and also such vegetables as seakale and chicory, which demand the use of a greenhouse. Peas, beans, spinach, tomatoes, salads, brussels sprouts, and sprouting broccoli are among the most profitable crops for a little family garden. All are of the cut-and-come-again type; that is, they produce crops over a long period if well managed, and none of them need glass culture—except tomatoes, sprouts and broccoli in the early stages, while seedlings that have passed this stage are not expensive to buy.

The following figures are not to be regarded as maximum figures.

but merely averages for small garden culture of vegetables in the hands of novices. Many will scoff at the quantities, but the average gardener is not an expert exhibition grower.

A pint of runner beans will sow a row 160 ft. long, and from such a row one would gather at least ten pounds of beans on most days during the cropping season. A pint of dwarf French beans would perhaps yield nearly as many pounds, but the cropping season is much shorter; say, three weeks instead of six or eight weeks.

A row of four dozen tomato plants growing in the open would produce at least a hundred pounds of good fruit in a sunny season. These would ripen from the middle of July onwards until the frosts —an average of ten pounds a week.

An ounce of spinach will sow 200 ft. of row. Assuming that it is sown in succession, 10 ft. at a time, there should be a cutting sufficient for two meals for a family of five from each sowing.

Two dozen brussels sprouts and one dozen purple sprouting broccoli would provide greens for a family meal two or three times a week during the winter; in some seasons they will provide much more.

These estimates are given merely for the convenience of the new garden owner. Experience is naturally a more reliable guide to the quantities required by his own family. A table of vegetable sowing times will be found at the end of the chapter.

THE PROBLEM OF THE SMALL ORCHARD

The garden owner who can spare a part of his ground for vegetable cultivation rarely needs much encouragement to do so, but a great many amateur gardeners who could well plant a small but useful mixed orchard are afraid to venture into this department of horticulture. Undoubtedly, the reason is that the amateur is nervous about the use of a pruning knife.

It does *not* need very great horticultural skill to grow good fruit. Neither does it need a great expenditure of time or money, certainly no more than to grow good roses or good dahlias. If you can afford the initial expense of plants that are already " formed " into bushes, standards, or cordons, according to your tastes, fruit growing is one of the simplest of garden operations.

The pruning of established fruit trees is quite simple, and its principles can be mastered in a very short time. Some fruits actually need very little pruning at all when once the mature shape of the tree has been formed. The only pruning on old standard cherries and plums, for instance, consists in cutting away broken or diseased branches and occasionally taking out a branch if overcrowding threatens.

What, therefore, should the owner of a spare plot of ground do to convert it into a small home orchard? First, the home orchard

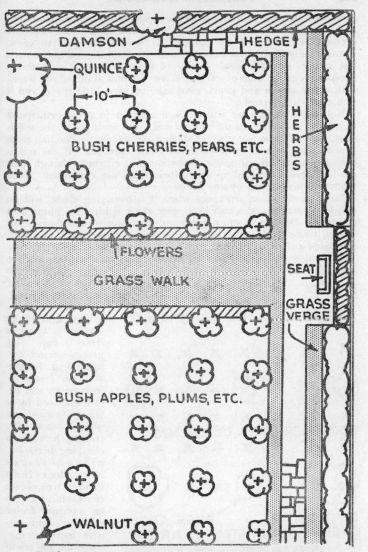

Fig. 8.   Spacing and general arrangement of a small orchard.

should be planned with an eye to the aspect of the ground available, and to the type of soil that exists. Planning should also take into account the needs of the family. It would not pay to grow, commercially, fruits that were not well suited to the soil and aspect, but it does pay the small family to grow a little of everything, irrespective of the kind of soil they have. A plot of mixed soft fruits, with a few apples and pears, need take up very little space, and is well worth the trouble.

Naturally, the owner will be well advised to grow principally fruits that are suited to the natural soil. For instance, if the soil is damp, even if it is waterlogged during the winter by flooding from a near river, it will grow excellent black currants. If the soil is light and warm, it will grow raspberries and currants, though light soil will need some feeding where these fruits are cultivated. Poor sandy soil is not liked by any fruits.

Light sandy loam, especially when it is overlying chalk, will do well for cherries, and a stiff loam over chalk is ideal for plums and damsons. Damp soils suit quinces and the raspberry and loganberry family, while strawberries like a rich soil in good heart, i.e., well cultivated and well drained.

A small fruit orchard can be arranged to take a great variety of fruits if it is well planned. A walled enclosure is ideal, since apricots, nectarines and other slightly tender fruits can be grown against the south wall. Failing walls or fences, a fruit patch can be well enclosed by a wire fence on which can be trained the various climbing berries— blackberries, loganberries, veitchberries, etc. Or fan-trained or cordon fruits can be used on wire fences if the site is not too open and exposed.

GOOSEBERRIES & CURRANTS

STANDARD CHERRY, PLUM ETC.   BUSH APPLE, PEAR ETC.

Fig. 9.   Spacing in an orchard, where intercropping of soft and tree fruits is desired.

Where there is any choice of site, a slope facing to the east should be avoided. Frosts are less dangerous if the early morning sunshine does not fall directly on the trees, and fruits on an eastern slope will often be ruined by a slight frost when those on a western, or even a northern, slope remain undamaged.

Shelter can be provided for the orchard by planting a row of damsons or of myrobalan plums along the side where winds are troublesome. These fruits are pretty hardy, and even if they do get damaged, the loss is less than if the more choice fruits, such as pears, were ruined by cold winds.

Reference to the orchard plan in Fig. 8 will assist the gardener to arrange his fruits to

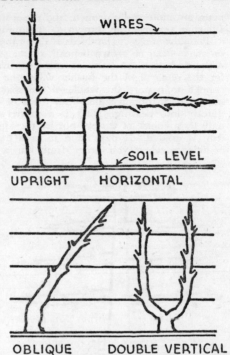

Fig. 10.   Four ways to train fruit trees on to cordons, which are useful for screening.

the best advantage, but it is quite impossible to give the ideal arrangement, since so many local factors are always involved. The best procedure to adopt is this : first see to the boundaries, arrange protective planting if necessary, or build walls or fences. Allocate plants according to site, but with due allowance for the amount of time available for cultivation. Cordon and other trained trees are far more exacting than loganberries, for instance, though the gathering of soft fruits is somewhat troublesome in the season of their ripening.

Next consider whether the plot is large enough to allow for standard fruits, or whether bush fruits are preferable. Standards are decorative, and when fully grown they are extremely profitable, but bush fruits are generally considered a better commercial proposition where a quick return is wanted. Bush apples and pears are more easily pruned, and the fruit is more easily gathered. Cherries are generally grown as standards.

The advantage of standards is that other crops—small soft fruits or salads—can be grown beneath them. A common practice with orchards is to plant standard and bush fruits alternately, allowing for the removal of the bushes when the standards become large enough to require the whole of the space. In such a case it is important to obtain small bush fruits of the kind that will come quickly into bearing. This is a matter which is controlled not only by a choice of variety but by the kind of stock on which the fruit is grafted. It pays then to take the nurseryman into your confidence when you order fruits for a new plantation. Fruit growers will willingly look at your planting plan and make suggestions if you ask them. It is always better to make a plan on paper, to scale, so that the plants are properly spaced.

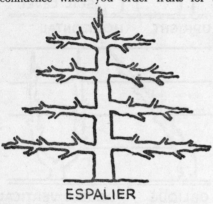

ESPALIER

Begin to fill in the details of your planting scheme by inserting first the fruits that appear to you to be most important. In this family tastes must be considered. A further point that affects this first choice is that some fruits such as apples can be bought in good condition in the markets, while soft fruits such as raspberries and currants, are difficult to obtain in prime condition. Moreover, the finest of these fruits are never grown for market, because they are too soft skinned to travel well.

FAN TRAINED

Fig. 11. Espalier and fan-trained fruit trees are a development of cordon training (Fig. 10).

Finish the planting

scheme by adding as many varieties and kinds as possible, so that you have a little of everything. A glut of one kind of fruit is often an embarrassment in the home garden. When that particular fruit has a " good " season, it is impossible to sell at prices which pay for the labour of gathering, and there is not much fun in gathering fruit that you could buy at about a penny a pound ! On the other hand, if you have a variety of apples and pears and cherries, some flowering early and some later, you are pretty sure to have some fruit even in a bad season, for the frosts that kill the blossom on one tree will not touch the others. At harvest time you get a further advantage, since the season of ripe fruit

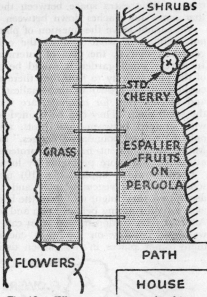

Fig. 12.   *Where a separate orchard is out of the question, tree fruits can be grown in the flower garden, as suggested in this plan.*

is greatly extended by having several varieties, which will fruit in succession, not simultaneously.

In arranging the fruits, try to make the best possible use of the site by intercropping, on the same principle as intensive culture of the vegetable garden. For some years at least, soft fruits could be grown between bush and standard apples and pears and cherries and plums, assuming these larger fruit trees are planted at the distance apart which will allow them to reach maturity uncrowded (Fig. 9). In the same way, when a plot of currants or goose-berries is planted at the proper distance apart, i.e., with 5 ft. or more between bushes or rows, there will be available space for a season or two between the rows, and strawberries might with advantage be grown there. Better still would be a few rows of salads interplanted, as the strawberries, while they would not crowd the other fruits, might be rather shaded by the bushes and so fail to ripen well.

A point to be kept in mind is that when soft fruits are used for permanent interplanting, i.e., to remain as undergrowth to standard trees, a little extra space between the standards is advisable, so that some sun reaches down between the rows.

We cannot leave the question of planning the fruit garden without mention of what is often the only possibility for the home gardener, that is, the plan of intermixing fruit with the flowers. In a very small garden it would be absurd to allocate any part of the plot entirely to fruit, but there are a great many fruits that could well be grown in the smallest garden plot. Loganberries and blackberries, for example, are very good subjects indeed for the small plot. They can be trained to walls, fences, or to simple wire strained between stout posts, and in this fashion they not only make good boundary " hedges," but also serve to break winds. Many an allotment has been protected, as well as made more attractive and more profitable by loganberry screens of this type.

Cordon-trained apples (Fig. 10) make a particularly effective screen between vegetable plot and flower garden. Thick and decorative, they might well form the background to a flower border, with a path running behind them and serving the vegetable garden. Alternatively, cordon-trained trees can be grown against boundary walls, or possibly on the walls enclosing tennis courts, and in many other places in the garden design. Espalier-trained fruits (Fig. 11) may be grown on to a pergola as in Fig. 12.

In a smaller garden still a single specimen standard tree set in the lawn might be of a fruiting character. There is little doubt that a well-grown cherry or apple (particularly the pink-blossomed apples such as Cox's Orange, James Grieve, etc.) is as decorative as any of the so-called "flowering" trees, and when in fruit it is particularly lovely. Fig. 13 shows how the corner of a small garden may be made attractive by the use of standard fruit trees.

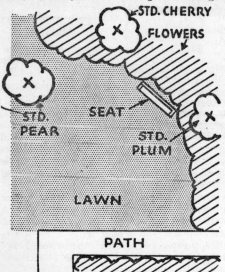

Fig. 13. *This plan shows how fruit trees can be used decoratively in border or lawn.*

Large gardens might frequently include an orchard belt between two sections of the flower garden, or a group of orchard trees might be used to separate the flower garden from any unsightly but necessary feature, such as a potting shed or greenhouses. Without going so far as to say that fruit trees should always be first choice, one might say that fruit trees should be considered first, and the purely ornamental trees only substituted after careful deliberation.

The various types of fruit trees, as illustrated in Fig. 14, all have their special use in a mixed planting scheme. Let us consider these types, and how they are formed.

A standard tree is a tree which is restricted to a single stem where it rises from the ground level, but is allowed to branch out and form a bushy, spreading head at some distance from the ground. For general convenience certain height classifications are

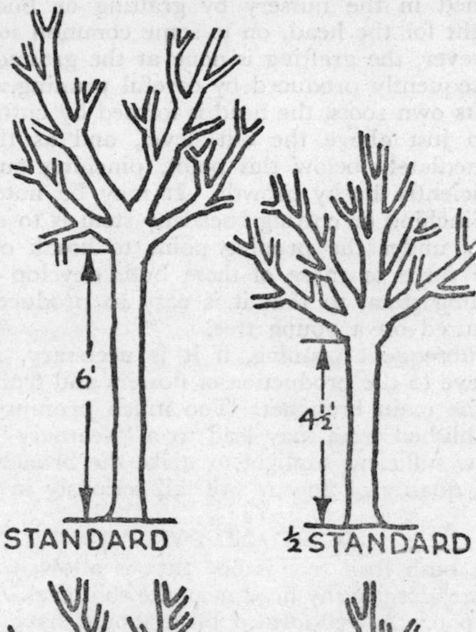

Fig. 14. *How to distinguish the four types of untrained fruit trees.*

universally adopted. For instance, a standard fruit tree usually has a bare main stem up to a height of 6 ft., while the term " half-standard " refers to a tree with about $4\frac{1}{2}$ ft. of bare stem.

As a rule a fruit tree grown naturally will not be a standard but will be of rather bushy character, and the standard is therefore an **artificial** production. In a great many cases standards are formed in the nursery by grafting or budding, at the required height for the head, on to some common stock (Chapter III). If, however, the grafting is done at the ground level, and a standard subsequently produced by careful pruning, or if the tree is grown on its own roots, the head is formed by cutting the top of the main stem just above the 6-ft. level, and as the side shoots develop immediately below this point, pinching out the tips to induce a sufficiently bushy growth. It may be noted here that the effect of pinching or cutting back any stem is to cause the buds immediately under the pruning point to break out into growth. As a rule three or more of these buds develop in place of the single, leading stem, so that it is easy to produce as many branches as required on a young tree.

Subsequent pruning, if it is necessary, is generally done with an eye to the production of flowers and fruits, and to the extension of the main branches. Too much pruning of the leaders on old-established trees may lead to a " feathery " growth that does not allow sufficient sunlight to strike the branches, and the production and quality of flowers will fall seriously in consequence.

BUSH AND PYRAMID FRUIT TREES

A bush fruit tree is one that is allowed or encouraged to form a spreading bushy head near the soil level. Fig. 15 shows how this is done. A well-formed bush should have several stems radiating from the main stem near to the ground level—generally 18 in. or 2 ft. from the ground, as such bushes are more easily managed. It is difficult to cultivate between bushes that have no clear main stem. In the proper bush type of tree there is no central trunk to the head of the tree, but only radiating branches with an open centre that allows plenty of sunshine to reach all parts of the tree.

A pyramid tree is somewhat similar to the bush type, but in this case the central main trunk is retained, and side shoots spring from this at various points, making a pyramidal silhouette to the tree.

The single-cordon tree (Fig. 10) is the simplest form of trained tree. In this the growth is restricted to a single main stem, and all side branches are cut away. Properly grown a cordon should be studded closely with blossom and fruit " spurs " throughout its entire length. Neglect of pruning for a single season will ruin a cordon-trained tree, and no grower should embark on this form of fruit culture unless he can give the necessary small attentions at the right season. The pruning is not difficult, and is an interesting hobby. Moreover, it results in fruit of the finest possible quality, and plenty of it.

Other trained trees are merely variations of the single cordon.

The double or treble cordon is, as the names imply, just a tree with two or three cordons instead of one.

Fan-trained trees (Fig. 11) are trees grown in a single plane, to train on walls or fences. The cordon-like branches radiate from a point near the ground, fan-wise. Espalier trees (Fig. 11) are trees with an upright central stem and side branches at regular intervals trained horizontally, giving the effect of a double staircase.

Most fruits can be grown in any of these ways, but the slightly tender fruits that need warm sunshine to ripen them, such as nectarines, apricots and peaches, are generally best as wall-trained trees on a south wall, since this gives them a warm situation. Cherries, except the Morello cherry, are not very suitable for wall culture, and stone fruits generally are better grown as fans than espalier trained. The Morello cherry does very well indeed on the north side of a wall.

Before turning to the details of culture of each fruit, it is worth while to mention a point which affects chiefly the grower of a single specimen tree. Certain varieties of various fruits are not self-fertile. That is to say, if they are grown by themselves, and not near to any other fruit trees whose blossom is open at the same time, they do not set their fruit, the reason being that the pollen from their own flowers will not fertilize the waiting stigma. They require pollen from some other different tree and in some cases only certain varieties will cross-pollinate successfully. Cherries are particularly difficult in this matter, and the Morello (cooking)

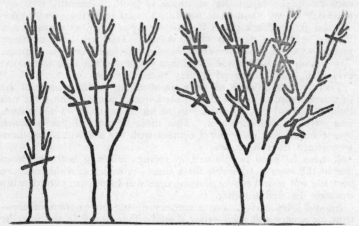

Fig. 15. *Where to prune a bush apple for the first three years, to obtain the necessary thick bush near the ground.*

cherry is the only variety that is completely self-fertile. Sweet cherries should only be planted where they can be planted in pairs, or where a neighbour grows cherries too. In districts where a good deal of fruit is grown this difficulty does not often arise, but in thickly populated areas, where perhaps only a few isolated fruit gardens exist, care should be taken over selection. Any fruit grower will advise on this point as far as he is able (full statistics on every variety are not available), and will suggest trees that are self-fertile for specimen planting.

Fruit trees are deciduous trees, and the planting season is therefore at any time from about October until March. Early winter is certainly the best time, as the roots can establish themselves during the resting season. It is sometimes thought that roots are not active during the frosty weather, but this has been proved wrong. Plants grow a little even under a mantle of snow, and when frosts do not penetrate far into the soil, the roots are active even though there is little visible top growth. Planting a new orchard should thus be regarded as an October or November task.

PREPARING THE ORCHARD SOIL

All soils should be prepared in the usual way described in Chapter II, with the object of bringing the surface soil layer to the state of maximum fertility, and if the depth of fertile soil is considerable, the fruit will be all the better. Digging should, therefore, be done to a minimum depth of nearly 2 ft., and great care should be taken that drainage is good. Generally it is not necessary to use manure at planting time, but in the case of poor dry soil it is advantageous if a heavy layer of rotted manure can be put in below the top 18 in. of soil. This will hold moisture in dry weather, and prevent loss of plant food through seepage. The manure should never come into direct contact with the roots; even if it is well decayed it may cause damage.

Fruit trees are best if set on a slight mound in the middle of the prepared deep wide hole, and staked immediately. The roots can then be spread out like the ribs of an open umbrella all round, and covered with fine soil. This must be pressed firmly down over the roots, as only direct contact with the soil will allow them to perform their function.

If trees have to be planted in spring, watering both overhead and at the roots is advisable for a time. A mulch of stable manure over the soil round newly planted trees will help them considerably through the first summer.

Should trees arrive from a nursery during inclement weather— frost, or a very wet spell—they should either be left in the packing straw for a couple of days or, if the bad weather continues, they can be taken out and " heeled in " to some moist frost-free soil in a sheltered corner of the garden. It is important that the roots should not become frosted or dry out completely, but it is not wise to set them in water, as this may cause them to decay.

When you stake a fruit tree, arrange the ties so that the bark is not rubbed. A piece of rubber tyre bound round the tree trunk before the tie is made is useful. All newly planted trees—even bushes—are best staked. If they sway only a little in the wind some of the finer root hairs are torn, and the tree suffers accordingly.

A point to watch as you plant is to see that the roots are not torn or broken, and if there are damaged roots to cut them cleanly away with a sharp knife. Ragged wounds allow disease spores to enter, and set up decay.

One item that sometimes puzzles amateurs is the question of the age at which a fruit tree may be safely moved. There is no rule about this, as so much depends on the history of the tree. In nurseries, trees for sale are frequently moved and induced to form fibrous roots near the main stem. Such trees can be moved without serious damage to the root system. Trees that have grown in the amateur's own garden for many years are more likely to be damaged fatally in the course of removal, for they have probably made a wide spreading root system. The fine root hairs are the parts of the root that actually feed the plant, and if these are torn, the plant must suffer temporarily.

DANGER OF MOVING OLD TREES

It is scarcely possible (without the special machinery which landscape contractors use to remove large trees) to move a well-established tree and to keep soil intact over the fibrous roots. Generally the thick roots have to be cut through in order to move an old tree at all. Then it is more or less a gamble as to whether the tree will be able to make more fibrous roots near the main stem with sufficient rapidity to recover from the shock.

For the sake of easy reference, and to help small garden owners, who may consult this chapter only for the sake of one or two trees, the essentials of cultivation, pruning and feeding various fruits are given here, the fruits being arranged in alphabetical order. Some of the facts will have to be repeated, as they apply to most fruits, but this procedure seems to make for simplicity.

Apple. Apples can be grown as bushes or standards, 10 or 12 ft. apart, according to the intention of the grower. If it is intended to establish a small orchard, and not to prune more than is necessary, 12 ft. should be allowed. In the small garden 10 ft. is ample, but the nurseryman should be asked to supply trees on dwarfing stock.

Apples can also be used as espaliers, horizontally trained to walls and planted 15 ft. apart, or as cordons planted only a yard apart.

Winter pruning of bush and standard apples is most important when once a proper skeleton of radiating branches has been formed. It consists of cutting back the small new side growths of the previous summer to leave two or three leaf buds. A leaf bud is distinguished from a flower bud by the fact that it is more pointed. At the same time, leading growths are shortened a little.

On an established fruiting apple there should also be at the base of the previous summer's growth a number of dormant flower buds, on the short " spurs " left after the last season's pruning. Summer pruning, when practised, is designed to encourage the tree to form such flower buds on the spurs. Summer pruning is done about August Bank Holiday, but the exact date for pruning is a matter for experienced judgment. When you summer prune, you pinch out the growing tip from the side growths, and leave four or five good leaves only. If you prune too early in the season, the tree will merely branch out again into unwanted feathery growth, but if you prune at the right moment it will begin to form fruiting buds or spurs as desired. Some apples are shy of spur formation, and fruit best if left to grow as naturally as possible. A good rule to remember is shorten the leaders or main branches in winter, prevent crowded growth, and try to keep the apple to a skeleton of cordons radiating from the main trunk so that the sunlight reaches each one.

Winter pruning can be carried out when convenient, but not later than February and not when there are very severe frosts about.

FERTILIZERS FOR APPLES

The feeding of apples is important, particularly potash feeding. Generally speaking, you can tell what foods are deficient in the soil by watching the trees. If a tree grows well and makes long new tips to its leaders and plenty of leaf growth, it has a sufficiency of nitrogen. If it flowers well it has sufficient phosphates. If it appears generally healthy, free from disease and with plenty of colour in flower and foliage and fruit, it has sufficient potash. If the edges of the leaves turn brown, potash is probably lacking. If the centres of the leaves turn brown, the tree needs phosphates.

An annual dressing of lime in the winter, and of kainit in autumn or winter, is advisable on apples, and both supply potash (kainit contains potash, and lime releases it from the soil).

Sulphate of ammonia or nitrate of soda applied in spring will supply nitrogen. Basic slag in autumn on heavy, rich soils, or super-phosphate of lime in spring on light soils, will supply phosphates.

Apples fed and pruned carefully are not troubled so readily by pests and diseases, but a certain amount of preventive spraying should be done. Bordeaux mixture or lime sulphur are useful for mildew and similar diseases, but care should be taken not to apply these too strong.

Pests include such general pests as greenfly and woolly aphis.

Greenfly is controlled by any ordinary insecticide used as a spray or dust. Woolly aphis, which resembles bits of cotton-wool on the bark, is best attacked by painting the patches with methylated spirit or petrol. The maggot of the apple sawfly causes fruits to drop in early summer. The remedy is to dust Derris powder over the branches and leaves in the late evening.

Codlin moth causes fruit dropping later in the season, and this is a troublesome pest to eradicate. The use of soil fumigant in early spring, tar-oil winter wash, and traps of sacking are ways to treat it. Sacking should be folded fanwise and pushed into the fork of the branches in August. In winter the sacking can be removed and burnt or dropped into strong insecticide. The alternative treatment for codlin moth is to use arsenic spray before and after the flowers open, but as there is a slight danger of the spray remaining after the fruit ripens, this should be considered only as a last resort in the home garden. (For varieties of apples, *see* lists.)

Apricot. Apricots are grown only as wall trees in most British gardens, preferably fan trained and 15 ft. apart on a south wall. They like rather dry soil in summer. To encourage fruit, allow one stem of one-year-old growth to remain at each joint on the main stems. The fruit should form on this stem, and when the flower has opened, all leaf buds, except one at the tip and two at the base, should be rubbed away. After the fruit has stoned, the top can be cut away and the basal buds will grow into fresh shoots. Both or one of these can be retained again when winter pruning is done.

While the tree is young, some new growth should be allowed on the leaders, but long spindly new growths at the tip should be shortened severely, and the feeding of the tree adjusted accordingly (*see* "Apples"). The use of stable manure often causes vigorous growth, but too rapid expansion may mean that too much wood remains between the joints, so that fruits are sparsely situated on the mature tree.

Cherry. Cherries are grown as standards, pyramids or bushes, and as fan-trained trees on walls. A full-grown standard cherry takes up a great deal of room—30 to 40 ft.—and the cherry in this form is therefore not very suitable for small gardens. The Morello cherry, which makes an ideal fan-trained tree to grow on north walls, is on the contrary one of the best of small garden fruits.

Cherries, like most stone fruits, should be pruned as little as possible, and it is best to prune only young wood. If an old branch must be cut away, the wound should be clean and lead paint or other preservative which will exclude moisture and germs should be used immediately over the scar. This will prevent disease from entering. Such cuts on stone fruits are inclined to " bleed," and should only be made where absolutely necessary.

Sweet cherries are particularly infertile when planted as isolated specimens, and they should always be planted in pairs (*see* lists). Morello cherries can be pruned as already advised for apricots. They are self-fertile.

The cherry sawfly is the chief pest that attacks cherries. Derris dust used over the foliage when the maggot is first seen is a useful deterrent. Arsenate of lead sprays are also effective, though arsenic is generally to be avoided in the small garden. Soil fumigants help to keep down the pest.

Lime is essential for success with cherries except where they grow on chalky subsoil. Other artificials can be used as recommended for apples.

Peach. Peaches and nectarines are, in most districts, only suitable for south walls. They are usually fan trained, though occasionally cordons are obtainable. They are cultivated and pruned like apricots, but whereas apricots after a few years of pruning begin to make spurs like apples, nectarines and peaches do not do this but fruit along the wood of the last summer's development. These trees prefer plenty of soil moisture, and a mulch of stable manure in summer is a help. Otherwise use fertilizers according to the condition of the tree as described for apples.

Pear. Pears are grown as pyramids, bushes, standards, espaliers or cordons, the distance for each being similar to that needed for apples. They will grow well on walls facing east or west, and though the instructions given for pruning apples also apply to pears there is often little need after the " head " has been formed.

The pear sawfly is sometimes very troublesome, and is difficult to cure. It attacks the pears early, and the maggot causes the young pears to drop. Dressing a soil fumigant over the soil surface when the blossom is open is a deterrent to the fly which causes the trouble.

Plum. Plums and damsons are definitely labour-saving fruits, since they need a minimum of pruning when once the skeleton of the tree has been formed. They are best grown as standards or bushes, from 10 to 15 ft. apart. Finger and thumb pruning in the early stages of the tree's life is the best pruning, as these fruits are very liable to gumming. Kainit and basic slag in winter, with an annual dressing of lime given also during winter, preferably a month later, is good for plums. Tar-oil as a winter wash is desirable, to keep down pests.

Gooseberry, Currant and Raspberry. These soft fruits are best grown in separate plantations. When planting they should be spaced about 5 ft. apart each way, the raspberries being set in groups of three canes with this distance between the groups. Alternatively, the raspberries can be grown in lines, allowing 5 ft. between the rows and 18 in. between every two canes.

Fertilizers can be used according to the behaviour of the plants, remembering the need for potash as well as for leaf-forming nitrates and flower-forming phosphates. Liberal use of stable manure as a summer mulch pays with all these fruits.

Gooseberries and red currants are pruned in winter, side growths of the previous summer being cut back sufficiently to keep a cordon-like skeleton of branches.

Black currants fruit on new wood of the previous season's growth. After the fruits are gathered, as much old wood as possible should be cut right away, leaving only new stems to carry the next season's crop. Unless water and food supplies are good, there will not be sufficient new growth for the purpose, and stable manure as a summer mulch is therefore particularly good for black currants.

Raspberries fruit on new canes. The way to prune them is to cut out entirely all the old canes when the fruit has been gathered, and then to pull out any canes that are not required to take their place, leaving only about half a dozen canes to each stool.

The chief pests of these soft fruits are big bud and raspberry maggot. Big bud is a mite that causes black currant buds to swell instead of developing properly into leaf growth. It is kept under control by spraying with lime sulphur in spring when the foliage is the size of a shilling.

Raspberry maggot hatches from eggs deposited by beetles that visit the open blossoms. Dusting Derris powder well into the open flowers is the only satisfactory cure, but as the flowers open in succession for many days, the dusting must be repeated about every two days during the blossom time.

Loganberry and Blackberry and similar hybrid fruits are grown and pruned much like raspberries. That is, they develop long canes from the base, and these are cut away each season after they have carried their fruits, the new canes being tied into their place on the provided supports.

These fruits can take almost any amount of feeding, and will respond accordingly. A heavy mulch of stable manure in summer and occasional pailfuls of water at the roots will result in exceptionally good crops. The raspberry maggot also attacks these two fruits.

Strawberry. The strawberry is a fruit which commends itself to the home gardener chiefly on account of its superior flavour when freshly gathered. It takes a considerable amount of garden space, and must not be relegated to any shady, or even half shady, position. Strawberries do not last in full bearing more than three seasons, and the common practice is to plant one-third of the strawberry patch fresh each season. This is generally done in August or September after the crop, when freshly rooted runners are available.

The plants are set in rows $2\frac{1}{2}$ ft. apart, 18 in. being allowed between the plants in the row. They are grown on with ordinary care over hoeing until the flowers appear, and then clean straw is laid down along the rows, so that the fruits will not be damaged by mud splashes when rains occur. Any runners that are seen are cut away the first season, and in the second and third season only a few runners—sufficient to re-make one-third of the patch—are allowed to develop. These will root themselves naturally as a rule, but it pays to peg each one into the soil, and give it a little fresh sifted soil to help the roots to form. When this has happened, the new runners can be moved at once to their intended quarters, or, if more practicable, they can be potted up temporarily and grown on until the plot is ready for them.

Good fertilizers for strawberries are an ounce of sulphate of ammonia and three of superphosphate per square yard in spring, and an ounce of sulphate of potash in winter. Should growth be poor, use a little nitrate of soda in liquid form after the fruit has set.

Some of the less common fruits may commend themselves to the garden maker. Nuts of various kinds, quinces, mulberries, outdoor grapes, figs and medlars can all be grown with ease in most gardens. Pruning grape vines under glass is described in Chapter IX.

The ways and means of protecting fruit bushes from the ravages of birds is always rather a problem in the small garden. The best time to think about it is before the bushes are planted, as by far the most effective method is to build a wire cage over the whole fruit area. It should be high enough to allow a person to go right in and pick the fruit comfortably. Caging is illustrated in Fig. 16.

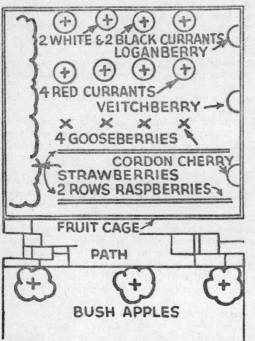

Fig. 16. *Planting soft fruits for caging. The cost of caging necessitates careful planning.*

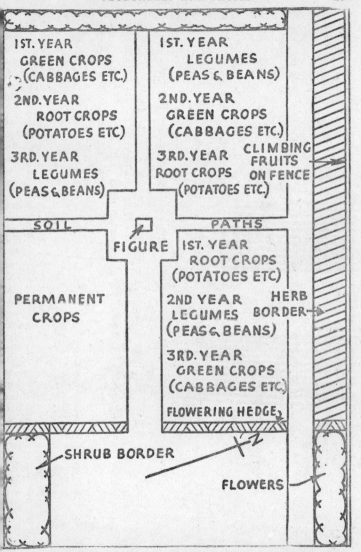

ROTATION OF CROPS IN THE KITCHEN GARDEN

VEGETABLE SOWING CALENDAR

Name	Time to sow or plant	When ready	Remarks
Artichoke, Globe ..	Plant March and April, 2–3 ft. apart	June to October	These do not bear well the first year; the flowerhead bracts are eaten.
,, Jerusalem	Plant Feb. to March, rows 3 ft. apart	Nov. to March	—
Asparagus	Plant April, 15 in. apart	Three years after sowing	Care must be given during the first few years, then it will bear prolifically for many seasons.
Bean, Broad ..	Sow Nov. to January, 2–3 ft. between double rows	June and July	Need well-manured soil.
,, Dwarf French	Sow May, rows 1½–2 ft. apart	June to July	Very early and late crops must be sown under glass.
,, Runner ..	May and June, rows 6–8 ft. apart	July to Oct.	Early crops should be sown in boxes and planted out in June.
Beetroot	Sow April to July, rows 4–5 ft. apart	Late autumn to October	Beet will grow on any soil; animal manure must be kept from the roots.

Broccoli, Autumn..
   ,, Winter ..
   ,, Spring ..
   ,, Summer ..
	Sow March to May Plant May to July, 12–15 in. apart	Sept. to June	All plants should be transplanted as soon as possible.

Brussels Sprouts ..	Sow March and April rows 2–3 ft. apart Plant May and June	Sept. to April	Should be picked after frosts. Do not cut tops until stalks have completely ripened.

Cabbage (Spring sown) (Autumn sown)	Plant early August	Sept. to Feb.	Requires a well-manured soil in good position. Should be hoed occasionally.
Carrot	March to May, rows 1½–2 ft. apart Sow March to early August	May to July June onwards. In October lift and store in ashes	Requires a well-cultivated soil.
Cauliflower (Spring sown) (Autumn sown)	Plant April to July, 2–2½ ft. between rows Sept. to February April, rows 4 ft. apart	All the year	—
Celery	Sow March, plant May 12 in. between rows	August to Oct.	Preferably grown in well-watered trenches.
Chicory	Sow May, 4 ft. between rows	October to Feb.	Blanch leaves by lifting plants and standing in a cool place in fine damp soil.
Cucumber (Outdoor)	Sow April, 12–15 in. between rows	August to Sept.	Requires plenty of manure and moisture.
Endive		June to October	Blanch by covering plants with flower-pots, three weeks before use.
Leek	Sow Feb. and March Plant May or June, 18 in. between rows	Can be left in ground until required for use in winter	Large specimens require plenty of manure. Blanch by covering with collars of brown paper.
Lettuce	Sow March, with successional sowing throughout the summer	June onwards	Moisture promotes rapid growth which is necessary. Soil should be prepared some time before planting.

VEGETABLE SOWING CALENDAR—continued

Name	Time to sow or plant	When ready	Remarks
Onion (Spring) ..	Sow under glass in Feb. Plant out in May, 9–12 in. between rows	September Finished off in dry open shed	Can be hung up and kept all the winter in a dry place.
" (Winter) ..	Sow in August, set out in February	June to Oct.	Useful for supplementing the spring-sown stock.
Parsley	Sow March to July, 12 in. between rows	All the year round	—
Parsnip	Sow Feb. and March, 18 in. between rows	Nov. to March	—
Pea (Early) ..	Sow February and March	June	Before sowing, soak seeds in paraffin to keep off the birds.
" (Second Early) ..	Sow March and April	June and July	—
" (Maincrop) ..	Sow April to June	July to Sept.	Deeply dug, well-manured soil. A mulch will help to retain moisture in latest sown crops.
Potato (Early) ..	Plant Feb. to March, 18–36 in. between rows	June	Potatoes should be sprouted before being planted.
" (Maincrop) ..	Plant April, 18–36 in. between rows	July, August, etc.	Soot is beneficial to the crops.
Radish	Sow March to Sept.	All the year round	—
" (Winter) ..	Sow June to August	—	—
Rhubarb	Plant spring and autumn, 3–4 ft. between rows		—

Seakale	Plant March and April, 2½ ft. between rows	November. Lift and store in moist sand	—
Shallot	February and March, 9–12 in. between rows	Lift in July when top withers; store until required	Will grow in any soil.
Spinach, (Summer) ..	Sow Feb. to August July to September, 12–15 in. between rows	May to January	—
,, (Winter) ..	April to July, 12 in. between rows		
,, (Perpetual) .			
Swede	Sow April to July, 15 in. between rows	Oct. to March	—
Tomato (Indoor) ..	Sow Jan. to March under glass	May to October	—
,, (Outdoor) ..	Plant out in May, 18–24 in. between rows	August to Oct.	—
Turnip	Sow March to August, 12–15 in. between rows	July to Nov.	Sow early crops in January in heat. Thin out as soon as possible. For "tops," sow in September and leave unthinned.
Vegetable Marrow .	Sow March, 4–5 f. between rows	July to Nov.	Allow plenty of moisture and manure.

FRUIT FOR THE SMALL GARDEN

(S.S.=Self Sterile   S.F.=Self Fertile)

Name		Variety	Picking time
APPLES	Culinary	Early Victoria (Bush)	Early August.
		Lane's Prince Albert (Bush)	Early October.
		Bramley's Seedlings (Half-standard)	Mid-October.
	Dessert	Worcester Pearmain (Bush)	Early September.
		James Grieve (Bush)	Mid-September.
		Ellison's Orange (Bush)	Mid-September.
		Laxton's Superb (Bush)	Late September.
		Cox's Orange Pippin (Bush)	Early September.
		Blenheim Orange (Bush)	Mid-October.
APRICOT	—	New Large Early (needs wall).	August.
BERRIES	Red	Loganberry	Early August.
		Phenomenal Berry	Mid-August.
		Veitchberry	August.
	Black	Bedford Giant Blackberry	Late July.
		Himalaya Berry	Early August.
		Parsley-leaved Blackberry	Late August.

CHERRIES	Dessert (Black)(White)	Black Heart (S.S.)	} All pollinate each other	July–August.
		Early Rivers (S.S.)		
		Napoleon (S.S.)		
		Governor Wood (S.S.)		
	Culinary	Morello (S.F.)		
CURRANTS	Red	Raby Castle (Late)	..	Early July.
		Earliest of Fore ands (Early)	..	End of June.
	Black	Boskoop Giant (Early)	..	Mid-June.
		Baldwin (Late)	..	July.
	White	White Versailles (Early)	..	End of June.
DAMSON	—	Farleigh Damson (S.F.)	..	Mid-September.
FIG	—	Brown Turkey (outside or under glass)	..	August.
GOOSEBERRIES	Red	Lancashire Lad (bottling, culinary or dessert) (Mid-season)	..	June.
	Yellow	Leveller (Mid-season)	..	June.
	Green	Keepsake (Late)	..	Early July.
MEDLAR	—	Nottingham ..	..	October to early November.
MULBERRY	—	Black (Common) Mulberry	..	August to September.
NECTARINE	—	Early Rivers ..	..	End July.
		Lord Napier ..	..	Early August.

FRUIT FOR THE SMALL GARDEN—continued

(S.S.=Self Sterile.　　S.F=Self Fertile).

Name		Variety	Picking time
NUTS	—	Kentish Cobs	End of September.
		Pearson's Prolific	End of September.
PEACH	Outside	Peregrine	Early August.
		Bellegarde	Mid-September.
PEARS	Dessert or Culinary	Williams's Bon Chrétien	Late August.
		Beurre Superfin } Bush or	Mid-September.
		Conference (S.F.) } Standards	Late September.
		Doyenne du Comice ..	Early October.
PLUMS	Dessert	Early Transparent Gage (S.F.)	Mid-August.
		Coe's Golden Drop (S.S.) ..	Mid-September.
		Czar (S.F.)	Early August.
	Culinary	Victoria (S.F.)	Late August.
		Green Gage (S.S.)	Late August.
QUINCE	—	Bereczki	August.
RASPBERRIES	—	Lloyd George (Mid-Season) ..	End of June.
		Pyne's Royal (light soil only)	Early June.
STRAWBERRIES	—	Royal Sovereign (Early) ..	Early June.
		Sir Joseph Paxton (Mid-Season)	June.
WALNUT	—	Meylanaise	September.

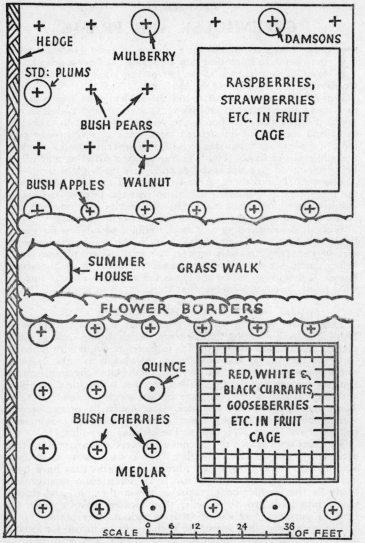

HEDGE

MULBERRY

DAMSONS

STD: PLUMS

BUSH PEARS

RASPBERRIES, STRAWBERRIES ETC. IN FRUIT CAGE

BUSH APPLES

WALNUT

SUMMER HOUSE

GRASS WALK

FLOWER BORDERS

QUINCE

BUSH CHERRIES

RED, WHITE & BLACK CURRANTS, GOOSEBERRIES ETC. IN FRUIT CAGE

MEDLAR

SCALE 0 6 12 24 36 OF FEET

A LAYOUT FOR A SMALL MIXED ORCHARD

CHAPTER IX

GREENHOUSE AND FRAME

THERE comes a stage in the evolution of most gardeners when they begin to think that they would like to have a greenhouse. Well, if you happen to be just at this stage, here are a few words of advice from one of the old hands.

First of all, think well all round the subject, and weigh up the pros and cons before you embark on gardening under glass of any kind. Frames and greenhouses are very exacting. You cannot go away and leave them unattended for a week at a time—nor even for a week-end—without danger of losing several months' work in a single night or day. (Plants in frames often suffer as much from being left closed on a sunny day as open on a frosty night !)

If you can afford them, there are electrical and gas heaters that are controlled by automatic means, so that the heat is kept within defined limits, but even these cannot regulate the sunshine and ventilation, or spray the plants overhead when necessary.

Without recommending any special choice of subjects for greenhouses, it may be as well to run through the season, noting what sort of tasks are necessary among the various greenhouse plants before coming to any definite decisions, as to how to use the greenhouse. The novice will be able from this general survey to sort out what plants he *can* grow from what he *would like* to grow.

THE GREENHOUSE THROUGH THE YEAR

There is no New Year under glass—that is to say, there is no beginning to the season, since every month brings rest to some plants and maturity to others. Let us therefore begin with January.

At the turn of the year—i.e., when days begin to grow longer—the greenhouse shelves will be gay with late chrysanthemums (quickly passing), cyclamen *persicum*, freesias, poinsettias, primulas, and the earliest of the common bulbs—narcissus, hyacinth, etc. There may also be fibrous begonias, ericas of sorts, the orange-berried winter cherry, and perhaps some winter-flowering carnations, and pelargonium, otherwise known as the bedding geranium.

The chief work among the greenhouse flowers in January is starting such tubers as gloxinias, repotting soft wooded plants as needed, starting into fresh growth such shrubs as fuchsias that have been stored dry for the winter and are to be forced into new growth ready for the summer beds, restarting chrysanthemums and similar plants into fresh growth in order that cuttings may be taken for bedding purposes, and sowing seeds of various other plants.

The greenhouse that serves the kitchen will be in use for forcing chicory, seakale, and rhubarb. Seed sowing will also begin—

tomatoes, cucumbers, aubergines, leeks, and other vegetables wanted early, or for which a long period of growth is desirable.

Strawberries intended for forcing are brought into the greenhouse from the frames in January, but there is not much work needed among other glasshouse fruits.

To keep up the temperature without making the house unduly close is important in mid-winter. Ventilation should be given daily, but all windows should be closed an hour before sundown. Keep the glass as clean as possible, as this allows the maximum sunlight to enter. Light is more important than warmth.

Spring bulbs, cyclamen and heather, and a number of primulas are still with us in February. To these will be added the sweet-scented Boronia *megastigma*, arum lilies and lilies of the valley. The frames this month will give us plenty of sweet violets.

Most flowers under glass need a temperature of 40 to 50 degrees Fahrenheit just now, and the gardener will need some heat to maintain this in most seasons.

Propagation of bedding plants from cuttings, seed sowing, and the restarting of dahlias, begonias, fuchsias, geraniums and similar plants occupies the gardener's time very fully. The shelves above the warm pipes are needed to start seeds and tubers, but when growth is active the seed boxes will require all the light they can get. They will then be moved to the shelves nearest the glass—a high shelf only a few inches lower than the roof is desirable. Under the shelves which are full of flowers will stand the various boxes of seakale, rhubarb, chicory, and so on that need heat without light. Cinerarias and other plants coming into flower will take the place of the late chrysanthemums, which, as soon as they have developed fresh basal shoots, will be broken or cut into pieces for the propagating frame or pit.

FRUIT GROWING UNDER GLASS

Fruit growing under glass will be pruned, and cleaned as necessary. Fertilization of glasshouse fruits is important, and the use of a camel-hair brush to fertilize the flowers by hand is desirable, in the absence of bees and other insects.

Greenhouse pests often turn up in large numbers at this season, and fumigation should be carried out where necessary.

All kinds of vegetables can now be raised from seed, to grow on under glass or in the open.

Azaleas, camellias, genista, pyrus *floribunda*, lilacs, and spiræas are among the greenhouse shrubs in flower in March. Shrubs forced for the greenhouse shelves are usually grown naturally in alternate seasons, and only brought into the greenhouse once in two years. Cinerarias should now be plentiful.

Seed sowing and pricking out, repotting ferns and palms, pot plants, and the caring for all glasshouse inhabitants in the matters of moisture, warmth and ventilation are the work for the month.

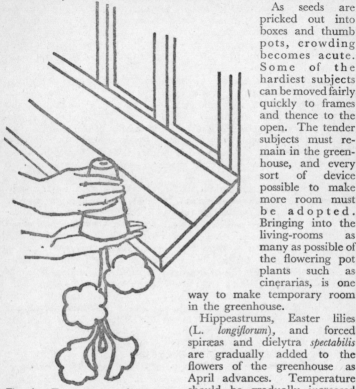

As seeds are pricked out into boxes and thumb pots, crowding becomes acute. Some of the hardiest subjects can be moved fairly quickly to frames and thence to the open. The tender subjects must remain in the greenhouse, and every sort of device possible to make more room must be adopted. Bringing into the living-rooms as many as possible of the flowering pot plants such as cinerarias, is one way to make temporary room in the greenhouse.

Hippeastrums, Easter lilies (L. *longiflorum*), and forced spiræas and dielytra *spectabilis* are gradually added to the flowers of the greenhouse as April advances. Temperature should be gradually increased (45 to 65), and water will be required by developing plants. Scorching may occur on hot sunny days, so shade seedlings and susceptible plants.

Fig. 1. To unpot a plant, turn upside down, supporting soil with right hand, holding pot with left.

Cuttings of new growth can be taken of dahlias, fuchsias, and other plants, and seeds of annuals, vegetables, melons, etc., can be sown. Fertilization of fruit blossom must receive attention.

The removal, in May, of half-hardy plants to frames for hardening off should ease the congestion in the greenhouse. Amateurs who use their glass only for seed raising and winter storage, and for occasional propagation by cuttings, will soon be able to empty it temporarily while shelves are scrubbed, paintwork renovated and the glass cleaned.

Strawberries forced in pots will be ready to gather, and other fruits will need a good deal of attention just now—syringing, fertilizing, finger and thumb pruning, etc. May flowers under glass include those of last month, with early roses, etc.

All bedding plants will leave the frames in June, and greenhouse cleaning and renovation need not be delayed. If tender subjects are flowering in the greenhouse, or coming into flower, they can usually be sheltered for a day or two during the hot weather in a frame, or under a south wall, while renovations take place.

Such good pot plants as torenias, salvias, and begonias are splendid for small greenhouses, and should make a brave show on the sunny shelves just now.

Expensive seeds of perennial and biennial flowers will be sown as other tasks permit, particularly seeds of primulas, cinerarias, cyclamen, etc., for next season (if not already sown in May).

Azaleas, hydrangeas, and other shrubs that have flowered in the greenhouse should be put outdoors in July until mid-September.

THE SECOND HALF OF THE YEAR

Potting on (i.e., moving a plant to a larger pot) of seedlings of cyclamen, primulas, cinerarias, etc., is work that must not be delayed. The correct way to remove a plant from its pot is shown in Fig. 1.

Carnations, ripening tomatoes, cucumbers, and other greenhouse crops are popular inhabitants of little greenhouses at this season. Many greenhouse annuals should be in flower.

Plenty of ventilation without draughts, and shading where needed are important.

The blue African lily (agapanthus), heliotropes, plumbago *capensis* (towards the end of the month), lilies and passion flowers are with us in August, side by side with pots of annuals and gladiolas.

August is a busy month where propagation is done on a large scale. All sorts of half-hardy plants such as heliotropes can be propagated from cuttings struck now under glass, and later grown on in the cool greenhouse for early flowering next season. For cuttings in a pot, *see* Fig. 2.

Freesias, and as soon as supplies are available, the Roman hyacinths and narcissi, wanted for Christmas flowering will be potted now.

Potting on into flowering pots will be required among cyclamen, cinerarias, chrysanthemums, and many other greenhouse plants.

August flowers continue into September, and are joined by the earliest of the greenhouse chrysanthemums and some of the late flowering heaths. Fuchsias are looking well this month, and such annuals as ricinus are glad of the shelter of the greenhouse towards

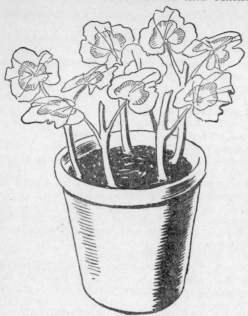

Fig. 2. Insert cuttings round side of pot.

the end of September.

Less overhead moisture, and possibly more heat, with shading removed, will be the chief alterations in procedure now.

All climbers, shrubs, and other plants that have finished flowering should be trimmed back and relegated to some part of the greenhouse where sunlight is less plentiful, while the lightest shelves will become occupied by chrysanthemums, winter-flowering carnations and other winter-flowering subjects.

More cuttings can be taken, and more bulbs must be potted up for early flowering. Stocks, pansies and other annuals sown in the garden in summer can be potted up to flower under glass.

Vegetables such as cauliflowers, etc., can now be sown as desired.

Begonias, crinums, camellias, and a blaze of chrysanthemums keep the October greenhouse gay.

Sweet peas can be sown now under glass to winter in the cold frames; arum lilies, and still more spring bulbs, including the bulbous irises, ixias, etc., can be potted up. Some of the shrubs—e.g. roses—to be flowered under glass can now be brought indoors.

Salads can be sown, and the first roots of rhubarb forced.

Chrysanthemums rule the greenhouse in November, though there are still some annuals, begonias, and the late pots of salvia that are gay. Salvia *splendens* and the scarlet schizostylis are two brilliant subjects for the November greenhouse. Lilies of the valley can be potted for forcing, and plants such as dielytra, spiræa, azaleas, may be potted up also for early flowering under glass.

French beans, and small salads, can be sown, but only where

plenty of heat is available. Salads that grow slowly are barely eatable. Seakale, etc., can be forced.

The first of the spring bulbs—narcissi paperwhite and Roman hyacinths—fill the greenhouse shelf in December. The earliest of forced shrubs are also coming into bloom, and Christmas roses (Helleborus *niger*) growing under hand lights or in the frames are opening their buds. More chrysanthemums and begonias and winter carnations are in bloom.

The early flowering bulbs can be brought gradually into more heat and forced into early flower. More potting of lilies of the valley for succession, and a start with the forcing of the main supply of small potted shrubs such as deutzias, lilacs and roses can be made.

A minimum temperature of 40 degrees should be aimed at in any greenhouse, and sharp watch kept for pests or diseases.

Fruits under glass are restarted into growth, and strawberries in pots are brought into the greenhouse now for early supplies.

The reader who has patiently read through the above resumé of greenhouse operations will have gathered that to take charge of a single greenhouse is an exacting task. If a constant succession of loveliness is our aim, we must be prepared to keep our plants ever on the move. This means also that space must be strictly apportioned and used always to the best advantage.

We might discuss here the various types of glasshouse, and show how much or how little space is available in each. Owners of single houses cannot usually exercise much choice in the matter, but they can exercise choice in the plants they try to cultivate, and it is very wise to limit that choice severely from the first.

The ideal one-structure glasshouse is a span-roof greenhouse with the ridge of the roof running from north to south (Fig. 3). The door should be on the south side, so that keen cold winds from north and east do not enter as it is opened. The heating boiler, if used, should be at the north end.

The width of a span-roof house generally varies from 9 to 12 ft. For tall plants such as carnations, a wider house, allowing for central staging, is sometimes built. There should be ventilation on each side of the ridge, and at the sides of the house, and ventilation below the staging is an advantage. All such ventilators should, of course, be controllable.

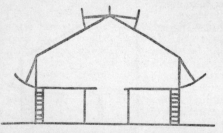

Fig. 3. Cross section of a span-roof greenhouse. The ridge should run north and south.

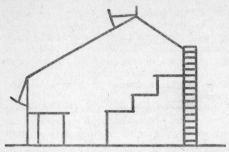

Fig. 4. A three-quarter span-roof greenhouse, the north side being house or garden wall.

A three-quarter span roof is the type of glasshouse erected where the ridge of the structure must run east to west (Fig. 4). The north side may be a house or garden wall, and if so, it is useful for the training of fruits and climbers. The front, or south wall is shorter, thus allowing for a large expanse of glass on this side exposed to the warmest of the sun's rays. Ventilation is usually under the south side ridge, and along the south side windows.

A lean-to greenhouse (Fig. 5) is often the best investment for the small garden owner, but if constructed against the house wall, care should be taken that there is a sufficient fall to the roof.

Staging inside the house is a matter of taste. Lattice wood is common, but a moisture stage where the plants stand on a 2 or 3 in. layer of small pebbles or crushed coke is useful for houses that cannot be sprayed too frequently in the warm weather. The pebbles hold moisture and keep the pots from drying out so rapidly.

Frames are regarded as accessories to the greenhouse, though in the small garden a frame is useful even where no greenhouse exists. Frames are of any convenient size and style, a single light frame being not more than $4\frac{1}{2}$ ft. from front to back. A frame is made so that the glass slopes slightly facing the south. There are three-quarter span frames built like the three-quarter span greenhouse. Frames are seen in Fig. 6.

A frame, like the greenhouse staging, can be filled with crushed coke or small pebbles, and pots and boxes can stand on this base. Alternatively, a frame can be filled with good rich soil, and seeds can be sown direct in this soil. Plants to be wintered under glass can also be planted in the soil bed of a frame, and if mats are available to ensure freedom from frost, no heat is required for chrysanthemums, etc.

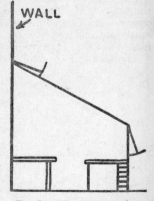

WALL

Fig. 5. A lean-to greenhouse against a wall is inexpensive.

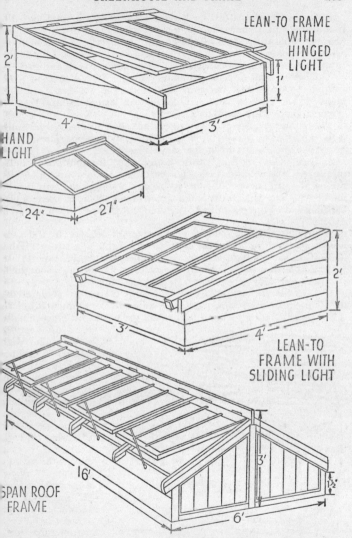

LEAN-TO FRAME
WITH
HINGED
LIGHT

2'

1'

4'

3'

HAND
LIGHT

24"

27"

2'

3'

4'

LEAN-TO
FRAME WITH
SLIDING LIGHT

16'

SPAN ROOF
FRAME

3'

1½'

6'

Fig. 6. *Four types of frame. Frames are necessary adjuncts to a glasshouse and are useful where no glasshouse is available.*

All glass structures can be heated by one of four methods, an it may be said at once that there are advantages in every kind heating apparatus. It is idle to go into the details of such method as any intending builder of a greenhouse can obtain full particula from the various firms concerned. The four methods are these :-

1. Coke or coal boilers and water pipes. An old method whic cannot be improved upon in the results it achieves. It doe however, necessitate considerable regular attention and care operate this system satisfactorily.

The running costs of coke boilers are low, and in large hous it is possible, by a system of partitions, to arrange for differer heats in different parts of the same structure.

2. Gas. Gas boilers, with automatic thermostatic contr minimize labour, and make for certainty. They are useful fc the owner gardener who wants to maintain a required temperatur in all weathers with a minimum of trouble. Gas is used outsid the house, and there should be no danger whatever to any of th plants.

3. Electricity. Electrically heated boilers operate in the sam way as gas boilers. The use of an electric cable is a newer metho of heating greenhouses and frames, and as the cables can be use in frames below the soil level, this method has much to commen it where the cost of electricity is not too high.

4. Oil heaters. Oil as a fuel for boilers is used on a large scal in commercial nurseries, which is sufficient recommendation fc this type of heating. Small oil heaters for use in little greenhous

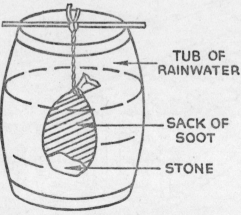

are also servic able. The sligh danger from fume scarcely exists wit some types of o heater, and th moisture content the air is kept u by the use of par of water over th heaters. For a except the rarest plants, I regar some of the moder oil heaters as ver satisfactory indee

Ventilation is matter for judg ment both in th greenhouse an

Fig. 7. The best way to make soot water. Its main use is in supplying mild nitrogen to plants.

ame. One point to remember is that ventilation should almost
ways be effected on the side of the frame or greenhouse away from
e wind. No young plants like draughts, but more plants under
ass are killed by coddling than by cold winds.

Ventilation and air moisture must both be considered. It is a
istake to allow air to become damp and stagnant : " damping
f " disease will inevitably result. Daily ventilation all the year
und should be aimed at, even if the ventilation is given for a
w minutes only.

Ventilation is particularly important when such plants as
matoes are in flower. If the air is moist, pollination will not
e effective, and the fruits will fail to set. That is why tomato
uses should always be opened about midday, and why, also,
e grower should tap each cane along the row about the same
me. Spraying overhead while the flowers are fully open is a
istake. In the case of cucumbers, it is not desirable that the
eds shall form, and spraying overhead is therefore permissible.

WATER FOR THE GREENHOUSE

Water supplies under glass are often mishandled. The best
ater supply is rain water from the houses themselves, brought
to a tank inside the greenhouse so that it is always at approximately
e same temperature as the soil of the pots. Failing an inside
nk of this description, care should be taken not to shock the plants
y watering with water at a temperature lower than that of the
reenhouse itself.

An open tank, or a bath under the tank, into which pot plants
an be stood occasionally for a thorough soak is advisable. Water-
g by immersion is ideal for most pot plants and for many seeds.

Soot water (Fig. 7) is a useful mild stimulant for flowers grown
nder glass or in the open garden. Besides containing a certain
mount of nitrogen which assists the growth of leaves and shoots,
ot tends to deepen the colour of the flowers and the green
f the foliage. Stimulants of any kind should be given only to
ants growing really strongly and should never be anything but
ery weak. A safe guide is to feed little and often rather than
nce with too strong a solution, and in the case of soot water the
quid should be dark brown.

The daily time sheet for heating, ventilation and watering is
ll important. Ventilators should be opened generally when the
n has warmed the house, and should be closed an hour before
ndown, so that the utmost use is made of solar heat. Boilers
ould be stoked at sundown, so that they will be giving good
eat in the coldest part of the night. Watering should be done
the morning in wintry weather, and not too freely except among
ulbs and other plants coming to maturity. Evening watering is

best in hot weather, as plants under glass should never have drop
of water standing on them during the day unless they are we
shaded.

Shading—blinds or whitewash—is important in most hous
during a part of the summer, but must not remain when unwante

It is not possible in a short space to go fully into the detail
cultivation of all kinds of greenhouse plants. They can, howeve
be roughly divided into groups, and their general treatment outline

Climbing plants come, I think, first, if only because these a
plants that the average amateur owner of a greenhouse neglect
The extremely decorative bougainvillea, with rose-purple or bric
red flowers—or, rather, bracts—is one of many highly spectacula
climbing plants suitable for the warm greenhouse. The blue passio
flower and the September-flowering plumbago *capensis* are suitab
for the cool greenhouse. The ideal way to grow such climbers
in a soil bed thick on the floor of a greenhouse, while the plan
themselves can be trained to the pillars or to wires strained horizo
tally along the walls of the lean-to greenhouse.

MAKING A GREENHOUSE BED

To make a bed in the greenhouse, the best way is to excava
deeply and insert as a bottom layer some crushed mortar rubble o
other porous material. Over this some decayed turf and garde
loam, the roughest at the bottom and finer compost at the surfac
will make a good bed for ordinary ornamental climbers.

Annuals for greenhouse culture are sown in boxes exactly a
described for outdoor annuals (*see* Chapter III) and pricked o
singly into small thumb pots. Some annuals are better sown dire
in the pots where they are to flower. Ordinary potting compost
used, and no special care is required in their cultivation. If annua
are required to flower in the winter, they should be sown ear
enough to catch a good deal of sunshine before the darkest day
as the flower production depends on sunlight.

The amateur is advised to use the tender greenhouse annuals-
torenia, schizanthus, etc., in preference to the hardy annuals, fo
the reason that they give a more luxurious air to the stages than o
such plants as nasturtiums and coreopsis.

Annuals can be sown at almost any time of the year, and freque
sowings under glass result in a good supply of young plants. Apr
May and August are possibly the best months for sowing.

As regards perennials, though a number of greenhouse plan
could be raised from seed, my candid advice is to buy plants whe
possible and to pay a good price for them. It is definitely a waste
time, space, heating and lighting costs to stock a greenhouse wi
inferior varieties. In a little greenhouse a single specimen of suc
plants as lippia *citriodora* (the lemon-scented verbena) or epiphyllu

Russellianum (the leaf-flowering cactus) is sufficient. Such perennials as the hanging bellflower, which may be desirable in numbers, for general decoration, can easily be increased if one good specimen is obtained. A good trade catalogue should therefore be obtained at once. A good way of potting a plant is shown in Fig. 8.

Bulbs under glass divide themselves easily into two groups, spring flowering and summer flowering. The ordinary spring-flowering bulbs are cultivated with great ease. They can be potted in ordinary potting compost in pots of sufficient depth to allow for good roots to form or they can be potted in bowls of moistened bulb fibre.

In either case they are mostly plunged under a thick covering of ash in a cold frame for a few weeks, and while there the roots begin to form. The bulb bowls or pots are then taken out, wiped clean, and brought into the cool greenhouse. Bulbs can be grown on in quite cool conditions, or heat can be gradually increased so that the bulbs are forced into early bloom. There is no particular secret of good cultivation beyond the general one of keeping to natural methods. That is to say, the bulbs are first in the dark, and in the cool, with enough, but not too much moisture. Then they are *gradually* given more light, more moisture, and more warmth, as they would be if left to develop naturally in the spring days.

A practice that is becoming increasingly popular is to plant quantities of bulbs in shallow boxes—i.e., boxes 4 or 5 in. deep and as large as available—and to grow them on in the frame or greenhouse until they are nearly ready to flower. They are then transferred to bowls, window boxes, or wherever wanted The advantage of this method is that the bulbs take up less space in the boxes than if they were planted separately in pots or bowls, but I do not recommend it, as root damage must inevitably spoil the splendour of the spring blooms.

Summer-flowering bulbs are grown in the same way as the spring bulbs, except that the gradual increase of light and heat is made easier by co-operation with Nature.

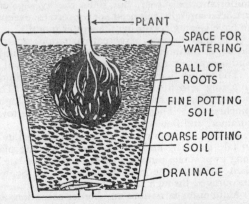

Fig. 8. *Potting a plant. This illustration shows a good soil and drainage arrangement.*

Now for the cultivation of just a few of the most popular of greenhouse plants—plants with which the novice would do well to make his first experiments in glass gardening, since they are profitable, comparatively easy, and on account of their popularity they are not too expensive.

Begonias. Horticulturally, begonias are of two groups, the tuberous-rooted and the fibrous-rooted kinds. Among the fibrous-rooted are several hybrids between the two groups.

Tuberous-rooted begonias include some dwarf bedding begonias, and those grown in pots for bedding or for greenhouse decoration. They can be grown from seed sown in February in a temperature of 65 degrees or from leaf cuttings. Tubers can be stored dry from season to season, and restarted into growth in trays of damp fibre in slight heat in February. If for summer bedding, the plants are hardened off during May and planted out about the first week in June, in moist, leafy soil in a sunny position.

Fibrous-rooted begonias are also grown for bedding and for greenhouse decoration. They are mostly rather tender, and more suitable for greenhouse culture than for the open. Increase is by means of cuttings. Some of this section are winter flowering, and many are grown as much for the beauty of their foliage as for their flowers. After flowering, they are kept in a lowered temperature, and with a minimum of water for some weeks, then restarted, and cuttings are taken from the fresh basal shoots.

Carnations. These are all-the-year-round flowering plants; that is to say, if you can give them a little heat in winter, you can have blooms from some of your plants all the season. Light is even more important than heat, but since the average amateur cannot use artificial sunlight, this need not concern us, except that it is important to have clean glass during the winter months.

For glass culture, perpetual carnations are potted up, as rooted layers, in autumn, in good clean compost containing sufficient sand and coarse grit to keep it open. Sterilized soil is preferable.

The young plants are grown on in cool conditions and repotted in spring into 6 and finally into 8 in. pots. They can stand in the open during summer, and when about 6 in. high the tops should be pinched out. They are brought under glass towards the end of the summer, and flower well for some time.

By layering fresh plants (or taking cuttings) in February and again in late summer, and by keeping back some plants in the open as long as possible, pinching them back rather late in the summer, and then bringing the pots under glass in September, flowers are encouraged through the winter months.

Malmaison carnations and border carnations are also increased by layering in July or August, the border carnations (hardy) being then wintered in the open or a cold frame for spring planting in the borders. Malmaison carnations, however, are grown all the year round in the greenhouse.

Perpetual carnations can be pinched back twice if bushier plants are desired, or if it is desired to keep them back, but Malmaison carnations should not be pinched more than once.

Chrysanthemum. The cultivation of late-flowering chrysanthemums can only be carried out where glasshouse protection is available, since the blooms come so late in the season that they would otherwise be ruined by frost. Very little artificial heat is needed, however, and the cultivation of Japanese late-flowering chrysanthemums is therefore an ideal branch of horticulture for the owner of the little, cool greenhouse.

These plants can be raised from seed sown in February, but the better named varieties are grown from cuttings. The cuttings are taken from the old stools, as soon as suitable new growths have been made, i.e., not too long after the flowers cease for the season. When the flowers fade, the flowering stems are cut down, and the pots kept moist to encourage the fresh shoots. These are taken off generally in February, though some may be taken earlier, and some later. They are rooted in sandy soil in a propagating frame or pit, and as soon as new growth commences on the cuttings, they are potted up singly into small thumb pots.

From then onwards, the plants are moved gradually to larger pots, as the roots fill the soil of the smaller sizes, until they finally reach 8 or 9 in. pots, in which they will flower. Two-thirds loam, rather lumpy, particularly at the bottom of the large pots, with the remainder made up of leaf-mould, or old stable manure, sharp sand, crushed mortar, bonemeal and soot make an excellent compost, but it is best to mix it well at the beginning of the season, and use from the stock gradually.

Staking and pinching and disbudding are three important

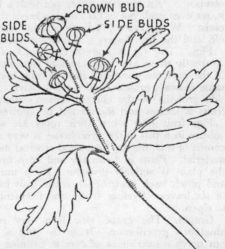

Fig. 9. Disbudding a chrysanthemum. The principle is to leave only one bud on each stem.

SSG—K

features in chrysanthemum culture. While pots stand in the open, i.e., from about April or May until September they must be protected from high winds, and a good way to do this is to stand the pots in a straight row, stretch wires along the row above the pots, and tie the stakes (three in a pot) to the wires. Winds will do no damage to plants staked in this way.

Pinching, i.e., the removal of the centre-growing tip, is recommended in all chrysanthemum culture. The flowers on the side branches that result after such pinching are better in form, and more gracefully placed than the central flower bud which might open if the pinching were neglected.

After pinching, disbudding may be needed to make a bushy plant. This means that one bud of those that develop on each stem is selected to remain and open, while all other buds are rubbed away as soon as they form. The question of which bud to retain is one that every grower will find by experience, though most nurserymen who specialize in chrysanthemum culture give detailed instructions on this point in their catalogues. Disbudding is illustrated in Fig. 9.

Convallaria. This, the popular lily of the valley, can be grown very easily indeed in the warm greenhouse. If early flowers are required, the specially prepared crowns for forcing should be bought about October or November, and potted up in ordinary potting compost. An inverted flower pot with a little coconut fibre inside it, set over each pot of lily crowns, keeps the soil and young growth moist. When the top growth is 2 in. high, the pot can be taken off, and the lily flowers will quickly open.

Figs. The fig is one of the fruits often grown under glass. Normally there are three crops of figs—one borne on young stems of the previous summer's growth, one borne on new stems of the same season's growth, and a third batch of fruits that grow on the side growths of the current season's stems. This third batch of fruits is useless and should not be allowed to remain.

Figs fruit best when their roots are somewhat confined, and culture in a tub in the greenhouse is very satisfactory. Soil should consist of turf, fibrous loam, and crushed mortar over good drainage material. Plant in February and keep up the water supply while the plant is actively growing. Keep unnecessary wood cut out, and pinch back growths when the fruit has set, to leave only five or six leaves. Syringe freely and frequently until the fruit begins to ripen.

Grapes. The grape vine is a very suitable climber for the amateur's greenhouse. It needs only a small amount of heat, but needs a maximum of care in pruning or feeding to make it a profitable investment. The vine can be planted in a border dug inside the greenhouse or, if more convenient, a vine can be planted outside the house, and brought inside through a special opening near the soil level.

Hard pruning for the first few years is desirable to form the vine into a skeleton of the desired shape. This will depend on the shape of the house, and the inclinations of the owner. A single vine is often allowed to make two main stems which are trained horizontally in opposite directions. From these, lateral stems are allowed to develop, on the upper sides only, so that they ascend to the roof of the house. During the period of forming the vine, unwanted buds are rubbed off immediately they appear.

Pruning is done annually at two seasons. In summer the side growths bearing the trusses of flowers are pinched back when fruits have formed, leaving only about two leaves beyond the fruits. In winter the side stems are shortened to leave one leaf bud only, at the base, pointing outwards.

On indoor grapes, some thinning of the bunches is desirable, and this is done by degrees, with sharp scissors, fruits being cut out here and there to allow the remainder to grow to full size.

Fertilization is important, and the use of a camel-hair brush, passed from flower truss to flower truss on a warm dry day, is advisable.

Heliotrope. The old-fashioned cherry pie, or heliotrope, should be more widely grown as a greenhouse shrub. In the beds it is used as a summer plant only, but under glass it will grow on from year to year and become quite a tall shrub. Its perfume alone justifies its inclusion. No special treatment is required, but if desired the plants can be hard pruned each spring.

Lilies under glass need very little special care. Deep pots should be used for them, with adequate drainage crocks, and good potting compost containing leaf-mould and sharp sand. Particularly in the case of stem rooting lilies, plenty of room should be left at potting time for further top dressings of fresh compost to be given as the plants grow.

Melons. Seed is sown in January, one seed to a pot of light soil. Press each seed $\frac{1}{2}$ in. into the soil, on edge. Further seeds can be sown at any time up to the end of June. Pot on into a 5 in. pot, in good loam with well-decayed manure. Pot firmly, with the soil surface sloping down towards the rim of the pot. Plant out into a prepared bed of two parts good loam, one part well-decayed manure (old mushroom beds do well) and a potful of bonemeal to each barrowload of compost. Grow on a main stem, with five or six side stems. Stop the side stems at every joint until a number of laterals are formed, each one having a female bloom. Stop the shoots one leaf beyond the flower. Melons need brisk heat at sowing time.

Fertilize the flowers at midday by carrying the pollen-laden centre of the male flower to the female. During this time do not spray frequently, but keep the atmosphere rather drier than usual. When the fruits are forming, thin out unwanted shoots, spray frequently, give plenty of water and liquid manure, and provide nets or other supports for the fruits.

Orchids. Because of the fact that these plants need special atmospheric conditions, they are not recommended for culture in the amateur's single greenhouse. There are a few that will succeed in the mixed house collection, and of these I should recommend Cypripedium *insigne*, Masdevallia *Veitchii* and Odontoglossum *crispum* —all fairly easy to manage and well worth the trouble. If the amateur remembers that sudden changes of temperature are objectionable, that a slight rest (not a complete drying off) after the growing season and plenty of water when fresh growth begins are all needed, he will find the cultivation of these plants simple enough. Repotting, when necessary, should be done just as new growth begins for the season, and the compost used should be fibrous loam, chopped fibre, and sphagnum moss with plenty of drainage material.

Palms and Ferns. These and other foliage plants are useful in the little greenhouse as in larger houses. Compost for these is merely ordinary potting compost with the addition of peat or leaf-mould. A very little fertilizer of a general character added to the water used during the active growing season is usually sufficient to keep these plants in good condition. Repotting, when necessary, should be done in early spring. A small pellet of sulphate of iron on the surface of the soil will prevent yellowing of the leaves on palms.

Peaches, Nectarines and Apricots. These are frequently grown under glass, for the sake of earlier and more certain fruits. They need a sunny, well-ventilated house, and a temperature of 45 degrees in very early spring to encourage the opening of the flowers. After the fruit is set, syringing should be done daily until the fruit begins to turn colour. Pruning is carried out in the same way as for outdoor grown fruits.

Richardia. The arum lily. Pot in compost of half fibrous loam, one quarter sand and one quarter leaf-mould, and keep in a cold frame through the summer. Do not allow the pots ever to become dry, and when the flowers are developing give plenty of water and weak liquid manure. From September onwards they should be brought into the greenhouse with a temperature of 40 degrees (minimum). They should flower at Eastertime.

Salvia. There are a great many salvias, and several of them (generally used for bedding) make good pot plants for greenhouse decorations. None is better than the blue salvia *patens*. This should be treated in the same way as dahlias, re-started into growth in the spring and stored dry during the winter.

Salvia *splendens*, a scarlet salvia, is grown from seed in the manner of any half-hardy annual, and makes a fine display of colour in the greenhouse, if grown on in 5 in. pots instead of planted out in June.

Violets. As subjects for frame culture, violets are ideal. They can be grown from single crowns, by dividing the plants immediately after they have flowered. These crowns can be planted out 10 in. apart on a prepared bed, and left outside all summer. In September they can be potted up and set into a frame, with old tan packed round and under the pots. Or, if preferable, a portable frame can be set over them without lifting the plants. The lights should be kept in position over the frames through the winter, but ventilation can be given so long as the temperature is above freezing point. Mats may be needed in severe weather during the night.

CHAPTER X

THE LAWN

I DOUBT if any phase of garden making causes more concern to the new garden owner than the construction of a lawn. The worst thing about it is that every neighbour offers good advice, and each neighbour's advice is different.

Let us, therefore, ignore for the moment the question of procedure, and consider what ideal soil conditions we aim at when we prepare the lawn site. First of all, we want the surface of the soil to be level. In a garden where the surface is roughly level already this will not be a serious problem, but in a garden of very rough ground, or on a site where a flat tennis lawn is to be formed on a steeply sloping hillside, the making of a lawn presents some difficulty. However, we will consider the problem later.

The second point in our ideal lawn site is that it should be well drained. We do not want water to collect on the surface and remain there long after rain has ceased.

Then, too, we want a lawn—not a patch of "weeds and concrete," as I heard one amateur gardener describe his tennis lawn after a week or two of drought. I can hardly stress too much the point that grass is a *plant;* that it needs to be regularly fed with air, water, and soluble plant food if it is to remain green and healthy; and that the soil in which grass is to grow must be "in good heart," just as if it was the soil of a border.

Well that, in brief, is the type of lawn site at which we aim. Now for the easiest and most effective way to secure it.

Levelling first. But we cannot consider levelling without also considering soil fertility and drainage. Fertile soil in any garden is the darker layer of soil which has been at the surface for years, and which contains decaying organic matter, bacteria, etc., that are not present in the under layers. We shall require this layer at the surface.

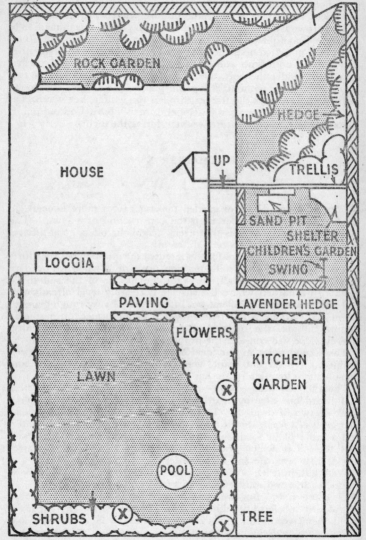

ROCK GARDEN

HEDGE

HOUSE

UP

TRELLIS

SAND PIT
SHELTER
CHILDREN'S GARDEN
SWING

LOGGIA

PAVING

LAVENDER HEDGE

FLOWERS

KITCHEN

GARDEN

LAWN

POOL

SHRUBS

TREE

A LAWN IN RELATION TO HOUSE AND GARDEN

On a very steep slope, the best thing to do is to strip off this surface layer and pile it somewhere on its own while the process of levelling is carried out. Naturally, if the lawn area is extensive, this is a troublesome proposition, but the trouble must be taken if success is to be won. A little care in selecting the right spot for temporary storage of the top soil—several heaps on each side of the lawn site might be wise—will save unnecessary labour.

Having found and reserved the fertile soil, we must survey the plot and calculate roughly where we want to move soil from, and where we want to move it to, in order to produce a level surface. The best method of levelling has been described in Chapter I.

HOW TO DRAIN THE LAWN

While you level the site, you can also attend to the matter of drainage. And at this stage you must consider the nature of your soil. If the subsoil is of an open porous nature, you need not worry about drainage. On a sandy site, for instance, you are not likely to be troubled by waterlogging; the opposite is more likely to be the case, and you may need to dress the soil well with leaf-mould, old manure or other humus, to help it to retain moisture. But on a clay subsoil, water is very likely to collect during rainy spells, and if water collects it will almost certainly collect more in one place than another, and that one part of the lawn will become sour, the grass will fail, and the lawn will be unsatisfactory.

Take care therefore. If, when you leave a hole open during heavy rain, the water remains there for a day or two, you may know that special drains are needed. Very rarely indeed it may be necessary to put in agricultural drainpipes (which are special drainpipes that carry away surplus soil water). Usually it is enough to take out trenches at intervals of about 15 ft., making the trenches perhaps 15 in. deep, and half filling them with porous material before replacing the soil.

Where agricultural drains are necessary, they must be packed round with rough breeze, so that the holes do not get clogged. Such pipes must, of course, lead to a suitable sump or main drain.

A point to note here is that when a flat lawn is made from a sloping hillside, there is more danger of water collecting at the end of the lawn where excavation was made than at the other end, as this part receives the drainage from the hillside above. A trench across this end of the lawn is a wise precaution.

Having roughly levelled, and properly drained the subsoil, it is time to turn our attention to the top layer. Let us remind ourselves again that grass is a plant, and also that it is a dwarf plant. We cannot expect it to fight its way among large stones, and still present the soft even appearance we want from it. It is important that the surface layer of 2 or 3 in. should be fairly free from large stones, and of even texture, fine and crumbly, capable of being rolled hard without caking into a solid cement-like pan. We also want it free of weeds.

The first thought of the amateur is to sift the top soil. This is not necessary, in fact it is rarely advisable, for the reason that the transition from fine surface soil to lumpy or stony subsoil should be gradual. If the soil is put down in definite layers, there is a tendency for it not to bind well, but to remain in layers that crack easily under the influence of dry spells, frost, etc. So the best method is to distribute the soil as evenly as possible over the site, removing any large, tap-rooted weeds at the same time. Then, if you can, leave it for a time, rough as it is, to weather.

Soil prepared in late spring, and left through the summer without sowing is in ideal condition for surface preparation when the first September rains come. It has generally grown a crop of seedling weeds by that time, and these can be hoed, raked or forked, so that they do not endanger the young grass. Alternatively, a site prepared roughly in September would be ideal for seed sowing in March or April. This also would have weeds present (weeds grow in all weathers !) but they are very easily destroyed before the lawn is made, and to allow a crop of weeds to germinate while the soil lies bare is one good way to rid the soil of many weed seeds that would certainly germinate later if left.

SEED OR TURF?

As long as we have lawns, we shall have discussions between amateur gardeners as to whether seed or turf should be used for their construction. Those who spend their lives among lawns can give the best answer. If expense is no object, and you want a quick lawn, then lay turf, but use the best Cumberland turf. Lay it in the winter, if you can, or use plenty of water after it is laid.

But the better way of making a lawn, provided you have the patience to wait and do not expect quick results, is to sow seeds. You have first to wait for the ground to mature, and then to wait for the seed to germinate and grow to a thick carpet—say eighteen months altogether before you have a really first-class lawn. But then it will compare with the finest lawn from turf, and will have cost you far less.

If you don't want to wait as long as that, then there are two other alternatives. The first, and best, is that you sow the lawn immediately you have prepared the site, without allowing a period for maturing, and by constant endeavour for the first six months you keep it weed free. Then you will have a usable, and perhaps almost as good a lawn as if you could wait the eighteen months. Or—and this is not what I advise as a rule—you can use second-rate turf, which may work out even cheaper than a lawn from seed, and will give you a lawn of sorts fit to use the first season. I don't advise second-rate turf, because it never gets to quite the pitch of perfection that a lawn made from seed reaches. The turf is bound to contain weeds, and the quality of the grass is doubtful, so that results are not uniform, as they are with good grass seed. However, the question is one for each owner to decide after consideration of costs and needs.

Let us then outline the procedure for both types of lawn. It is not essential that so much care should be taken over the layer of fertile soil when turf is to be used, as the grass is already established and can be fed from above. But it is an advantage if the soil preparation is carried out thoroughly, as the even distribution of the fertile layer makes for evenness in the quality of the turf after it has been in use for a time.

HOW TO LAY TURF

Turf is best laid during the winter months, but it can be laid at any time if due attention can be given later to watering. Turves are cut about 2 in. thick, and should be trimmed before use to an even thickness of $1\frac{1}{2}$ in. This is obtained by the use of a gauge box, which is a box 1 ft. square (or larger if the turves are larger) and $1\frac{1}{2}$ in. deep inside. The turf is laid upside down in the gauge box, and then trimmed off level. The prepared, rolled soil surface is disturbed very lightly, and the turf then laid by inverting the gauge box. Four corners are not allowed to meet, the turves being set brickwise, as this encourages it to bind better. After laying the turves, it is best to beat them well down with a turf mallet (or the spade), but the beating should not be too drastic, especially if the soil is inclined to be sticky.

It is a great help to newly laid turf if a barrowload or two of finely sifted soil is prepared and mixed with a little grass seed, the mixture being scattered over the turf and brushed well into the cracks. Watering, or rainfall, turns the turf quickly into a fine lawn that goes from strength to strength.

A lawn made from seed can be used fairly quickly if it is a lawn made for ordinary outdoor teas and deck-chairs sort of use, but it will be some time before the grass is strong enough to stand the wear and tear of games. The two best sowing months are September and April, but weather must serve as a guide. A lawn site prepared as already described, with the fertile soil redistributed over the levelled subsoil, needs alternate rolling and raking to bring it into the right condition. This rolling and raking can only be done when there is some moisture in the soil, but not enough to make the top layer sticky; so that it will be found impracticable to keep to any certain date in the calendar.

Sowing must take place on a day when the rake can be used

with ease, and preferably on the day before warm showers are to fall—a chance for weather prophets !

To estimate the quantity of seed required for a rectangular lawn, measure it both ways, in yards, multiply the figures together, and divide by eight : this gives you the number of pounds of grass seed needed. Thus, if the lawn is 8 yds. by 10 yds., the amount of seed needed will be 10 lb.

If you try broadcast sowing without dividing the seed first, you will probably find that you have sown three-quarters of the supply on the first half of the lawn, so here is a good way to ensure even sowing. Begin by stretching a line down the lawn, 1 yd. from the edge, thus marking off a yard strip, say 1 yd. by 10 yds., if the lawn is the size mentioned above. Use ten ounces of seed, and sow it as evenly as you can along this strip. Now mark off a second yard strip, and sow a second ten ounces. Continue across the site in the same manner.

After you have finished this, take the line and this time stretch it widthways across the lawn, marking off a strip 1 yd. by 8 yds. Use 8 oz. of seed to this strip and sow again as evenly as you can. Then mark another 1 yd. by 8 yds., and so continue sowing in a direction at right angles to the first sowing. You will use up the remainder of the seed, and the result will be a much more even distribution of the seed than if you sowed it all at once. This method is illustrated in Fig. 1.

Next take the rake, and with a light touch rake the fine soil surface, so that the seed is more or less covered : you cannot actually cover it entirely by raking, as you must not let the teeth penetrate deeply.

Pass a light roller over it at this stage, if you have one, and then dust a very little finely sifted soil over the surface to cover the seed completely. Protect the seed, if your lawn is not too large, by threading black cotton between twigs about 6 in. above the ground.

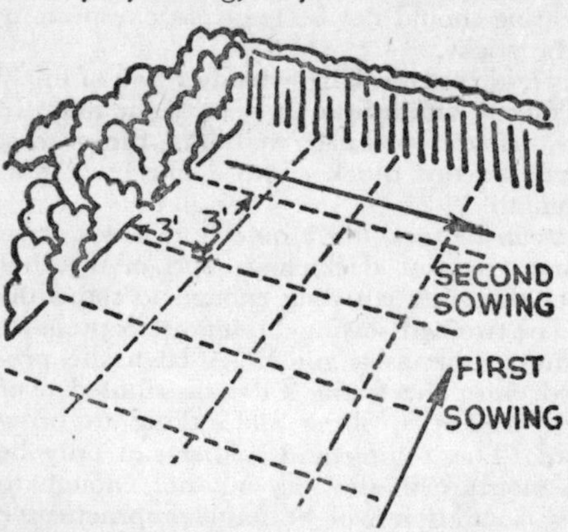

At some time, varying from ten days to three weeks, after sowing the lawn will quite suddenly take on a fine green film, and if the weather is warm and rains frequent,

Fig. 1. Lawns should be sown in thin strips, a second sowing being made across the first.

the grass will thenceforward grow very rapidly. If the seed is sown in September, the first rapid growth will soon cease, and it is probable that no cutting will be necessary until the spring.

Rolling is necessary, however, even on a newly sown lawn. Rolling is done for a definite purpose, and that is not, as many amateur gardeners seem to think, for the purpose of levelling the surface. That cannot be done by rolling, except where the lawn has been disturbed and must be reconsolidated. Rolling is done because it " tillers " the grass; that is, by bending down the growing blades it makes several grow in place of one, and the grass becomes thicker.

Grass should not be rolled too heavily while it is young. Probably when it is about 2 in. high, or a little less, there will come a day that is dry and sunny, after showers. The roller will then pass over the new lawn without pulling up lumps of soil and grass roots, and without so hardly pressing down the young grass that it is " sealed " into the wet soil.

THE FIRST MOWING

After the first use of the roller, wait two days and then set a sharp mower so that the blades are lifted 2 in. from the ground, and just skim off the tiny tips of the grass. This first cut is another ticklish operation, for which the right moment must be chosen. If the roller or mower seem to be injuring the grass in any way, wait for a more favourable opportunity.

The first cutting should be followed by a second according to the growth of the grass, and gradually the blades of the mower can be lowered to normal.

Probably long before the grass seed appears, and certainly before it has been rolled and cut many times, weeds will appear. This is inevitable. The first task on the lawn may therefore be to pull out, by hand, every tiny weed that can be seen. To do this you have to walk over the lawn, and it is advisable to use a plank to take the tread of your boots. Some lawn workers tie short planks to the soles of their shoes, but this, in actual practice, makes one's feet so clumsy that I doubt its advantage. A movable plank is, however, useful in protecting the soft soil and the new grass.

To be sure you rid the lawn of weeds, mark it off in strips as you did when sowing, and weed one strip at a time. It is an exacting job, but if you do it at this stage you will never have so much trouble again.

From thence onwards, cut the lawn as often as you can—even in winter a lawn should be cut if it has grown—and roll it often, too. Do not ever roll when the soil is really sodden with rains : such rolling merely makes the surface cake hard and subsequently it will crack. Moreover, grass (again, remember that it is a plant) needs air at the roots and hard rolling on wet soil prevents air from entering the soil. Avoid rolling, too, in frosty weather, when the blades of grass would be easily injured. Roll as often as you can in showery weather, or whenever there is moisture in the soil, but no water-logging.

If the natural soil of the garden is sandy, or if chalk is very near the surface and the layer of fertile soil is very thin and not very fertile, it is wise to add plenty of humus to it when the lawn site is prepared. Any kind of decaying vegetable or animal matter is useful.

On a garden where the soil is of clay, I should always use lime when preparing the site. Lime eases the gardener's labours by helping to break up hard sticky lumps of soil. It actually causes the fine soil particles, of which the clay is formed, to cling together in tiny groups, and this gives them the loose shifting quality of sand.

Another reason for the use of lime on heavy soil is that it discourages worms, and worms can be objectionable if they are present in too large numbers under the grass.

WHAT FERTILIZERS TO USE

But apart from these general measures which the gardener will take during the process of soil preparation, what fertilizers will be needed? And when should they be used? The answers to these questions are linked up with the question of existing soil. On light, congenial soil, where a fine grass mixture can be used (grass mixtures are dealt with later in this chapter), I should adopt the method of treating the soil only with sulphate of ammonia—no lime and no general fertilizers.

There should be no need for fertilizing at seed-sowing time, but as soon as the grass is well established and the mower can be used in comfort, the treatment with sulphate of ammonia can begin. As the sulphate is very liable to burn tender young grass, unless the weather is very showery and the application made very carefully, the gardener will be wise not to begin too early. A regular dose, once in three weeks, allowing only from ¼ oz. to ½ oz. of the sulphate to the square yard, is useful. To allow for even distribution, mix the sulphate with sand or fine soil before spreading it on the lawn, brush it well in between the blades of grass, and then immediately water it in unless the weather is showery. This treatment results in a very fine, thick turf, provided, of course, that the best grass seed is used for sowing.

On heavy stiff soil, where lime is used during preparation, I should use a rather coarser grass mixture and should feed the young grass with some prepared lawn fertilizer (sold by all sundriesmen). The proprietary mixtures are not very much more costly than home-mixed fertilizers, and they have the advantage of thorough mixing, which is very difficult to achieve in the home. If you prefer to do your own mixing, you can use sulphate of ammonia and superphosphate of lime in the proportion of one to three as a spring fertilizer, at the rate of 2 oz. to the square yard. In the autumn, if you do not dislike clover, you can use 1 oz. to the square yard of basic slag.

Clover is not objectionable on some lawns, and it has one big advantage over grass, that it keeps green in dry spells for a longer time. Clover does, however, make an uneven lawn, i.e., greener in the clover patches than elsewhere, and it is not liked by tennis players because it soils the balls. Basic slag encourages clover because it is a phosphatic fertilizer, and clover is a plant that needs phosphates and does not need nitrates. Sulphate of ammonia in small frequent doses through the growing season discourages clover, as it feeds the grass and allows it to oust the clover from the lawn.

At the beginning of winter, a lawn generally requires a little extra attention, and it can then be fed with guano, or old decayed manure, mixed with fine soil and brushed well into the grass.

The treatment of weeds on lawns is a matter of judgment in more ways than one. We can, however, roughly divide the weeds into two different types.

First there are the large, tap-rooted weeds, such as docks, dandelions and the broad-leaved plantain. It is not much use to pull off the tops, or destroy the leaves of these weeds if they are well established in an old lawn. The old method of digging each out separately has much to commend it, but if a pocket knife or a weed grubber is used there will nearly always be a small portion of the root left in the ground, and this will inevitably grow again and replace the old weed with a new one.

A PINCH OF LAWN-SAND

Fig. 2. Tap-root weeds can be killed by lawn sand dropped into their centres.

The best way to treat large tap-rooted weeds is to drop into the heart of each a spot of lawn sand (Fig. 2). This can be mixed at home, but again I should prefer to buy it ready mixed for use on the small lawn. Good lawn sand contains probably seven parts of sulphate of ammonia, three parts calcined sulphate of iron, and as much sand as both chemicals together. Equal parts of sulphate of ammonia and sand will make a nearly as good a substitute.

THE PROBLEM OF SPREADING WEEDS

The other chief type of troublesome weed is the kind with broad spreading leaves over the soil surface, or with a matted, creeping habit, so that the foliage and stems both spread out through and over the grass. Clovers, trefoil, speedwell, buttercup, daisies, yarrow, chickweed, pearlwort, plantain, self-heal and ribwort, with several kinds of moss are of this type. These weeds can be eradicated by surface applications of lawn sand made up of three parts sulphate of ammonia, one part calcined sulphate of iron and twenty parts sand. One application may not be sufficient, and it is important for success that the applications should be during dry weather, as rain following immediately will render the application useless as a weed destroyer. For a weedkiller of this kind to be effective, it must be scattered thinly over the leaf surfaces of the weed. It will do little harm to the vertical grass blades.

Even if the grass leaves are a little damaged, and a blackened appearance follows, the grass will quickly recover, and be all the better for the extra plant food that the weedkiller contains, whereas the weeds will take longer to recover, and so will be crowded out by the grass. A very weedy patch may take some time before it becomes reasonably weed free.

Before considering the small lawn repairs that constantly crop up on all kinds of lawns, let me say a word here concerning the reclamation of a lawn from old meadow grass, or an old neglected lawn. I have known many gardens that were made on old pasture land, where the owners have desired to economize both time and money in the making of the lawn, and to use the grass at once, and be spared the cost of either seed or turf.

If such be your desire, then the first thing that you must do is to rake off all the old, brown grass, if such is present, or to mow down the tall new grass if you happen to take over the garden in late summer when the site has become a hayfield. Large stones and other rubbish will come off with the rake, and the surface left will probably be bare, brown, and only roughly level.

If there is no rain, water this well, and wait a week or two for the grass to begin growing again. The big weeds will come along first, probably, and these you can cut out and treat with a spot

of lawn sand as already described. Meanwhile, prepare a few
barrowloads of fine sifted soil, mixed with sifted ash if you like,
and as convenient, distribute this over the grass, filling up slight
hollows and so making the surface of the lawn gradually more
and more level. Use the roller between showers, and use the mower
after rolling has made this possible.

Gradually, a yard width at a time, tackle the weed problem
seriously, spot treating the larger weeds, and using lawn sand
over the whole area. Also tackle gradually the problem of the
lawn surface, repairing bare patches and filling hollows, lowering
hillocks, replacing very coarse lumpy tufts of grass by fresh pieces
of turf from elsewhere in the garden or by re-sowing the patch with
grass seed.

This gradual method will, in time, give you a good lawn in
place of your meadow, but though you spare yourself the weeks
of bare disturbed soil that are associated with sowing or turfing,
you do not really save much labour in the end. However, it can
be done.

The re-sowing of bare patches is a repair that becomes necessary
on every lawn at some time. Where lawns are in constant use
for games, the common practice is to keep a reserve patch of turf
from which pieces can be lifted when needed, to replace old worn-
out patches. This is not a practical proposition in many gardens,
and re-sowing is an alternative. Bare patches may result from
wear, and also from the destruction of weeds, but if they are the
result of chemical applications, the patch should not be re-sown
until the effect of the chemicals has had time to be washed away.

RE-SOWING WORN PATCHES

To re-sow a worn patch, first lightly fork the surface 2 or 3 in.
of soil, press it down again, sow the seed, allowing two or more
ounces to the square yard, and rake lightly over the patch. Protect
the seed from birds, and keep the sown patch watered if the weather
is not showery.

If the edge of a lawn meets a gravel path or flower border, and
a 2-in. " ditch " exists (to allow for trimming the lawn edge) a few
careless steps from lawn to path may cause a ragged edge. The
most satisfactory way to repair this is to take out a square of turf,
including the ragged portion, turn it round so that the ragged edge
is inside, and replace it. The bare piece can then be re-sown,
and the repair will soon be unnoticeable. This operation is
illustrated in Fig. 3.

New lawns are very liable to sink unevenly during the first
summer, unless care and skill went to their making. To repair
an indentation in the lawn surface, take out a square of turf, add
some finely sifted soil, sufficient to restore the level, and then replace

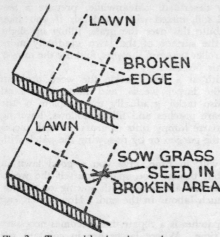

Fig. 3. *To mend broken lawn edges, reverse the turf, then re-sow the worn part.*

the turf and roll well. In the same way, should a hillock exist on a lawn, take off the surface turf, remove a layer of soil, replace the turf, and roll well. Remember to water such patches well for a time afterwards, so that the turf settles back firmly into place.

Purposely, I have said little about grass mixtures, beyond a reference to coarse and fine grasses. The best plan for a small garden owner is to ask advice from the seedsman. There are special mixtures for various purposes. The finest mixture of all is sold only for use on bowling greens and where a similar perfection of lawn is required. (Bowling green construction is a matter for expert advice.)

All lawn seeds sold are mixtures, and in some there is a good proportion of rather coarse grass. This is cheaper and makes a serviceable lawn for children's play. Then there are mixtures that contain an extra large proportion of annual grass, and these are usually sold for town gardens, where grass does not live well through the winter. But if you tell the seedsman the kind of soil you have, and the kind of lawn you want and how you intend to use it, he will give you the most suitable mixture for your purposes.

I do not propose to describe lawn tools here. I would just remind you that good tools make for good and easy work, and that good tools are worth taking care of when you have bought them. A lawn of more than a quarter of an acre is worth a motor mower of sorts, and a lawn of less than that size is worth the best hand mower you can afford to buy. And, finally, the best tool you can afford, or even the worst old second-hand tool, will work better if it is kept clean and oiled and not left out in all weathers.

CHAPTER XI

WATER IN THE GARDEN

A NATURAL water supply in the garden is an asset with which few are blessed. With a stream that meanders through the garden, or just a spring, it is possible to make a really delightful water garden; but failing a natural supply, the water can still be introduced artificially.

Water in the garden layout is used in one of two ways. It can be treated quite formally, as in a pool or canal, with fountains if desired, or it can be allowed to follow more natural lines, as streams in the wild garden, or cascades in the rock garden. Where room permits, these streams can be widened out into informal pools here and there.

Let us consider first water in the garden in formal surroundings. As will have been seen in Chapter I, our garden is divided into separate parts each having its interest, and it is possible to link water in some form with any of these. In the rose garden, for instance, the central feature could be a circular pool with a simple fountain playing into it (Fig. 1); on the terrace a rectangular pool would be more

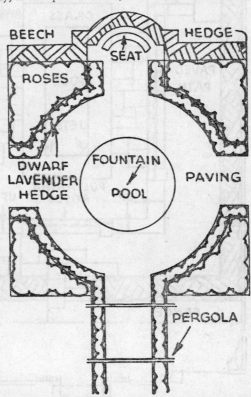

Fig. 1. A circular fountain pool approached by a pergola fits well in the rose garden.

305

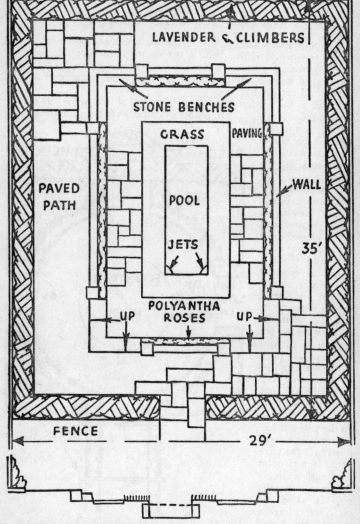

Fig. 2. A design showing how a formal setting, incorporating paving, hedging, etc., suits a rectangular pool.

suitable; and even more interest can be given to the herbaceous walk by the introduction of a pool as a terminal feature or at a point where paths cross. In such a position various designs are possible, determined by the space available and personal taste—rectangular, circular, a combination of the two, or octagonal. Rectangular pools on the whole look best in a formal setting (Fig. 2), but if you have a pool set in the lawn near the house, then a winding shape is pleasant.

Formal treatments of this kind should be kept near the house and away from overshadowing trees, although a certain amount of reflection in the surface of the water adds to their charm. It is in the autumn when the leaves are falling that trouble arises. If they are allowed to fall into the water and left to rot, they turn the water stagnant and dirty. Nearby planting should be in keeping with the formal outline of this part of the garden. Bedding plants are particularly suitable near formal water, and conifers or clipped trees in preference to the ornamental types. In the spring, beds of daffodils, hyacinths, or tulips would make a bright display to be followed in the summer by antirrhinums, asters, salvias, or zinnias.

It has already been mentioned that fountains can be used in connection with the formal pool, but where space is limited it is sometimes possible to introduce a wall fountain as the main feature, the pool at its feet to catch the water being only of secondary importance. For instance, where a flight of steps ascends towards a bare brick wall, the otherwise uninteresting face can have a gargoyle spouting water, or a ledge holding a figure from which water descends, or a simple stone vase from which water

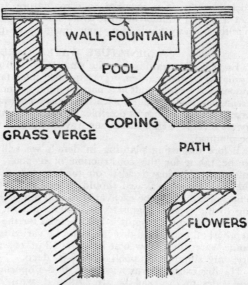

Fig. 3. *A fountain incorporated in the terrace wall is best if combined with a pool at the lower level.*

tumbles. Behind the wall a small pump could be fitted to circulate the water over and over again.

A similar wall fountain can be introduced on terraces, but here it is usual to have a formal pool at the base of the wall, as seen in Fig. 3.

For fountains of all types there are various designs of pumps on the market, simple to install and that could be run at a very low cost. Electricity is the usual means of power.

For informal pools we are able to utilize our natural streams, but failing them, water introduced artificially can be made into a delightful water garden. It is important that the informal pool should be away from the house and in surroundings that are in no way formal. The two should never be combined. A garden where there are considerable numbers of trees and shrubs makes an ideal setting for a water garden of this type, especially where it is possible to plant the banks and surrounding areas. Undulating ground, too, lends itself to this informal treatment.

It does not follow that water must always be used in conjunction with rock work. A stream, whether natural or artificial, lends itself to the construction of a fascinating water and wild garden. As in rock gardens, it is essential to copy nature as much as possible. Let a stream wander at will; avoid hard, straight lines and formal planting of any kind. Let your imagination play.

A MINIATURE WATER GARDEN

Even if your garden is quite small, you can probably manage a miniature water garden. Perhaps the inlet tap could be hidden among a few rocks built as a natural outcrop and then a little stream created to feed a small pool a little distance away. Let the stream take as long a course as possible, perhaps skirting a group or two of dwarf shrubs. Fig. 4 shows one way in which a water garden might be planned.

Before discussing planting in detail, we will consider the steps to be taken for the construction of a pool, whether formal or informal. Having decided on the exact position in the garden, the area to be excavated should be marked out by means of pegs. The soil must then be excavated to a depth of 9 in. to 3 ft., according to the type of plants to be grown, and the quantity of fish (if any) to be kept. Also, it is not essential for the pool to be an equal depth at all points and this can again be varied to suit circumstances. Some water lilies grow best in about 12 in. of water, whereas others are only suitable for pools 2 or 3 ft. deep.

Having excavated as necessary, it is important that the bottom and sides of the pool be strengthened with brickbats, or other solid material, rammed firmly into the soil if it is of a light nature, in order to obtain a firm base on which to place the concrete.

It is important, too, to make the concrete of good quality materials. Portland cement, sand which should be clean, coarse and graded, together with a coarse aggregate are the three materials used. A good aggregate is crushed stone such as granite, gravel or graded ballast, although sometimes clinker and broken bricks can be used with satisfactory results. These should be mixed together in the following proportions: cement, one bucket; sand, two buckets; coarse aggregate, three buckets; water, half to three-quarter bucket. This should be mixed so that it is neither too stiff nor very wet; a handful should retain its shape when squeezed.

The floor of the pond is constructed first, pegs being used to indicate the finished level. These are removed as the work proceeds; in order to obtain a good join between the walls and the floor it is advisable to leave the latter rough at this point. When the base of the pond is set, shuttering made of stout timber must be set up to make the walls, leaving about 4 to 6 in. between it and the soil in which to place the concrete. The boards must be put in firmly to prevent bulging as the concrete is placed in position and, to prevent it from setting to the boards, first give them a coat of limewash. In large pools it will be necessary to reinforce the concrete, using iron rods or strong wire netting. To ensure a solid wall with no air pockets, consolidate the concrete with a shovel or piece of stout timber.

The shuttering must remain in position until the concrete is thoroughly set, which usually takes about a week. Having removed the shuttering the surfaces should be washed over with cement grout, made by mixing equal parts of sand and cement with water until they

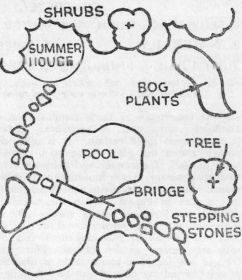

Fig. 4. A layout for a small water garden. The pool can be fed from a hidden inlet.

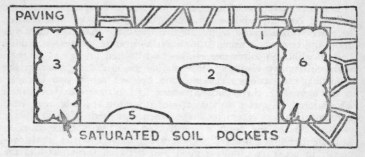

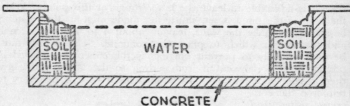

1. FLOWERING RUSH   4. WATER FORGET-ME-NOT

2. WATER LILY   5. SWEET FLAG

3. MIMULUS & PRIMULAS   6. MARSH MARIGOLD & IRIS

Fig. 5. (Below) *How soil pockets are made;* (above) *Suggested pool planting which will give variety and colour to the garden.*

are the consistency of thick cream, in order to make the pool absolutely watertight. A proprietary substance can be used to make even more certain. It is often desirable to have soil pockets round the edge of the pool. These are made between two " walls " of concrete, and being entirely surrounded thereby have no drainage, retain moisture, and are suitable for water-side plants. Such pockets, and a general scheme for formal pool planting, is seen in Fig. 5. When the main constructional work is finished, the surround can be made. The most attractive finish to the pool is to place paving round the edge and slightly projecting. This will hide all irregularities in the concrete, and link the pool with the general garden design. This paving can have small crevices left for rock plants such as dianthus and saxifrages or, in very formal lay outs, it can be left quite clear.

After constructing the pool, time must be allowed for the whole to sweeten, especially if there are to be fish in it. There are properties in newly made cement work that are deadly poison to animal life and harmful to vegetation, and which must, therefore, be removed. This is easily done by filling and emptying the pond three or four times before stocking it. As an extra precaution potassium permanganate can be added until the water is wine colour. After leaving it for three days, empty and refill with clear water. The pond should now be quite ready for stocking.

Preparations prior to planting are of great importance. If they were not made when the pool was first built empty away the water about the middle of April so that you will be ready for planting in May. Place on the bottom 6 in. of heavy, screened loam from which all organic fibre has been removed and mix bonemeal with it. Ram the soil down firmly or it will work loose when water is added. The aquatics should then be planted in the positions desired.

When filling the pool with water care must be taken only to increase the depth with the growth of the plants. As the stems increase in length so more water can be added.

Another method of planting is to fix the plants in baskets, or to strap them between two turves and lower into the water.

QUEEN OF THE WATER GARDEN

For either formal or informal pools, the water lily, perhaps, should be the first considered, for it is the queen of the water garden. The first essential for successful cultivation is still water. Water-lilies found growing wild are always in the backwaters of rivers away from running water. They must also have plenty of sun and air, and are therefore admirably suited to our formal pools. The leaves should be given adequate water surface, so that they do not become crowded, for the water lily increases in size very rapidly, sometimes doubling its growth in one season.

The compost for water lilies is the same as already mentioned for aquatics in general. Peat and leaf-mould must be avoided, as also must sand. When planting be sure to make the roots very firm and only fill the pool by degrees, as the stems extend in length. It is advisable to leave the same water in the pool for as long as possible, only changing it if it becomes really dirty, as the older and stiller the water the more luxuriant the growth.

As the plants become too big for their position they can be lifted and divided, this operation being carried out in May; otherwise the plants can be left in position throughout the year.

Reeds are favourite plants for the formal pool, the tall, erect growth contrasting well with the floating form of the water lilies, but there is an exceedingly large variety of aquatics suitable for the pool, whether it be formal or informal.

Water plants are divided into three groups. First, there are those that live entirely under the water and are known as oxygenating. These, as the name implies, give off oxygen which is beneficial to animal life in the water. This process is counteracted by the carbon dioxide given off by the animals and absorbed by the plants. It is obvious, therefore, that the ratio between the plants and animals in the pond must be balanced.

The next group is the floating aquatics in which the whole plant floats, and the last section is the aquatics that grow with their roots under water and throw foliage and flowers well above the surface.

PLANTS UNDER THE WATER

Of oxygenating plants, the most important are the Canadian water weed, water milfoil, and water crowfoot.

Elodea *canadensis* (Canadian Water Weed) is the most popular submerged plant, growing very rapidly. It will be necessary to reduce it periodically, by pulling out handfuls.

Myriophyllum *spicatum* (Water Milfoil) is another excellent submerged plant, which makes very good spawning ground for fish. It has dainty feathery foliage.

Ranunculus *aquatilis* (Water Crowfoot) is very attractive with floating leaves and miniature white flowers in addition to its submerged foliage. It therefore serves a double use, as it not only acts as an oxygenator but is ornamental, too. It also has the advantage of growing successfully in either swift-running water or a still pool.

Floating aquatics are less popular for the outdoor water garden than they are for indoor aquariums. Duckweed is perhaps the most well known and yet unfortunately proves a nuisance, as it increases so rapidly. It has one advantage, however, in that nearly all hardy fish are very partial to it as a green food. If it becomes a nuisance it can easily be skimmed from the surface.

Frog-bit is a native floating aquatic with a profusion of small dark, green leaves and small white flowers.

Plants for the edge of the water are very numerous and our selections must be confined to the most popular. Some require about 9 in. of water, while others only need to have their roots just covered. The following list will give a representative collection.

Acorus calamus (Sweet Flag). This is a strong-growing grass with sword-shaped leaves similar to the iris. The variegated form in which the green foliage is striped with cream and rose is perhaps even more attractive. This plant requires only a few inches of water.

Aponogeton distachyon (Water Hawthorn). This is a very great favourite, as it is easily grown and bears sweetly scented flowers which are in bloom for a long season, often as late as October. The leaves and flowers are both floating, and suitable for any pool.

Butomus umbellatus (Flowering Rush). This is a handsome reed that bears attractive umbels of pink flowers during summer. It stands out of the water to a height of about 3 ft. and requires to be planted in water 2 or 3 in. deep.

Caltha palustris. (Marsh Marigold). This is the wild marsh marigold or kingcup which many will have seen growing wild. It flowers early in the year and bears a mass of golden yellow blossoms, which give a continuous show for three or four weeks. The leaves, too, are quite attractive and, as it is an exceptionally easy plant to cultivate, it should find a home in every pool. There is a double-flowered form if this is preferred.

Iris pseudacorus. This is the wild yellow water iris which only requires shallow water and will grow on the banks of a stream.

Menyanthes trifoliata (Marsh Buckbean). This is an attractive little water plant with a profusion of white flowers which, when in bud, are bright rose colour. The trifoliate leaves are also quite attractive. This is another plant for shallow water.

Mimulus luteus (Water Musk). An attractive dwarf spreading plant for marshy ground that bears numerous rich yellow flowers throughout the summer.

Sagittaria japonica (Arrowhead). A handsome plant with a profusion of snow-white flowers on slender stems.

Scirpus zebrinus (Zebra Rush). This rush has curious green and white bands up its stems; hence the name. It will grow 4 to 5 ft. high.

Typha latifolia (Great Reed Mace). This giant reed often erroneously called bull rush, needs no description.

As with water lilies these plants all need plenty of sun and air, and a growing medium of rich loam. It is important to watch the plants, for if they tend to become overcrowded they must be reduced in quantity.

No reference has yet been made to the bog garden. It is usual, particularly in the informal water garden, to construct the waterway so that the water can lap over the sides here and there into bays of good rich soil. In these, numerous plants will flourish which otherwise, if completely submerged in water, would rot away. Primulas are, perhaps, one of the most important plant families suitable for bog and marshy conditions, and with these alone it is possible to get a variety of colours and flowers at most seasons of the year.

In bog gardens it is important to plant in drifts or colonies, for single plants do not give a good effect, unless it be such large specimens as gunnera. Drifts of plants alone, however, do not comprise the ideal bog garden, for a background of trees or shrubs is necessary to enhance the colourful planting and, of course, these give shelter from winds. Shrubs such as bamboos, willows and dogwood are particularly suitable. Of the many bog plants the following are a few of the best.

Astilbes. These should be planted in groups, close to the water, so that their graceful feathery plumes may be reflected. They are at their best in July and August. Some of the best varieties are amethyst (purplish-rose), diamant (pure white), King Albert (pure white), and gunther (brilliant pink).

Cimicifuga racemosa. The tall branching spikes of white flowers in August and September grow to a height of 5 ft.

Hemerocallis (Day Lily). These bloom from June to September. The foliage is long and narrow, and the flowers vary, being yellow, orange, red or apricot. They require plenty of moisture and good vegetable soil. Good varieties are George Yeld (orange, with inner petals orange scarlet), and Kwanso *plena* (reddish bronze).

Iris Kaempferi (clematis-flowered Japanese Iris). The flowers are often 8 or 9 in. across and they come in June and July. Their colour ranges through all shades of blue, crimson, red, white and purple. They require plenty of water in the growing season.

Lythrum salicaria. These have carmine blooms and grow from 3 to 4 ft. high. The spikes contrast well with dark foliage.

Primulas. All the members of this family require a sweet, moist and well-drained soil, with leaf-mould and peat. Some varieties well worth growing are : primula *Beesiana*, rosy-purple, 2 ft.; P. *Bulleyana*, which pass through shades of apricot, orange, and scarlet, 2 to 2½ ft.; P. *capitata*, purplish-blue flowers, May to July, 1 to 1¼ ft.; P. *denticulata*, lavender, April and May, 1 ft.; P. *japonica*, crimson, June, July and August, 1 to 1½ ft.; P. *pulverulenta*, crimson, May and June, 1 ft.; P. *sikkimensis*, yellow, 1½ to 2 ft.

FERNS BY THE WATERSIDE

There are a few species of ferns particularly suitable for waterside cultivation, the most important being the royal and lady ferns. Adiantum *pedatum* (hardy maidenhair) has graceful feathery fronds and grows to a height of 1½ to 2 ft. Athyrium *filix-foemina* (lady fern) is a very easily cultivated fern that looks very attractive in crevices of stonework. It has graceful and delicate green fronds and grows 3 to 4 ft. in height. Osmunda *regalis* (the royal fern) reaches a height of 5 ft. and sometimes even 8 ft. The fronds are of a delicate green shade which become bronze in the autumn.

Funkia *fortunei* looks attractive in clumps beside the water, with its heart-shaped leaves, veined, green, glaucous blue, or yellowy green. The purple flowers are borne on spikes 2 ft. high. Gunnera *manicata* (Chilean rhubarb) has huge leaves shaped rather like an umbrella. These die as soon as a sharp frost comes, after which they should be cut off and placed over the crown to protect it. When they rot they make an excellent mulch. Rodgersias have very handsome foliage and grow best in partial shade. The spiræa-like flowers are white or pink.

INDEX